John:

How blessed we are
to have you as friends living
under the cover of grace.

With love,

Jeff Leetheam

GRACE LIKE RAIN

SOAKING UP GOD'S BEST
(EVEN WHEN WE'RE AT OUR WORST)

Jeff Petherick
With Karl Nilsson

Elk Lake
PUBLISHING™

www.ElkLakePublishing.com • Elk Rapids, Michigan USA

GRACE LIKE RAIN

Published by Elk Lake Publishing, Inc.

Copyright ©2011 by Elk Lake Publishing

ISBN: 978-0-9793543-2-8

Scripture texts cited in this book are taken from: The Holy Bible: New International Version (NIV) ©1978, 1984 International Bible Society. The Message (MSG) ©1993 Navpress. The New Living Translation (NLT) ©1996 Tyndale House Publishers. The Amplified Bible (AMP) ©1965 Zondervan. The New American Standard Bible (NASB) ©1995 The Lockman Foundation. New King James Version (NKJV) © 1982 Thomas Nelson. The Holy Bible, English Standard Version (ESV) ©2001 Crossway. All used by permission. All rights reserved.

Cover design: Evan Jones
Interior design: Kevin Stoddard
Proofing: Jennifer Troeger
Printed in the United States of America

Acknowledgements

Heavenly Father, we thank you for our wives, our families, our pastors, our Savior. We dedicate this work to all who will accept and extend your greatest gift. To them we say: Grace is the rain that washes the dust off our soul, nourishes our hungry heart, and quenches our thirst for everything except more and more of You. We gratefully acknowledge that this book was written Dei gratia *— by the grace of God.*

"God owes us nothing. Anything this side of hell is pure grace."

— Puritan proverb

Contents

Preface — Why Me?

"Grace? Are you sure? Aren't there already a million books about it by theologians and PhDs? I've read a stack of them and I'm still not sure I understand it. How can I bring anything fresh to this divine reality? No offense, God, but I'm pretty sure you picked the wrong guy."

No matter how much I argue with God, he always wins. When he wants me to take on a project, he drops it on my heart and it sits there until I do something about it. Even if it doesn't make sense. Even if others seem far more qualified.

I became a Christ-follower over ten years ago. Since then, I've seen God radically change people from all walks of life. These mind-blowing conversions weren't something I heard about or read on Facebook. I was there. And that's how it is with grace. It's always been a tough concept to grasp. But after being personally exposed to its transforming power, my understanding increased by quantum leaps. So while I don't bring huge doctoral credentials to the subject, I do bring an eyewitness perspective. Maybe that's my calling. To make God's truth accessible by sharing real-life encounters. *Grace Like Rain* is just that — a compilation of true stories about God's grace in my life and in people I've met.

All my "God stories" begin with an invitation. For example, I've been to India seven times. Why? Because my Indian friend, Jaya Sankar, invited me to "come and see." That's the same invitation Jesus gave to the disciples. He simply invited them to come, to become active participants in history's most incredible display of God's grace. And that's what God wants for all of us. With whispers, nudges and promptings, his Spirit invites you and me to get off the bench and into the game — to be his hands and feet as he moves in the lives of others.

And to experience his grace in action.

Prologue — Season of Grace

"Who are you and what have you done with my kids?"

It was obvious that aliens had abducted my sweet children and replaced them with some kind of incredibly irritating creatures. Although the pod people looked exactly like my offspring, their bizarre antisocial behavior was proof positive that the *X-Files* were on to something.

Fortunately, my wife and I discovered a relationship with Jesus Christ just as our son and daughter headed full steam into their terrible teens. I've often described these non-wonder years as the time when human beings are at their most irrational and self-absorbed worst.

Before Copernicus, scientists thought the universe revolved around the earth. Now we know it revolves around teenagers. Parents, teachers, traffic, total strangers — all orbiting the giant teenage hairball. The only way teens will spend one nanosecond thinking about others is if it meets their needs, boosts their ego or makes them happy. And because teens lack the emotional maturity to match their cognitive powers, formerly sane adults find themselves having ridiculous arguments with the same kids who used to think mom and dad knew everything.

Of course I'm exaggerating. But I can't tell you how many times my wife and I would look at each other and ask, "Is it too late to trade them in?"

We survived the teenage years, but only by tapping into God's power. Jesus said he would send his Holy Spirit to be our guide and counselor, and we leaned on that promise daily (sometimes hourly). It was in those trying times that we learned the most about our faith, and how to have the *"peace of God which transcends all understanding"* amidst the chaos.[1]

But the most important lesson we learned was not about staying calm or hiding the car keys or helping with homework. It was about grace.

What's grace?

For now, let's just say it's the "undeserved love and salvation of God." While the whole earth was busy sinning, God launched his cosmic plan to settle the score for our misbehavior. Not by hurling down fiery lighting bolts of judgment, but by leaving heaven to be born in a smelly stable, living among us for 33 years, and then voluntary taking the punishment for our sins. And he did it all knowing in advance that the very people he was coming to rescue would torture him, spit in his face and impale him on a cross.

Jesus came, knowing we would spit in his face and impale him on a cross.

That's grace in a nutshell.

Since the day my wife Gina and I first put Jesus at the center of our lives, we have believed in the transformational power of grace. After all, we were living proof that it works. Before Christ, we were self-centered children, yuppie brats who did not deserve forgiveness. So by the time the teen years hit the fan, we knew from experience that God's grace can redeem, restore and renew.

It had saved our marriage from blowing apart. And we believed it could get us through parenting, too.

But *believing* in grace and *practicing* grace are two entirely different animals. Especially when it comes to our kids. What better parallel exists between us and our Creator than in our similar role as parents? Nothing wounds a mom or dad's heart like a struggling son or daughter. And nothing wounds the Father's heart more than seeing one of his children go astray. Being parents gave us a far better understanding of God's infinite patience and the power of his grace.

Our reliance on that grace was really put to the test when our teens began sowing the seeds of their independence. Stepping out like the Prodigal Son, they each experienced life apart from God and the consequences of rebelling. We had hoped (naively) that just being Christians would spare them from making the same mistakes as other kids. But how realistic was that? How silly to think the instant Jesus enters our heart, the old self disappears completely! Even the Apostle Paul — the guy who wrote over half of the New Testament — continually struggled with his old sin nature, *"What I want to do I do not do, but what I hate I do."*[2]

Well, that's at least *one* thing adults and teens have in common.

When I was a brand new Christian, I was told the path of a believer would always be easy. No detours, no speed bumps, no road construction. But it doesn't work that way. Although God's roadmap was perfect, I wandered and wobbled from side to side despite my best efforts. For years, I felt frustrated and guilty every time I had to adjust my route and make a course correction. Today, my goal is not to be perfect, but to keep from wandering so far that I'm unable to swerve back onto the pavement. By praying, listening to God and studying scripture, I've developed an internal navigation system. Call it my spiritual Garmin. When I stray more than a few degrees from the straight and narrow, a voice tells me "Recalculating your route. Turn around and try again." And that's my realistic hope for our kids as well.

When our teens tested their wings (and our patience), God used it to teach us more about grace. In fact, I call this tantrum time "our season of grace." By extending grace to our children, its transforming power boomeranged and hit us, too. Especially me. I'm hard wired to be judgmental. My career as an investor hinges on my ability to make snap judgments, often without complete facts. This skill is good for sizing up portfolios but can be rough on relationships.

> I've developed an internal navigation system. My spiritual Garmin.

On top of my tendency to be judge and jury, there's something in my DNA (and maybe yours) that constantly whispers "people should get what they deserve." You know, the Barney Fife gene that wants to make a citizen's arrest when you witness someone littering or double parking. When someone snitches a grape at the produce counter, I want to toss 'em in the slammer. If God hadn't taught me about grace, I'd still be a self-righteous finger-pointing Christian.

Not a pretty picture.

As a spiritual baby, I was drawn to rules and regulations, and the deeper I dove into my faith, the more legalistic I became.

Without grace, I'd still be a self-righteous finger-pointing Christian. Yuck.

I saw things in black and white, and my advice to other believers was heavily laced with tough love, short on the love. I wielded Bible verses like a holy nightstick. I thought being self disciplined and following the rules were the way to spiritual maturity.

Today, I still believe that spiritual practices and obedience can help draw us nearer to Christ. But I also see the risk. When pride replaces love, we try to bring others up to our own standard of holiness, forcing our rules on them. Then, when trouble comes (which it inevitably will), we make three typical mistakes. We *judge*: "You are a spiritual failure." We *compare*: "You should be more like me." And we *blame*: "You brought this mess on yourself because you (fill in the blank)."

To the relief of God — and the human race — I eventually took off my holier-than-thou robes and came down from the mountaintop. Over time, I began to understand that Christianity is about receiving and giving grace, not keeping and enforcing rules. And I learned that God's grace is so different from human nature that we have difficulty even understanding it.

Fortunately, God knew we'd have trouble getting our brains around a concept as big as grace, so he spelled it out. The Jewish rabbis had 613 laws, but one stood far above all others as the "greatest commandment." It was originally delivered by Moses in the final months of his life just before the Israelites crossed into the Promised Land. Six centuries later it was quoted by a young teacher named Jesus at the temple courts in Jerusalem.

This ancient confession of faith, the *Shema,* still opens every synagogue service and is recited twice daily by observant Jews. In it, God revealed that his utmost desire for all people at all times is that we love him totally, with every fiber of our being: *"Hear O Israel, the Lord our God is one. Love the Lord your God with all your heart and with all your soul and with all your mind and with all your strength."* [3]

When Jesus quoted the *Shema,* everyone smiled and nodded in agreement. But he wasn't through yet. He looked the religious leaders straight in the eyes and added a second part — the knockout punch that scuttled the existing religious system and shifted the paradigm from legalism to grace: *"Love your neighbor as yourself"* [4]

> God's desire is that we love him totally, with every fiber of our being.

That second part sounds simple enough — "love your neighbor." But it's hard. So hard, in fact, that it's absolutely impossible to do through human effort. Only God's grace can give us the ability.

So there it is. *Love God and love others.* The Royal Combo. You can embrace it or ignore it. But you can't say you never heard it.

Before we jump into chapter 1, let me get real serious. Like country singer Lynn Anderson, God never promised us a rose garden. Quite the contrary. He promised us trials and tribulations. If you don't *accept* his grace, you won't make it. And if you don't *extend* his grace, you'll hurt everyone you come in contact with.

It's that important.

Growing through our family's "season of grace" has matured us, humbled us and stretched us. We're just beginners, novices really, but we're practicing what little we do know about grace. Not perfectly, not every second, but we're trying. And even though we screw up sometimes, we see its transformational effects in the people around us.

I pray this book helps usher in your own season of grace.

○   ○   ○

"God is not proud. He will have us even though we have shown that we prefer everything else to him."

— C.S. Lewis[5]

I: AMAZING GRACE

1: AMAZING GRACE

CHAPTER 1:
I Know It When I See It

"War. What is it good for?"

In 1970, singer Edwin Starr asked that musical question to a nation deeply divided over the Vietnam War. To President Nixon's dismay, the answer was the controversial but catchy chorus: *"Absolutely nothing."*

As a native Detroiter, it's only natural that I paraphrase the Motown classic to ask, *"Grace. What is it good for?"*

If you're short on time, I can save you some reading by giving you the answer right now: *"Absolutely everything."*

Maybe I'm weird, but God's ultimate, all-encompassing gift to humanity makes me think of other ultimate, all-encompassing gifts. Like my Swiss Army knife with 27 functions including a corkscrew (in case I'm lost in the jungle but just happen to have a bottle of Chardonnay). Or Windex. In *My Big Fat Greek Wedding*, the bride's father used a spritz of the blue stuff to treat poison ivy, psoriasis and a wedding day zit the size of a golf ball. And don't forget duct tape!

But all the MacGyver gadgets in the world can't do what grace can. Because grace is, well, uh ... that's the question: What exactly *is* grace?

The three-word definition most Christians can reel off is: "God's unmerited favor." Not bad. Or maybe like me you've memorized the five-word acrostic: "God's Riches At Christ's Expense." Again, not bad.

These clichés are not incorrect, but they fall short.

Wikipedia (don't laugh) does a better job: "Divine grace is a Christian term for gifts granted to humanity by God that he is under no obligation to grant. Grace describes all of God's gifts to humankind, including our life, creation, and salvation."

Okay, too much info. But here's the important point: *Grace is a gift we can't earn and don't deserve, but get for free anyway.*

My Greek language skills pretty much end with ordering flaming goat cheese at a restaurant. But experts in the vernacular dialect of that era say the word translated "grace" in the New Testament is *charis,* and it means: "That which affords joy, pleasure, delight, sweetness, charm, loveliness, good will, and favor. The merciful kindness by which God turns people to Christ."[1]

That's a mouthful. But it basically means that grace deals with *all that is wonderful and beautiful and worth celebrating.*

So of all people, Christians should be grinning and throwing parties and rejoicing like crazy because God has given them his wonderful grace. In fact, that's another way we could define grace: *all the good gifts we enjoy freely in life.*

> Of all people, we should be grinning and throwing parties and rejoicing like crazy.

Good start, but we're only scratching the surface of something a zillion miles deep. If you've studied ethics or philosophy or law, you know there are many intellectual concepts that defy easy explanation, even by mental giants. Back in 1964, a brilliant Supreme Court Justice named Potter Stewart ended his protracted legalese definition of pornography by saying, "I shall not attempt to further define obscene material — *but I know it when I see it.*"

Whew. Thank goodness. "I know it when I see it" means there's hope for mortals like me with sub-Einstein IQs (Albert's was 170, minus ten points for his crazy hair). Otherwise, we're stuck sifting through ages of undecipherable debate on the meaning of grace. Ask 100 theologians to define grace and you'll get 101 (not a typo) different answers.

And it's not only *grace* that's a biblical brain buster. Christian doctrines like the resurrection, the virgin birth and the Trinity are theological mysteries, beyond unaided human understanding. I mean, who can get their head around the incarnation of Jesus? The concept of Almighty God coming to earth and living as a person both *fully human and fully divine* is mind-boggling. Mysteries like that can only be glimpsed — but never fully grasped — through the eyes of faith, and then only by divine revelation.

Is God keeping secrets from us?

No, but it might seem that way for two reasons.

First, he's smarter than us. Infinitely smarter. *"As the heavens are higher than the earth, so are my ways higher than your ways and my thoughts than your thoughts."*[2] Can your ego live with that? In the book of Job — believed to be the oldest book of the Bible — we find a man just like us grappling with life's unanswerable questions. After arguing with God about how he was running the universe, Job recognizes that we humans cannot fully know the plans or motives of our Creator. After 42 chapters, he finally concedes that God's purposes are supreme: *"I know that you can do all things; no plan of yours is ever thwarted ... Surely I spoke of things I did not understand, things too wonderful for me to know."*[3]

When we try to figure out God, we are — with apologies for the unflattering analogy — like the flea on a dog trying to understand the dog.

Second, God works according to his timetable, not ours. Let me break it down for those of us not invited to the Mensa picnic: *God has a master plan known only to him, and he is actively working it out behind the scenes. He is not in a hurry. He is not nervous about the outcome.* Throughout history, God has been revealing this divine strategy to mankind stage by stage, a little at a time. Abraham got a piece. David got some more. Isaiah, Jeremiah, Daniel, and so on all got clues.

God's progressive revelation was incremental for centuries, but it made a giant leap ahead when a man named Paul took a roundtrip to paradise, and I'm not talking about Club Med. Sometime after Christ's ascension, the Apostle Paul was *"caught up to the third heaven,"* where he *"heard inexpressible things."*[4] After being granted unprecedented insight into the mysterious unseen, he told the early church: *"The mystery was made known to me and I was allowed to comprehend it by direct revelation."*[5]

It's not a mystery in the Sherlock Holmes who-done-it sense.

He wasn't describing a "mystery" in the Sherlock Holmes who-done-it sense. He was describing profound truths that had been temporarily hidden but were now revealed. This once secret knowledge would be available — not to mystics or religious cults, but to anyone who would read and believe what God was saying through Paul: *"In reading this, then, you will be able to understand my insight into the mystery of Christ, which was not made known to men in other generations."*[6]

Today, Paul's inspired writings (he wrote 14 of the 27 New Testament books) help us comprehend more of what the ancient prophets who lived before Jesus desperately yearned to know. But even with the entire Bible at our disposal, Paul says our current understanding is incomplete: *"Now we see things imperfectly as in a cloudy mirror, but then we will see everything with perfect clarity. All that I know now is partial and incomplete, but then I will know everything completely, just as God now knows me completely."*[7]

And that's how it is with grace.

Frustrated theologians have been trying to define it for over 2,000 years. They've succeeded only in muddying the waters by thin-slicing it into confusing categories like sanctifying grace, habitual grace, sacramental grace, actual grace, *yada, yada, yada.* Which is why I chose the simple art of story-telling to help us understand and apply this wonderful, mysterious gift.

This side of heaven, no one will fully pin it down. But hopefully, by reading accounts of people who've had head-on collisions with grace, we'll become like Justice Stewart — and *know it when we see it.*

○   ○   ○

"I do not at all understand the mystery of grace — only that it meets us where we are but does not leave us where it found us."

— Anne Lamott[8]

I: AMAZING GRACE

CHAPTER 2:
Prisoner Number 24601

According to the Justice Department, 67 percent of inmates released from state prisons are back in jail within three years. So I shouldn't have been surprised when I heard the story of a repeat offender who went back to his old ways.

Out of jail for just 48 hours, the former prisoner blew into town like an angry wind. He'd spent most of his adult life behind bars and it showed in every line etched into his rugged face. Standing over six feet tall with wide shoulders and huge hands, he had the menacing stance of a predator and the scars of a man who knew violence firsthand. Women and children scurried inside to avoid him. Men gathered in groups and watched him suspiciously. Obviously a stranger to civilized society, this hardened criminal was a man with no friends and no job. Maybe even no conscience. Ignoring the whispers, he banged hard on the door of a senior citizen's home. For some unknown reason, the 75-year-old man allowed him to enter. Ignoring the old-timer's hospitality, he robbed the defenseless man and fled the scene under cover of darkness. Within one hour the cops had arrested him.

If it was up to me, I'd lock the bum up and throw away the key. In my book, ripping off an innocent stranger who's trying to help you is about as low as you can get. Even lower if the Good Samaritan is an old man.

I felt disgusted inside; I wanted to punish the thief myself. Trouble is, I couldn't. Not unless I ran up on stage. You see, I didn't hear the story on the evening news, I heard it at the theatre. If you're super-religious, fasten your seatbelt, because our first example of grace in action isn't found in the Bible but on Broadway.

o　　o　　o

When it opened in Paris in 1980, the musical *Les Miserables* was an instant hit with French audiences. The Broadway production opened in 1987 and was nominated for twelve Tony Awards, winning eight, including Best Musical. That was the beginning of a global marathon of packed-out performances that still continues.

Why are audiences around the world so mesmerized by this story?

Because it's about grace.

The Broadway smash is based on Victor Hugo's 1862 novel *Les Miserables*, and its 900 or so pages tell a story of redemption and revolution on a grand scale. But for our purposes, we'll zero in on three characters who epitomize the differences between grace (God's free gift of salvation) and legalism (man's attempt to earn it).

The novel begins with a brief biography of Charles Myriel. Born into an aristocratic family, the wealthy Myriel flees to Italy during the bloody French Revolution. Years later, he returns to his homeland as a simple priest. In a chance encounter with Emperor Napoleon, Myriel is appointed to the prestigious office of bishop. When he moves to the French diocese of Digne, he discovers that the church has placed him in a luxurious palace. Embarrassed by the opulence of his new home, he notices the patients at the hospital next door are living in dangerous, filthy conditions. In a shocking move, Myriel switches houses with the incredulous hospital inmates.

Even more unheard of, he gives 90 percent of his church salary to the city's poorest residents. Traveling on foot, he feeds the poor, ministers to the sick and comforts the dying. Ignoring his personal safety, he insists that his front door always remains unlocked as an invitation to those in need.

By 1815, the tireless Myriel has been bishop for nine years and lives with his sister and a single elderly servant. The only reminders he has kept from his wealthy past are nine silver items — six knives and forks, one soup ladle, and two beloved candlesticks.

Then, on a cold night in October, a rough-looking vagrant walks into Digne. He has money to spend but despite his pleas, the hotel and inn keepers refuse him food and shelter. The villagers insult him with threats and curses, telling him to leave town. When he tries to take shelter in an abandoned kennel, a ferocious farm dog attacks him. Freezing and hungry, the unwelcome visitor cries out, "I am not even a dog!"

Seeing his despair, a local passerby suggests he go to Bishop Myriel for help. Expecting rejection, the traveler gruffly introduces himself as Valjean, and admits that he is an ex-convict just released from prison. To his surprise, the bishop doesn't slam the door, but welcomes him in, offering him supper and a warm bed for the night. Despite the danger to himself, the clergyman treats the angry, hostile Valjean with courtesy and kindness.

As they talk, we learn the stranger's pathetic story. His full name is Jean Valjean, a former tree-trimmer who has spent the last nineteen years doing hard labor in a maximum security prison. His crime? Stealing a loaf of bread to feed his

He served 19 years for stealing a loaf of bread.

widowed sister's starving family. That petty theft cost him five years; he spent fourteen more on the chain gang for trying to escape.

By the time he is finally released, this once decent, gentle man is full of hatred for society. The beatings and brutality he suffered in jail are matched by the cruelty he experiences in the outside world as an ex-convict.

Knowing his reputation has preceded him, Valjean is surprised when the bishop asks him in for dinner. When he's invited to spend the night he is even more confused. The bishop's unexpected kindness moves Valjean profoundly, but two decades of breaking rocks have embittered him against everyone. Silently slipping out of bed in the middle of the night, he searches the modest home for valuables. Finally, in a cupboard right above the sleeping bishop's head, he discovers the silver cutlery and stuffs it in a pillowcase. If the old man wakes up he is determined to kill him without flinching.

While escaping with the loot, the local police catch him and drag him back in handcuffs to the bishop. As a repeat offender, this theft will bring him life imprisonment without hope of parole. However, in an act of grace that defies imagination, Bishop Myriel tells the police that he had actually *given* the silverware to Valjean as a parting gift and that he is totally innocent. Valjean is shocked. The aged priest then puts his beloved candlesticks into the thief's bag — his last possessions of any value. To further convince the police, he even scolds Valjean for forgetting to take this important part of his intended "gift."

After sending the puzzled *gendarmes* on their way, the bishop tells Jean Valjean that he has used the silver to purchase his soul for God. As Valjean is leaving, he reminds the pardoned thief, "Don't forget that you promised me to use this silver to become an honest man."

No wonder Jean Valjean was stunned. He expected to get jail, but instead got freedom and a small fortune in silver. What the law required was judgment, but what the priest gave him was *grace* — a wonderful gift that he did not deserve or earn.

This gift of grace was life changing. After a brief misstep, a weeping Valjean returns to pray on Myriel's doorstep, vowing to become a righteous man. Adopting a new identity, he starts factories, becomes a mayor and brings prosperity to many. He saves a prostitute, protects his workers, adopts an orphan and constantly serves the poor. From that night on, the hardened criminal lives to help others and eventually sacrifices his own life to save a young man.

That is grace in action.

At the opposite end of the grace spectrum, a zealous policeman named Inspector Javert makes it his life's work to track down and recapture Valjean for a parole violation. Despite Valjean's obvious redemption and rehabilitation, Javert is obsessed with enforcing the letter of the law and ruining his new life. His inflexible sense of justice demands punishment without mercy. Unyielding and rigid, this self-appointed watchdog of the social order can neither forgive nor accept forgiveness.

Finally, after years of being pursued by Inspector Javert, a chance meeting allows ex-con Valjean to save his tormentor's life from an angry mob of revolutionaries. He pretends to march Javert away to execute him, then secretly releases him. But instead of thanking Valjean for his mercy, the humiliated policeman commits suicide.

That is legalism in action.

In the gentle bishop and in the reformed convict we see humble men pursuing unconditional love. In the police inspector, we see a self-righteous man pursuing moral perfection.

To his last breath, *Les Miserable* author Victor Hugo himself modeled grace. Before he died in 1885 at the age of 83, his final wishes were, "I leave 50,000 francs to the poor. I wish to be taken to the cemetery in the hearse customarily used for the poor ... I believe in God." Despite his wish for a pauper's ceremony, his body lay in state under the Arch of Triumph, guarded by horsemen with flaming torches. On the day of Hugo's burial, a million spectators followed his funeral cortege.

> **A million spectators followed Victor Hugo's funeral cortege.**

There's an old theological definition of grace that seems to drive the plot of this classic novel: *The mercy of God as distinguished from his justice, like a criminal pardoned by a judge.*

Hmmm. Pardoned by a judge. Sound familiar?

o   o   o

"Your worst days are never so bad that you are beyond the reach of God's grace. And your best days are never so good that you are beyond the need of God's grace."

— *Jerry Bridges*[1]

CHAPTER 3:
Déjà Vu All Over Again

"What goes around comes around."

It's more than a cliché — it's the guiding principle behind many world religions including Hinduism, Buddhism, Sikhism and the westernized hybrid called the New Age movement. Originating in ancient India, this concept of eternal cause and effect is known as *karma* and it's the functional worldview of billions.

Here's how it works: Everything we think, speak or do shapes our present and future experiences. The results — or fruits — of our thoughts, words and actions are called karma. Positive deeds result in a good karma, negative deeds result in a bad karma. The fruits of our karma may be seen immediately in this existence or delayed until our next life.

Racking up *good* karma points may mean rebirth into a higher station, such as a superior human or a godlike being. Accruing *bad* karma points could result in rebirth as an inferior human or a lower animal. I've been to India, and I've seen how belief in reincarnation allows wealthy "high caste" Hindus to conveniently justify their lack of compassion for poor "low caste" souls who've been recycled to live as orphans or beggars like in the Oscar-winning *Slumdog Millionaire*.

This endless cycle of birth, death, and rebirth inspired a cynic to write: "I know a guy who believes he's coming back after he dies. If he does enough good he'll come back as a higher life form. But if he blows it, he might come back as a rat or an insect and have to work his way back up the ladder. But what if he's a bad ant? What's lower than that? Does he come back as a bacteria?"

Duh, how about a politician?

Kidding aside, much of the world's population believes in this cosmic circle of life. In Disney's animated blockbuster *The Lion King*, the song "Circle of Life" extols the *"the wheel of fortune"* that *"keeps great and small on the endless round."* And why not? It's an attractive belief system. I've often attended funerals of friends or loved ones who didn't know Jesus and secretly wished they could somehow have another chance to come back and find God.

But that's a false hope. Scripture clearly declares we only go around once, *"Man is appointed to die once, and after that to face judgment."* [1]

The heavenly harmonies of folk-rock legends Crosby, Stills, Nash & Young burned the lyrics of their song "Déjà Vu" into my brain, *"We have all been here before."* But despite the constant tugging of pop culture to embrace eastern mysticism, most Christians still firmly reject the idea of reincarnation.

Unfortunately, we *don't* reject the idea of karma.

We talk like Christians but live like Hindus.

You could say, we talk like Christians but live like Hindus. When I'm on a spiritual roll, I pat myself on the back. I think that because I've helped somebody or went on a mission trip or donated money, I've created enough "good karma" to *win* God's acceptance. Other times I kick myself in the pants, thinking that because I've cussed or lost my temper or watched an R movie, I've created enough "bad karma" to *lose* God's acceptance.

In his hit single "Instant Karma," John Lennon sang, *"Instant karma's gonna get you. Gonna knock you right on the head."* And that's how I view my life. On the bubble. At risk. Trying to avoid the knock on the head by staying on God's good side.

But the truth is, God's love and acceptance of me is nonstop, unconditional, and totally independent of my actions, good or bad.

What the what?

Let me explain. When my kids disappoint me, I don't stop loving them. And I sure don't stop being their father. Likewise (and more so!) nothing we can do will make God love us any less or stop him from being our heavenly Father.

But what about "a man reaps what he sows?" [2]

That is true in the physical world, but not always in the spiritual. If I drink too much, I'll get drunk. If I drive off a cliff, I'll die. While we are on this earth there will be physical consequences for physical actions. That's Newton's third law of motion. But God's grace transcends physics and our short life on earth. His forgiveness erases the eternal consequences of our actions. A man may go to jail for robbing a bank. That punishment is society's justice. But if he repents and trusts God, he is forgiven. The eternal consequences of being a bank robber are gone, but the temporary consequences remain. He will *reap* 20 years in prison for *sowing* a crime, but not in eternity — or some future life on earth.

That's grace. And it's the polar opposite of karma.

The person who helped me understand this best wasn't a theologian or a scholar, but a rock & roll superstar from Dublin, Ireland.

In his remarkable book, *Bono in Conversation*, author Michka Assayas asks the pop singer if he doesn't think "appalling things" occur when people become religious. Bono answers, "It's a mind-blowing concept that the God who created the universe might be looking for company, a relationship with people, but the thing that keeps me on my knees is the difference between grace and karma." [3]

The rock journalist asked him to explain. "At the center of all religions is the idea of karma. You know, what you put

It's mind-blowing that the God who created the universe wants a relationship with people.

out comes back to you: an eye for an eye, a tooth for a tooth, or in physics — in physical laws — every action is met by an equal or opposite one. And yet, along comes this idea called grace to upend all that ... Love interrupts the consequences of your actions, which in my case is very good news indeed, because I've done a lot of stupid stuff."

Knowing Bono's wild history, Assayas presses him for details. "That's between me and God. But I'd be in big trouble if karma was going to finally be my judge. It doesn't excuse my mistakes, but I'm holding out for grace. I'm holding out that Jesus took my sins onto the cross. I don't have to depend on my own religiosity."

When the interviewer balks, Bono clarifies, "The point of the death of Christ is that Christ took on the sins of the world, so that what we put out did not come back on us, and that our sinful nature does not reap the obvious death. It's not our own good works that get us through the gates of heaven."

Bono is known for peppering his music with cryptic hints of spiritual wisdom. And musicologists say the last song on any U2 album is carefully chosen for those seeking a glimpse of God. On *How to Dismantle an Atomic Bomb*, it's "Yahweh." On *No Line on the Horizon*, it's "Cedars of Lebanon." On *All That You Can't Leave Behind*, it's a haunting ballad called "Grace." In it, Bono suggests that God's grace comes into this dying world and transforms it: *"She takes the blame, she covers the shame, removes the stain ... Grace finds goodness in everything ... Grace finds beauty in everything ... Grace makes beauty out of ugly things."*[4]

This album alone has sold a staggering 12 million copies. And besides containing a startlingly good definition of grace, it has a subliminal message. A hidden clue to what Bono calls "God's phone number."

Here's the secret: The cover is a photograph of the band standing in the Charles de Gaulle Airport in Paris. In the background, a departure sign clearly reads "J33-3" — a sly reference to Jeremiah 33:3, *"Call to Me, and I will answer you, and show you great and mighty things which you do not know."*[5]

Right. Mighty things like *grace*.

○　　○　　○

"Grace isn't a little prayer you chant before a meal. It's a way to live. The law tells me how crooked I am. Grace comes along and straightens me out."

— Dwight L. Moody[6]

1: AMAZING GRACE

CHAPTER 4:
Living in Graceland

"The beauty of grace is that it makes life not fair."

That puzzling lyric from "Be My Escape" by the rock band Relient K has angered some, pleased others and confused just about everyone who's heard it. After all, how could anything as kind and loving as grace be unfair?

Because God's unconditional mercy is so, uh, *unconditional*, that it ticks us off, that's why.

I mean, how is it fair that good people (think Mother Teresa) and bad people (think Charles Manson) could both wind up in paradise — regardless of their conduct on earth? Sometimes when I can't sleep, I dream up extreme hypothetical cases. Cases of dudes so bad to the bone that they would stretch God's grace to the limit. Except then I remember God's grace *has* no limit.

And that's what ticks me off.

Okay, I know that John 3:16 says *"For God so loved the world that whoever believes in him shall not perish but have everlasting life."* But God, that must be a typo, how could that pesky "whoever" clause possibly include really, really, bad people like...

Adolf Hitler — His Nazi death squads systematically killed up to 14 million innocent civilians, including 6 million Jews in concentration camps. Then, as Berlin was being invaded by

> **How can Mother Teresa and Charles Manson both wind up in paradise?**

the victorious Allies, Hitler and his wife, Eva Braun, committed suicide in the secret underground *Führerbunker*. Eva took cyanide; Adolf shot himself through the right temple. But what if instead of grabbing a Luger pistol, Hitler grabbed a Bible and asked God for mercy?

Joseph Stalin — The greatest mass murderer to ever live was responsible for 40 to 60 million deaths. In one day, the cranky leader assassinated 100 members of his own parliament. Killings reached their peak in the Great Purge of 1937, when 700,000 Russians were executed. Millions more died of starvation in Stalin's network of labor camps that stretched across 12 time zones. But what if he accepted Christ and became a believer during the last week of his life in 1953?

Pol Pot — Portrayed in the movie *The Killing Fields*, this Marxist leader killed one in five of his own countrymen. From 1975 to 1979, his Khmer Rouge soldiers murdered 1.7 million Cambodians, or 21 percent of the population. Never captured, Pot died peacefully in his sleep in a jungle hideout. To the end he showed no regret, saying only "My conscience is clear." But what if instead of denying his genocide, he had repented of his sins before God?

And what about China's Mao Tse-Tung, killer of at least 50 million? Or Saddam Hussein? Could God's grace be sufficient for them?

Closer to home, what about criminals like Jeffrey Dahmer? This American serial killer committed his first murder at age 18. He went on to torture and kill 16 more men and boys. His shenanigans were particularly gruesome, involving dismemberment, necrophilia and cannibalism. In 1994, Dahmer was savagely beaten to death by a fellow inmate in prison.

You probably knew about his repulsive crime spree. But did you know he became a Christian before he died?

Before his own untimely demise, Dahmer heard the gospel and was baptized in a whirlpool tub by a Wisconsin minister named Ray Ratcliff. In his book, *Dark Journey, Deep Grace: Jeffrey Dahmer's Story of Faith*, Ratcliff tells how he came in contact with the infamous killer and shared the saving message of Christ.

After murdering 17 people, serial killer Jeffrey Dahmer accepted Christ in prison.

Those of us who believe the New Testament agree that God's grace is available to any person — no matter how bad he has been — if the person accepts Jesus as his Savior. Or *do* we? Plenty of Christians choke on the idea that anyone as evil as Dahmer could enter heaven.

Ratcliff concurs, "One of the most common questions put to me about Jeff has to do with the sincerity of his faith. And I usually hear this from Christians."

The question irritates Ratcliff. "Jeff was judged not by his faith, but by his crimes. The questioner always seemed to hope I'd answer: 'No, he wasn't sincere.' The questioner seemed to be looking for a way to reject Jeffrey as a brother in Christ instead of seeing him as a sinner who has come to God. Such ungraciousness is contrary to the Christian spirit."

Ratcliff responds to those who don't want Dahmer as a heavenly roommate: "Was Jeff saved? Were his sins taken away? Is he a Christian believer? Did he repent of his sins? Or was the blood of Christ shed on the cross somehow too weak, too thin, too anemic to cover his sins?"[1]

And that is the ultimate question: Can God's free offer of salvation apply to the monsters of history? And if it does, how can that be fair to the rest of us who never hurt a fly?

Here's the answer: Christianity teaches that our salvation is not based on our work on the earth, but on God's work on the cross. The Apostle Paul explains, *"For it is by grace that you have been saved, through faith — and this is not from yourselves, it is the gift of God — not by works, so that no one can boast."*[2]

This "grace" is the central bedrock truth of the gospel —

that faith in Christ is the only means of being made right with God. No amount of human effort or good deeds can contribute anything toward our salvation. And since it's an absolutely free gift from God, none of us can take any credit for it!

Virtually all Christians embrace this half of the equation. But they do not always accept the other half — *If no amount of good deeds can get you into heaven, then no amount of bad deeds can keep you out of heaven.*

God is not Santa Claus, checking to see if you've been naughty or nice.

God is not Santa Claus, checking to see if you've been naughty or nice. He is not a cosmic bookkeeper adding up your good deeds on one side of a scale versus your bad deeds on the other. Whether you've lived as a saintly grandma or a sleazy crook, your only route into heaven is by putting your faith in Jesus Christ. And whether that happens at a young age (like Billy Graham) or on your last day on earth (like the thief on the cross), God's offer of complete forgiveness stands.

Think back to *Les Miserable* in chapter 2. No one can qualify for salvation by *keeping* the law (like Inspector Javert) and no one can be disqualified from salvation by *breaking* the law (like ex-con Jean Valjean). It all boils down to "Did you or did you not accept God's free offer of salvation?" Even if we can't fully understand this apparent inequity, God's grace is available equally to every man and woman, *"For the grace of God that brings salvation has appeared to all men."*[3]

Notice that God's grace has been extended to "all men." Saints and sinners. Cops and criminals. Everyone. So how come everyone's not a believer? We can't blame God; after all, the whole purpose of Jesus coming to earth was to *"seek and to save what was lost."*[4]

Okay, if it's not God's fault, what's the problem?

We are.

Each man has a free will to choose or reject God's too-good-to-be-true free offer. Unfortunately, the trouble with free offers is that sometimes we're too proud to accept them. Especially when it comes to salvation. We'd rather work for it. As humans, we pride ourselves on being self-sufficient, self-reliant, self-motivated, self-disciplined — do you see a trend here? So it's a matter of swallowing our pride and admitting we need help. And not everyone's ready to do that.

Whenever and wherever somebody asks for help, God listens. And whether those cries of repentance come from a jail cell on death row or a church pew on Easter Sunday, he responds exactly the same way — with *unlimited, unmerited, unconditional favor.*

The kind of unmerited favor that includes dictators and drug dealers and dorks. If that seems unfair, consider this: If God were fair, we'd *all* be punished — Sunday School teachers and vicious criminals alike — because we've all *"sinned and fallen short of the glory of God..."* [5]

God's unmerited favor includes dictators and drug dealers and dorks.

That's the bad news.

But the good news is found in the very next phrase *"...and are justified freely by his grace through redemption that came by Christ Jesus."* [6]

Whoa. Time out. We just saw that God wants everybody everywhere to accept his free offer and be justified and know him and enjoy his abundant life. Here's my question: *If everybody everywhere is welcome to the Biggest Party of all time, why aren't people busting down our church doors to get in on it?*

Because we turn people off.

Think about it. Jesus loved people. And people loved him. Drawn by his compassion, multitudes followed him from town to town as he ministered to widows, orphans and oppressed workers. At every level of society he was known for helping the poor, feeding the hungry and healing the sick. He reached across the racial, religious and gender barriers of his time to the marginalized people of his day — lepers, tax collectors, prostitutes, outcasts of every description. He was approachable, gracious and kind.

Today, his followers are perceived as being *just the opposite*.

Big chunks of modern society think Christians are hateful, judgmental and bigoted. Instead of being warm and welcoming, we're seen as cold and snobby — out of touch party-poopers who live isolated lives behind church walls. Our role model isn't the joyful Jesus who turned water into wine, but the uptight "church lady" from SNL who squelches fun and wouldn't know joy if it hit her in the face.

Big chunks of modern society think Christians are hateful, judgmental and bigoted.

Don't believe it? In his book called *unChristian*, author David Kinnaman found today's Christ-followers don't represent their founder, and often do more harm than good for his cause. According to research by the Barna Group, Christians are best known for the hot-button issues they stand *against*, instead of the blessed hope they stand *for*. After interviewing thousands of young adults, they found that most un-churched (or de-churched) people now perceive Christians as "hypocritical," "insensitive," "overly political" and "judgmental."[7]

And I have to agree with them. We can be pretty obnoxious.

○   ○   ○

What is it about religious people that draws them to self-righteousness? Why is it the closer we move to God, the more pious and pig-headed we can become? Shouldn't the opposite be true? Shouldn't we become more loving and forgiving and accepting? Of all people, we should be known for opening our arms, not looking down our noses.

Author Ken Yancey talks about inviting a prostitute to church. Her response was, "Church! Why should I go there? I'm already feeling terrible about myself. They'd just make me feel worse." Ouch. The rejection she anticipated is what Yancey calls "un-grace."

If we want our hearts to be like God's heart, we need only to examine the life of Jesus: *"Anyone who has seen me has seen the Father."*[8]

And what do we see — a harsh judge? Or a merciful servant? In case after case, Jesus refused to judge, even though the Father had given him complete authority to do so. Instead of scolding people, he offered grace and redemption. In fact, the only time we see Jesus angry at anyone is when he lashes out against self-righteous religious leaders. He considered judgmental hypocrites to be the greatest threat to his Father's plan of love and forgiveness.

They still are.

○   ○   ○

Until he returns to close out history, Jesus has commanded us to proclaim his kingdom and share the good news with everyone we meet. Not only to the ones we deem worthy or think would make good neighbors in heaven, but to *everyone.* Our job is not to act like "bouncers" at the Pearly Gates, screening out the undesirables. Our job is to extend grace — *the unmerited favor of God* — to the flawed and broken people we meet.

God is in the business of restoration, and no one is beyond the redeeming power of his grace. Even if *we* think they're too messed up to salvage.

Here's what I mean: It's estimated the song "Amazing Grace" is performed 10 million times a year. Published in 1779, it may be the most recognizable song in the English language. It's been recorded at least 12,000 times. No other hymn in history has been recorded by so many stars, including Johnny Cash,

Aretha Franklin, Rod Stewart, Willie Nelson and Elvis Presley. Mahalia Jackson sang it in Carnegie Hall. Arlo Guthrie sang it at Woodstock. And a version played on bagpipes became the best selling instrumental ever. It has inspired and comforted generations. But the hymn's author, John Newton, was not an angelic saint living in an ivory tower.

The writer of "Amazing Grace" was the hard-drinking captain of a slave ship.

He was the hard-drinking hell-raising captain of a slave ship.

In fact, Newton wrote "Amazing Grace" while docked in an African harbor waiting for a fresh shipment of human cargo.

On Newton's ship, the prized payload was 600 slaves, laid out side-by-side and chained to each other in holding pens just 24-inches high. They wore neck collars, handcuffs and leg irons. Half of them died from disease, malnutrition and the unbearable heat below decks. There were no toilets and no ventilation during the long voyage from Africa to the Caribbean plantations. The stench onboard was so bad that ships downwind of a slaver could smell it for miles. Each morning, corpses were tossed overboard, and sharks followed the floating prisons across the Atlantic. Beatings and brutality were common, and to keep the underpaid sailors from rebelling, Newton allowed his crew to rape the slaves at will — after he had enjoyed his pick of the helpless women.

During a near-fatal storm, Newton cried out to God and he became a believer some years later. He soon quit the slave trade and spoke of its evil as "a business at which my heart now shudders."

But renouncing his profession was only the beginning.

He became a prominent minister and the primary mentor of a young Member of Parliament named William Wilberforce. When the youth came to Newton for guidance, he encouraged the rookie to stay in politics and "serve God where he was."

Over the years, Newton lost his eyesight, but the blind preacher continued to write sermons and hymns that changed England's spiritual climate. Ironically, his most profound influence on history was his opposition to the slave trade, a cause he transferred to his protégé. Inspired by Newton's passion, Wilberforce worked his entire life to abolish the moral blight of slavery. His Slave Trade Act of 1807 abolished the slave trade in the British Empire and led to the Slavery Abolition Act of 1833.

God rescued the kind of man I would have condemned.

All because God rescued the kind of man I would have condemned.

○   ○   ○

"Amazing grace! How sweet the sound that saved a wretch like me. I once was lost but now am found, was blind but now I see."

— John Newton[9]

I: AMAZING GRACE

CHAPTER 5:
Huey Lewis Got It Right

Ever wished you had a time machine?

Since I was a boy I've dreamed about going back in time to witness historical events. Imagine watching Jesus give the Sermon on the Mount or Lincoln deliver the Gettysburg Address. Or how about zipping ahead to the future? I would love to pick up the cure for cancer and bring it back. As an investor, I'd be tempted to see where the Dow Jones is headed, but that's another story. Anyway, my fascination with time travel made *Back to the Future* a special treat.

This comedy classic is the story of teenager Marty McFly (Michael J. Fox), who is accidentally sent back to 1955. He meets his future parents in high school where (gulp!) his own mom falls in love with him, and if that's not a creepy thought, I don't know what is. Much of the movie (and its two sequels) is a blur, but I'll never forget the amazing song "The Power of Love" by Huey Lewis. Ironically, this megahit was the last song added to the movie's soundtrack — finished just two days before the final mix of the film.

You may not remember that Doc Brown's plutonium-powered DeLorean had to hit 88 mph to generate the 1.21 gigawatts of power required for time travel, but I bet you do remember the lyrics to Lewis' song: *"It don't take money and it don't take fame, don't need no credit card to ride this train. Tougher than diamonds and stronger than steel, you won't feel nothin' till you feel the power of love."*

My fellow movie lovers, God's grace (not a flux capacitor) is the real power of love. And as the Reverend Huey sang, this power can *"Make a bad one good and a wrong one right."*

Unfortunately, many well-meaning religious people focus on the power of *judgment* instead of *love*. They preach an angry gospel that stresses repentance instead of grace. Their fiery message is basically "Stop sinning! Follow the rules! Repent or burn!" To paraphrase *The Godfather*, they're making an offer you *can* refuse. And it's kept people away in droves.

Their fiery message is "Stop sinning! Repent or burn!"

So is it wrong to teach repentance?

No, but you can't put the cart before the horse. Repenting means "turning away from sin," and it should be the natural, inevitable outcome of following Christ. Repentance is a divine work that begins *after* we understand the love relationship that's available with Jesus. You can't turn away from sin with human effort alone. Will power and good intentions are not enough. You can only change on the outside (behavior) by the grace that God gives you on the inside (transformation).

That's the power of love.

o   o   o

In the Greek language of the first-century writers, there are four separate, distinct words translated as "love." Three of them describe an emotional, romantic, or sensual attachment. But the fourth is used exclusively to express the "God kind of love" as described in the New Testament. This unique word *agape* means the "divine, unconditional, self-sacrificing love" that is the fundamental characteristic of grace.

The early church used *agape* to not only describe the love of God for mankind, but — and this is super important — the love of Christians for each other. This kind of selfless love is so amazing, so unexpected that the word sometimes means "to stand with your mouth wide open as in wonder or awe."

And that's what the world does when it sees grace in action.

In his book, *Repenting of Religion*, Greg Boyd writes that *agape* love is the "act of unconditionally ascribing unsurpassable worth to another at a cost to oneself."[1] Simply put, it's thinking about others more than ourselves. And to make sure we don't miss the point, God gives us a word picture, *"This is how we know what love is: Jesus Christ laid down his life for us. And we ought to lay down our lives for our brothers."*[2]

> **Unconditional love is the fundamental characteristic of grace.**

As I said earlier, raising kids is a crash course in the power of love. If you're like me, you may have tried bullying or "guilting" your child into obedience. Instilling fear or using force can produce temporary behavior change, but it will come at a high cost. Side-effects may surface as rebelliousness in the teen years or show up in college as wild behavior. But try love and forgiveness instead and you'll see a more positive transformation. Love is a slower process than fear, but it carries long-term rewards — a productive, well-adjusted life.

In the great debates over fear versus love, politicians often quote Machiavelli's *The Prince,* published in 1532. When asked whether it is better to be loved than feared, the author wrote, "It would be best to be both loved and feared. But anyone compelled to choose will find greater security in being feared than in being loved."

Plenty of governments and parents have tried to lead according to this Machiavellian model (think Mussolini, Darth Vader). Trouble is, commitments made in fear are only kept by fear. Sooner or later, ruling over anyone (soldiers, nations, spouses or children) by fear is doomed to fail. As soon as those being ruled get the opportunity, they will escape or overthrow the one in power.

Fear results in resistance, subversion and stubbornness.
Love results in compliance, loyalty and willingness.

○   ○   ○

In a famous story from John's gospel, Jesus is put in a tricky situation by religious leaders who want a basis for accusing him. To test him, they drag in a disheveled woman caught in the act of adultery. They remind Jesus that Jewish law demands she be stoned to death. The woman is guilty. She knows it. Jesus knows it. The crowd knows it. If Jesus says "Stone her" he will be in conflict with Roman law. If he says "Release her" he will be in conflict with Mosaic law.

The trap was set. The Pharisees were licking their lips. But Jesus refused to take the bait. He knew that grace was more powerful than any law.

> **The woman is guilty. She knows it. Jesus knows it. The crowd knows it.**

The religious leaders were outraged by the woman's behavior. Jesus was outraged by their lack of compassion. When they demanded he judge her, he demanded they judge themselves instead. In a pronouncement that still echoes through the centuries, Jesus told the self-righteous accusers: *"If any of you is without sin, let him be the first to throw a stone at her."*

Hearing this, the men dropped their stones and slipped away, one at a time, until only Jesus and the woman were left. *"Woman, where are they? Has no one condemned you?"*

She replied, *"No one, sir."*

"Then neither do I condemn you," Jesus declared. *"Go now and leave your life of sin."*[3]

The power of love is transformational. When Jesus spoke to the woman, he placed a high value on her life by showing compassion and respect. He didn't lecture her, shame her, or point out her long history of sexual immorality. Only after he affirmed her worth as a person did he go on to deal with her behavior, *"Go and sin no more."*

Jesus could have reacted with judgment and condemnation. Instead, he showed grace — *the unmerited favor of God* — to this flawed and broken woman. Instead of judging her, he restored her dignity and self-worth.

Incidentally, he offered the *same* forgiveness to the religious leaders. But they didn't receive it. They knew they were sinners. That's why they dropped their stones. But apparently the lesson didn't sink in. They came back more self-righteous and more determined than ever to stop Jesus. On the other hand, the fallen woman understood the lesson fully and became one of Christ's most devoted followers.

That is grace in action.

But what about her sinful behavior? Did she get off Scot free?

To set the record straight, Jesus reminded the crowd (and us) that we're *all* guilty of sin — not just the adulterer, but her male partner (it takes two to tango), her neighbors and her accusers. Everyone is guilty of something. And everyone is in need of forgiveness. When Jesus stooped to write in the dusty ground that day, some speculate he was writing the Ten Commandments. By the time he got to number ten, no human could honestly say he hadn't broken one of them.

> **Sin is sin. It's not a question of degree; it's a question of forgiveness.**

Some had disobeyed a few. Others had broken them all. But in the light of God's holiness, sin is sin. It's not a question of degree; it's a question of forgiveness.

Now imagine the same story if Jesus had publically condemned her behavior. The mob would have pulverized her with a hail of rocks. And if she somehow survived the public humiliation, she might have taken her own life out of guilt.

So if the power of love is able to transform lives, why do we quickly forget about it and turn to *judgment* instead?

There are three reasons:

1. We judge because we don't fully understand grace. (Don't feel too bad, the concept is virtually inconceivable from the human perspective.)

2. We judge because our parents judged. And *their* parents judged. And their parent's parents judged. All the way back to the Garden. Satan promised Eve and her hunky husband that eating the forbidden fruit would give them God's ability to judge right and wrong: *"When you eat of it, your eyes will be opened, and you will be like God, knowing good and evil."*

When Adam and Eve bit the apple, they felt guilt and fear for the first time. They immediately hid from God and then lied to cover up their sin. They blamed each other, the serpent, and their rotten childhood. Instead of showing grace to his wife, Adam judged her on the spot: *"The woman you put here with me — she gave me some fruit from the tree, and I ate it."* [4]

As soon as they knew the difference between right and wrong, they began to judge each other — in essence, doing God's job — and we've been doing it ever since.

3. We judge because we're afraid. Grace is a very threatening concept. Especially to religious leaders. To them, preaching "salvation by grace" seems like giving people license to sin. They're afraid people will take advantage of God's mercy — that they'll "sin today knowing they can ask forgiveness tomorrow." But that would be a very dangerous game. Toying with sin is flirting with disaster. It's been said, you can pick your sin, but you can't pick your consequences. *"Do not be deceived: God cannot be mocked."* [5]

Adam and Eve blamed each other, the serpent, and their rotten childhood.

If we're sincere Christians, we won't deliberately live in a way that's repugnant to God. We may have temporary lapses (nobody's perfect), but we do not sin brazenly or habitually. And we sure won't use pop culture as our barometer of behavior. Author Jerry Bridges says, "God has not called us to be like those around us. He has called us to be like himself. Holiness is nothing less than conformity to the character of God." That echoes Paul's take on the Jesus life: *"If anyone is in Christ, he is a new creation; the old has gone, the new has come!"* [6]

If we're sincere Christians, our goal is not to see how much we can get away with and still sneak into heaven, but to see how much we can please God. When you love someone, you don't take advantage of them, you willingly and enthusiastically serve them! How could anyone who *truly understands* the awful price Jesus paid to save them throw it back in his face?

The answer is: They can't.

But the key phrase is "truly understands."

Unfortunately, there are millions of nominal, cultural Christians who *don't* understand. To them, Christianity is a social club, a Sunday diversion. These are the kind of lukewarm churchgoers who supported Hitler back in pre-war Germany. In league with the Nazis, their state-sponsored churches chose safety and security over faithfulness to God. They even agreed to remove the Old Testament from the Bible to please the anti-Semites.

Our goal is not to sneak into heaven.

The thorn in their side was a fiery pastor named Dietrich Bonhoeffer, who dubbed their shallowness "cheap grace." According to Bonhoeffer, cheap grace is the failure of a church or individual to take seriously the depth of human sinfulness — and what it cost God to redeem us.

In his 1937 book *The Cost of Discipleship*, Bonhoeffer writes, "Cheap grace is the preaching of forgiveness without requiring repentance ... grace without discipleship, grace without the cross, grace without Jesus Christ." He contrasts it to costly grace, "It is costly because it condemns sin, and grace because it justifies the sinner ... What has cost God much cannot be cheap for us."[7]

Grace is free, but it is never cheap. Bonheoffer proved it. He was executed by the *Gestapo* for refusing to refute his faith. Before being arrested he wrote, "When Christ calls a man, he bids him to come and die."

So the fear of "too much grace" is unfounded, and honestly, a little far-fetched. If a person *does* use grace as a permission slip to keep on sinning, it's likely they never knew God in the first place: *"No one who lives in him keeps on sinning. No one who continues to sin has either seen him or known him."*[8]

Grace is free, but it is never cheap.

Ouch. That is not the most popular verse in the Bible. It may sound harsh, but I can't water it down. Genuine believers are tempted just like everyone else. And in a moment of weakness we may give in — temporarily — to sin. But we will not *continue* sinning without remorse. If somebody casually and continually practices sin, their conversion is in doubt. *"No one who is born of God will continue to sin ... This is how we know who the children of God are and who the children of the devil are: Anyone who does not do what is right is not a child of God."*[9]

Double ouch. Before reading further, ask yourself: Am I consciously struggling against my sin (addictions, porn, anger, gossip, greed) or just plain enjoying it? Am I repenting and asking God for help in my area of weakness (we all have one) or am I ignoring (or compartmentalizing) him so I can continue indulging?

Religious leaders were afraid of grace back in Paul's day, too. They thought it would cause formerly God-fearing people to stampede to the camel races and belly-dancing clubs. When they warned Paul that his message of grace was promoting sin, he responded, *"Shall we go on sinning so that grace may increase? By no means! We died to sin; how can we live in it any longer?"*[10]

Here's the bottom line: One day, all believers will stand before Almighty God face-to-face and discuss what they've done (or not done) in service to Christ. This "believer's judgment" described in Romans 14 does not determine salvation — that's already settled *"by grace through faith alone."* But make no mistake, *"Each of us will give an account of himself to God."* [11]

If you're still worried about cheap grace, or "easy believism," or people taking advantage of God's free offer, chill out. Nobody's getting off the hook. On that unavoidable day, God will judge the motives of every heart. But until then, remember this — judging is *his* job, not ours.

> Am I consciously struggling against my sin or just plain enjoying it?

o   o   o

When Christians are afraid of emphasizing grace, the pendulum swings to the other side and they emphasize works. These "legalists" readily acknowledge it was God's free gift that *purchased* their salvation, but they don't realize it's the same free gift that *maintains* their salvation! They think that keeping their ticket to heaven depends on good works. So they concentrate on following their own weird interpretation of God's rules (no dancing, no card playing, no movies, whatever).

Paul dealt with this "grace plus works" debate in his day, *"Here it is in a nutshell: Just as one person (Adam) did it wrong and got us in all this trouble with sin and death, another person (Jesus) did it right and got us out of it ... All that passing laws against sin did was produce more law breakers."* [12]

In other words, righteousness — a right relationship with God — does not come from keeping laws or anything else we do. Not from memorizing the Bible or praying seven times a day or fasting once a week. Nothing we can do can make us right with God. Not wearing a cross, not making donations, not joining a church.

Every other world religion says "do." Only Christianity says "done." The work of salvation has *already been done* for us through

Every world religion says "do." Only Christianity says "done."

the obedience of Jesus going to the cross and making us right with his Father, once and for all.

So if following rules can't earn my salvation, does anything go? Is every behavior and lifestyle choice okay?

No way, Mr. Loophole. When we fully understand how amazing God's gift is to us, we're automatically compelled to live differently — out of gratitude! Nobody beating us over the head with a Bible will make us change. Nobody shoving rules down our throats will make us change. Nobody screaming about eternal damnation will make us change. Only God's grace will motivate us to make the behavior adjustments he wants us to make.

Then why *does* God want us to change our lifestyle? To GET saved? Nope, we're already saved by grace. To STAY saved? Nope, we're locked in by grace.

I think there are two big fat reasons he wants us to change.

Number one is so we can experience a full life of abundance and significance: *"I have come so they can have life and have it to the full."* One translation reads *"a better life than they ever dreamed of."* [13] Foolish behavior or an ungodly lifestyle can ruin our health and happiness, preventing us from enjoying God's best. Somebody said, "God loves you just the way you are, but too much to leave you that way."

Number two is so we can effectively tell others about the Jesus life. Contradictions in our lifestyle can be a fatal distraction to nonbelievers. People who don't know God can (and will) use any inconsistent behavior in us as an excuse to reject the message of salvation: *"Be careful that the exercise of your freedom does not become a stumbling block to the weak."* [14]

This positive change in our behavior is called "sanctification" and it happens *after* "salvation." It's important we don't confuse the two words. Salvation occurs the moment we place our faith in

Jesus Christ and his sacrifice on the cross. It's instantaneous. But sanctification is a gradual, on-going process. Salvation does not involve human effort. Sanctification does. Salvation is positional. Sanctification is experiential. You could say sanctification is "a born-again believer partnering with God to become a godlier person."

Unlike salvation (a free gift we can't work for), we are actively involved in our own sanctification. We are told to "put on" this new way of life — by submitting to God's will, resisting sin, seeking holiness and trying to be more like Jesus: *"Be made new in the attitude of your minds ... put on the new self, created to be like God in true righteousness and holiness."* [15]

If all that seems complicated, think back to *Saturday Night Live*. Remember how Dana Carvey imitated George Bush? He copied him so well that the former president openly complimented the impressionist. That's what we should do: *"Be imitators of God."* [16] Another translation says, *"Watch what God does, then do it."*

> **Salvation doesn't involve human effort. Sanctification does.**

Make like Dana, and you're practicing sanctification.

○   ○   ○

In the prologue, we looked at the ancient super-commandment — the *Shema* — first uttered by Moses as the Israelites paused on the Sinai threshold to the Promised Land. [17]

For ages, orthodox Jews have regarded it as their most sacred verse. Some have embraced it with the kind of passion I can only wish I had. In 2006, an Israeli soldier named Roi Klein took it to the extreme. A major in the Golani Brigade of the Israeli Defense Forces, Klein was killed during the Lebanon War.

During a raging battle, a hand grenade was thrown into the house where Klein and his unit were positioned. Klein jumped on the live grenade and blocked the horrific explosion with his body. He was killed instantly but his soldiers were saved by his act of self-sacrifice. Here's the kicker: The soldiers reported that Klein was reciting the *Shema* (loving God) as he jumped on the grenade (loving others). Overnight, Roi Klein became a symbol for heroism in Israel.

And an example of grace in action.

○   ○   ○

"When the power of love overcomes the love of power, the world will know peace."

— Jimi Hendrix[18]

II: GRACE IS NOT...

II : GRACE IS NOT...

CHAPTER 6:
Grace Is Not Judgment

Did you know that Gatorade was named for the University of Florida Gators? Or that Florida flamingos get their pink color from the shrimp they eat?

Here's another fun fact: About half of all Florida residents arc Michigan transplants who hung up their snow shovels and headed south. So when our Detroit-based church decided to plant a campus in the Sunshine State, lots of members felt the tug of God drawing them to warmer climes. But after the initial rush of volunteers, we still needed additional helpers to move down and launch the new ministry. Then our creative team devised a new recruiting strategy — handing out plastic snow scrapers with the imprint "Suffering for Jesus in Orlando."

It worked like a charm.

In one short phrase, the clear alternatives were presented: *Motown or Mickeytown? Frostbite or suntan? Parkas or swimsuits?* Kidding aside, it's hard to imagine two cites (and climates) more different than Detroit and Orlando.

From sandy beaches to snowy mountains, God intentionally designed a world full of contrasts. Night and day. Oceans and deserts. And sometimes the best way to understand something is to study its opposite. So maybe the best way to understand what grace IS could be by looking at what it IS NOT.

For instance, God's grace is *not* something you earn. It's *not* conditional. It's *not* temporary. It's *not* an excuse to sin. It's *not* the little prayer you say at mealtime.

And it is absolutely, positively *not* judgmental.

In fact, grace and judgment are polar opposites. It's the perfect, holy nature of God to show grace; it's the fallen, sinful nature of humans to judge.

Is it always wrong to judge?

Depends on who's doing the judging and why.

> **Grace and judgment are polar opposites.**

We're all familiar with the judging in a courtroom. It determines the outcome of legal cases. And we're familiar with judging on a sports field. It determines the winner of a contest. But what about the judging that happens in our hearts? That's the ugly kind that makes evaluations as to *"worth, quality or fitness."*

When we judge somebody, we are actually saying they're not *worth* much, they're of poor *quality*, and maybe they're not even *fit* to live.

Brrrr — that's cold.

This kind of judging can happen anywhere. Spontaneously. Ever sit in a shopping center or an airport and watch people? It's one of my favorite hobbies. Only I don't just watch them, I judge them: *Fatso doesn't need a Cinnabon, he needs a salad ... Looks like this slacker's got a big hangover ... Nice lapels on that suit, pal. Welcome to the Eighties.*

Try it sometime and see if your mind doesn't wander to judgment: *Her dress is too tight because she's trying to look sexy ... He needs all those tattoos because he has low self esteem ... She wears Prada because she's a self-absorbed snob.*

Without really trying, my mind generates an endless string of negative opinions. It's easy to judge strangers in a shopping mall or waiting room because I'm not a part of their lives and I know nothing about their story. But God does, and his heart aches for every person I see. They are all created in his divine image, and their immortal soul will live on for eternity in heaven or hell, just like mine. A man who sensed this profundity was C. S. Lewis, author of *The Chronicles of Narnia*. He wrote, "There are no ordinary people. You have never talked to a mere mortal."

Why do we snub and insult God's magnificent, immortal children? Maybe we make harsh judgments about others to feel better about ourselves. Or maybe we do it because there's something in us that's far crueler than we care to admit.

> **Maybe we judge others to feel better about ourselves.**

Either way, it's in our nature to take cheap shots when we're at a safe distance. I learned that lesson when our church video team used a telephoto lens to film random people from a block away. As I viewed it, I began to make my typical snap judgments: *Too heavy, too old, too poor, whatever.*

Then the camera zoomed in. When I saw the same strangers close-up, I felt entirely different. Tenderness and empathy replaced my initial hard-edged appraisals. Distant figures became intimate portraits; faces that spoke volumes, eyes full of hope and smiles trying to mask the pain.

When we get closer, we begin to understand that we all have the same dreams, hurts and struggles. When we glimpse even part of somebody's story, we respond in a more God-like way, with mercy and compassion. Imagine if we knew their *whole* story — all the facts, all the evidence — like God. How different would our response be?

Unfortunately, today's society seems designed to keep us isolated from other people. We communicate online, live behind locked doors, travel in sound-insulated steel cocoons. Maybe it's this "safe distance" from other people — especially drivers — that lets me judge them so easily.

If you doubt that we're all trying out to be the next Judge Wapner or Judge Judy, think about your last time behind the wheel. Remember how terrible the other motorists were? Comedian

George Carlin said there are only two kinds of drivers on the road — jerks and idiots. Jerks drive too slow and idiots drive too fast. In my judgmental world, the only driver maintaining the ideal speed is me!

As a spiritual giant, I know I should turn the other cheek in traffic. But when a driver hesitates at a green light or cuts me off at a merge, I go ballistic. *How inconsiderate! How rude!* (My actual remarks are a bit more colorful and not fit for print.)

When I'm in a hurry, everyone else seems to be on Valium. So I ride the guy's bumper in front of me. But when someone tailgates *me*, I tap my brakes to teach him a lesson. If he refuses to back off, I slow to a crawl just to annoy him (Yup, I have this Christ-like thing mastered). Sometimes I wish Jesus drove the earth instead of walked it, so he'd have something to say about road rage. Well, okay, maybe he did: *"Anyone who is angry with their brother will be subject to judgment ... anyone who says, 'You fool!' will be in danger of the fire of hell."* [1]

I wish Jesus had something to say about road rage.

In our self-contained hunk of metal and glass, we're insulated from the other driver's world. We don't know their story, so we make one up — sometimes based on what they drive: *Gas-guzzling SUV doesn't care about the environment ... Wimpy hybrid is a tree-hugging wacko ... Rusty sedan is too lazy to get a job.*

Being in a car let's us make unfair, unfounded judgments from a safe distance.

My friend Craig Mayes is now the pastor of *Communitas* in New York City and has switched from automobiles to the MTA subway. But while living in Detroit, he had to rush his wife Chris to the hospital for the delivery of their first child. She went into labor quickly and seemed ready to give birth right in the backseat. It was 6:00 a.m. and he was racing through town like an adrenalin crazed father-to-be. Suddenly, he was blocked by a red light. The streets were deserted and there was only one other car waiting in front of Craig at the stoplight. Checking both ways, he pulled around the waiting Chevy, blew through the red light and hurried on his way. When the light turned green, the guy in the other car burned rubber to catch up. Speeding alongside, the offended driver began honking and cursing. Risking a crash, the furious driver flipped the bird at Craig, then swerved in front to block him.

If the angry Chevy had known *why* Craig ran the red light, he would have had a totally different response. Same for us when we pass judgment on other people. We never know what's going on "in their backseat." We never know the whole story. Only God does. The first-century Jewish philosopher, Philos of Alexandria, put it this way: "Be kind, for everyone you meet is fighting a great battle."

○　　○　　○

In our legal system, a judge is an impartial mediator, highly trained to render a fair and just verdict. He instructs the jury to convict only if there is evidence "beyond a reasonable doubt." Yet even with all the legal safeguards, mistakes do happen and innocent people are sometimes found guilty.

In 1992, the conviction of a man who had already served 11 years in prison for rape was overturned when the judge and jury were proved wrong by science. At age 34, Kerry Kotler was freed after a judge ruled that new DNA tests showed him innocent. Since then, DNA testing has freed hundreds of innocent prisoners who were wrongly accused — including dozens from death row.

Mistakes happen. Innocent people are sometimes found guilty.

Apparently, God is the only being in the universe who knows all the facts. Which is exactly why he tells us to leave the judging to *him*.

Jesus knows how easy it is for humans to judge and how it backfires on us. He warned: *"Do not judge, or you too will be judged. For in the same way you judge others, you will be judged, and with the measure you use, it will be measured to you."*[2]

Obviously, when earthly crimes are committed, earthly justice is required to maintain public safety. That's why we have police and prisons. But that is not the judging Jesus was talking about. He was zeroing in on our innate tendency to focus on the shortcomings — real or imaginary — of others. One translation says, *"Don't pick on people, jump on their failures, or criticize their faults — unless, of course, you want the same treatment."*[3]

Jesus goes on, *"Why do you look at the speck of sawdust in your brother's eye and pay no attention to the plank in your own eye? How can you say to your brother, 'Let me take the speck out of your eye,' when all the time there is a plank in your own eye? You hypocrite, first take the plank out of your own eye, and then you will see clearly to remove the speck from your brother's eye."*[4]

Jesus was using hyperbole to emphasize that unless we remove the big imperfections from our own life (planks), we can't possibly help someone else remove the small imperfections (specks) from their life. If we don't, our keen observations about others might be only the reflection of our own faults.

Is there ever a place for judgment in relationships?

God didn't commission me to be a "judge" but a "fruit inspector."

Yes and no. I like to say that God didn't commission me to be a "judge" but a "fruit inspector." Jesus said, *"By their fruit you will recognize them."*[5]

You might be asking: *But how do we know what fruit is good?*

Well, we can't exactly thump the melons or squeeze the peaches. Luckily, the Apostle Paul tells us what the good fruit is: *"love, joy, peace, patience, kindness, goodness, faithfulness, gentleness and self-control."* And he points out the bad fruit, too: *"sexual immorality, impurity, debauchery, idolatry, witchcraft, hatred, discord, jealousy, fits of rage, selfish ambition, dissensions, factions, envy, drunkenness, orgies … and rooting for Ohio State.*"[6] (I made that last part up. Mostly.)

As a fruit inspector, I am not to judge the motives of somebody else's heart. But if I see evidence of "bad fruit" in a friend or loved one, I can respectfully, lovingly approach them and offer to help. When I see sinful, destructive behavior, I need to get involved — but I am not to judge. My only job is to extend God's grace. Paul reminds us, *"If someone is caught in a sin, you who are spiritual should restore him gently … Carry each others burdens."*[7]

o   o   o

Often, the only difference between "being judgmental" and simply "making good decisions" is the *motive* behind our response. When we are using sound judgment, we're simply trying to assess whether something is good or evil. Right or wrong. Truth or lie. We are working through information step by step to determine the best course of action.

In life, we're required to make judgment calls every day. Whether it's in raising our kids, running a business or refereeing a soccer game, we need to assess the facts objectively, using our God-given abilities in a way that honors him.

I'll give two positive examples.

First, in my role as a portfolio manager, I meet with management teams from hundreds of companies. It's my job to judge their viability and potential for success. By analyzing their market position, track record and product offering, I judge whether their stock will be a good investment for my clients. That's what I get paid for doing. Our research is rigorous, but in the end, it's an imperfect process that requires relying on intuition, experience and gut feelings.

Second, let's say your daughter starts dating a guy with a history of abusing women. She insists he has changed, and urges you not to be judgmental. The guy admits he was once a raging alcoholic but promises he's a new man. You decide to give him a chance. Later however, you witness a verbal confrontation between your daughter and the boyfriend. You warn her, but she rejects your help and says you are simply "judging" him.

What do you do? You want to protect your daughter, but you also want to encourage a recovering addict. You look at the facts, ask God for guidance and conclude he is drinking again. With God as your guide, the motive behind your reaction is pure. It's simply to protect your daughter. After processing the information you have, you conclude it's best for her not to date this man until you're convinced his life is truly changed. This is not passing judgment, this is being prudent.

On the other hand, let's say you're prejudiced or paranoid or controlling. Then your motives are not pure, you're not seeing things clearly and you are probably judging your daughter's friend unfairly.

Here's a way to tell the difference: Using sound judgment means looking *up* to God. Being judgmental means looking *down* on a person. Looking *up* to God for guidance is done out of love and respect in a search for truth. Looking *down* on others is done out of fear and selfishness in a rush to judgment.

Apparently, our rush to judge is built in. The author of *Blink*, Malcolm Gladwell, studied our predilection for snap judgments: "The most common — and the most important — forms of rapid cognition are the judgments we make and the impressions we form of other people. Every waking minute that we are in the presence of someone, we come up with a constant stream of predictions and inferences about what that person is thinking and feeling."

Unfortunately, says Gladwell, these judgments are often faulty: "Mind-reading failures happen to all of us. They lie at the root of countless arguments, disagreements, misunderstandings, and hurt feelings."[8]

To help conquer my natural inclination to judge, I sometimes ask God to let me see people through his eyes. One day at the local shopping mall, a father became increasingly frustrated with his two young children. Finally, he scooped up one of the kids, grabbed the other firmly by the hand and marched them out to his car in the parking lot. While strapping them into their car seats, he spanked their legs and yelled so loudly that everyone could hear. I was appalled at the father's lack of self-control and immature response. So was everybody around me. Our condescending glares clearly spoke our disapproval. We nodded to each other in a way that made us feel better about ourselves. Silently, we agreed: *Can you believe this guy? What a lousy Dad. He should have never had kids.*

We need to see other people through God's eyes.

Then one of the women shoppers broke the silence. Watching from her car, she yelled sarcastically, "Do you need some help parenting your children?" The response that came back was totally unexpected: "Yes. My wife just died and left me alone with the kids, and I am totally lost right now." My heart sank, and my sanctimonious pedestal was yanked out from under me. I felt so embarrassed I wanted to disappear into the asphalt.

The story you just read was fiction. But how often does this happen for real? We think we understand a situation only to discover the "story behind the headlines" and realize how completely off base our assessment was. If we're honest with ourselves, most of us are natural-born judges. But what if we knew everyone's full history? Their circumstances going back to an abusive childhood or an alcoholic father or an absentee mom?

If we saw people as God's beloved children of unsurpassable worth, our response would be compassion, forgiveness and grace. American journalist Sydney Harris wrote, "We evaluate others with a Godlike justice, but we want them to evaluate us with a Godlike compassion."

Busted. *Mea culpa.* My bad.

Rather than evaluating people, God simply asks us to love them, regardless of our opinions or natural inclinations. This doesn't mean we shouldn't *"speak the truth in love"* when we detect bad fruit. We should. But we must do it only because we love that person too much to remain silent.

○   ○   ○

In Richard Stengel's biography of Nelson Mandela, *Mandela's Way,* he points out a character trait that is the very opposite of judging others: "Mandela sees almost everyone as virtuous until proven otherwise. He starts with an assumption that you are dealing with him in good faith. He believes seeing the good in other people improves the chances that they will reveal their better selves."

That's great advice: *Assume the best. Withhold judgment. Treat everyone as equals.* Following Mandela's principles would make the world an enormously better place. But the Bible takes grace one step farther. Not only should we refrain from judging and tearing people down, we should be intentionally building them up: *"Value others above yourself, not looking to your own interests but each of you to the interests of others."* [9]

Think about the people in your neighborhood or school. It's good to bite your tongue and not judge them. But how much better to open your mouth and encourage them? Now think about the people in your office or workplace. It's good to not hinder their chance at promotion. But how much better to give them a boost up? *"Don't push your way to the front; don't sweet talk your way to the top. Put yourself aside, and help others get ahead. Don't be obsessed with getting your own advantage. Forget yourself long enough to lend a helping hand."* [10]

Business author Seth Godin describes this self-effacing grace: "A graceful person gets things done, but in a way that you'd be happy to see repeated. A graceful person raises the game of everyone nearby. Graceful is the person we can't live without."

That's who we want to be. But Godin says something is holding us back. "Every day, we get a chance to give others the benefit of the doubt ... the opportunity to give our support, our confidence and our trust. And yet, most days, we hesitate."[11]

I can almost hear God saying, *"Don't hesitate!"*

So let's pile on the praise. Let's lend a hand. Let's go out of our way to help someone who doesn't deserve it and could never earn it. Humans *judging* each other will never lead to a transformed life. But humans *loving* each other can change the world.

○   ○   ○

"If you judge people, you have no time to love them."

—Mother Teresa[12]

II: GRACE IS NOT...

CHAPTER 7:
The 99 Sheep

A husband wants to divorce his wife so he can marry a 14-year-old girl. The wife refuses, because she won't be able to support herself. So the man conspires with the town's crooked leaders to frame his wife for a crime that carries the death penalty.

Sound preposterous? Couldn't happen?

Based on a true story, the violent and disturbing film *The Stoning of Soraya M* is about an Iranian woman falsely accused of adultery by a husband who wants her out of the way so he can marry a teenager. Difficult to watch and hard to believe, it reveals the horrors of a society where women are regarded as property and moral crimes are punished by torture. In the movie's horrific climax, the heroine, Soraya, is buried up to her waist and brutally pelted with rocks and stones — some thrown by her own husband, father and children.

After ten excruciating minutes, she's battered beyond recognition.

Grinning with victory, the husband walks up to examine his wife's blood-soaked body to make sure she is dead. As he prods her crumpled form for signs of life, one of Soroya's eyelids flutters. The stoning is promptly resumed.

This dark story is told in flashback. A French-Iranian journalist (played by James Caviezel, who was Jesus in *The Passion of the Christ*) is driving through a remote village when his car breaks down. While repairs are being made, he is approached by a local woman named Zahra. She is Soraya's aunt, and tells the journalist the harrowing story of her niece's savage execution the day before. Caviezel's character, the real-life Freidoune Sahebjam, went on to write the best-selling book on which this film is based.

Although it sounds like something from the Middle Ages, the grisly event actually occurred in August 1986 in the Iranian village of Kupayeh. Unbelievably, the barbaric practice of stoning "fallen women" is still carried on in areas of the Middle East and Africa today.

The practice of stoning "fallen women" is still carried on in some areas.

In modern America we don't actually stone people for sexual misconduct, but religious fundamentalists still punish the offenders with a fervor that suggests the Salem witch hunts of the 1700s...

○   ○   ○

Looking into her parent's eyes, the 16-year-old student could see and feel their disappointment. Just three years earlier, this Christian teen had made a pledge of sexual purity to her parents and friends. Now she was confessing how she had broken her vow of chastity.

Earlier that afternoon, her best friend had privately confronted the girl's parents, revealing their daughter's sexual encounter with a classmate. She said that if the girl did not voluntarily confess the incident, she would divulge the entire story. Her motives were right. She was genuinely worried about her misguided friend and fearful the teen would do it again if she remained silent.

Armed with this shocking information, the parents promptly summoned their daughter.

She was not always one to come clean on the first pass. But this time the girl told her parents the blunt truth. She had been alone with a young boy from her Christian school. He suggested

66

they experiment with the one thing all teenagers are curious about. Throwing caution and common sense aside, she engaged in an act that would have profound consequences.

Maybe it was the influence of movies and television. Maybe it was raging hormones or something she'd seen on the Internet. Whatever it was, her curiosity was piqued and she bit the apple.

Reeling from the details, her parents listened in disbelief. They could not hide their sadness as they heard how their child's innocence had been lost in one seemingly harmless night. They tried hard not to judge, because they had also experienced sexual intimacy before marriage. But they had desperately wanted life to be different for their kids. They believed to their core that God designed sex as a sacred gift for a husband and wife to give each other in the context of a lifetime marriage commitment.

> **They experimented with the one thing all teenagers are curious about.**

To them, virginity was not something to be embarrassed about but a treasure to be guarded. Sex was not a meaningless act that "everyone was doing" but a physical consummation of a spiritual union.

The parents personally knew many young men and women who had intentionally "saved themselves" for their future mate. Unhindered by the emotional baggage that comes from sleeping around before marriage, their sex lives were blessed. Without the guilt and suspicion (and inevitable comparisons) that having a prior sexual history brings, their marriages were strong. This was the hope they had held out for their children, but now that dream was shattered.

Regaining their spiritual composure, they told their daughter that God in his incredible grace would forgive this moral failure. They said he would honor anyone who came to him with a repentant heart. But, like Adam and Eve's blunder in the Garden, this mistake triggered tough consequences that wouldn't go away overnight — no matter how hard they prayed.

The parents also knew that once Pandora's Box had been opened, it would be more difficult to resist future sexual temptation. It would take a recommitted heart and a strengthened will for their daughter to stay pure again until marriage.

The consequences of this mistake wouldn't go away overnight — no matter how hard they prayed.

Through her sobs and hugs, it was obvious the girl felt terrible about what she'd done. Moved with compassion, the parents repeatedly told her how much they loved her. They stressed that God had not rejected her or written her off. They explained how badly they wanted her fully forgiven and restored. After buckets of tears, things began to look brighter.

They did not foresee the dark clouds on the horizon.

When the daughter returned to her Christian school that fall, there was plenty of whispering about what had happened that summer. Knowing glances in the hallway and snickering in the lunchroom tipped off the girl that her secret was out. Even though she had only confided with her closest friends, the entire student body seemed to know. Eventually the principal and headmaster heard the rumors and called her into their office. Confronted by the allegations, the girl confessed openly, apologized sincerely, and told them how she was working through the situation with her parent's help.

That act of confession and promise to never repeat her mistake could have — and should have — been the end of it. But according to the school's rulebook, the teen had committed one of the four "major sins." Smoking, drinking, drugs and sex were punishable by expulsion. The officials reminded her that every student had signed a contract, stating they would not engage in any of these acts. She had broken her covenant with them, and now she must face the punishment.

When the school called the father in for an unscheduled conference, he figured it was about his daughter's indiscretion. Driving to the school, he decided to simply tell the officials that he and his wife were aware of the situation and had

Smoking, drinking, drugs and sex were punishable by expulsion.

been dealing with it. He was ready to help his daughter accept whatever consequences they suggested, and was eager to get past the incident. He was confident that his brothers in Christ knew how deeply the family was committed to following Jesus, and how much they supported the mission of the school.

Knowing it was a Christian institution, the father expected a program of mandatory counseling or a period of conditional probation. What he expected was grace. What he got was judgment: "We are asking you to remove your daughter from our school immediately."

The expulsion was called "voluntary," but if he refused to pull her out, the leaders would seek board approval for an expulsion. In a menacing tone, they warned him the proceedings could get ugly. Real ugly. The father was shell-shocked. Nauseous. His choice was to yank his daughter out of the school she loved or have her dragged through the mud of a formal hearing. With tears in his eyes, he signed the form, withdrawing his daughter.

On the drive home his stomach churned. He was a mess of conflicting emotions. But he was sure about one thing — this was *not* the way Christ would have treated his daughter. It felt like she had been brought before a group of judgmental Pharisees and condemned for making a mistake that millions of teens — even Christian teens — commit annually.

In a moment of misdirected anger, the father lashed out at his pensive passenger, "Was your one night of fun worth this? Did you think about getting kicked out before you disobeyed God?" First she cried. Then she exploded in rage. Her reaction convinced the father that his approach was not working. Riding home in uncomfortable silence, he considered how Jesus would handle the situation.

And the word that came to him was "grace."

That afternoon, the family sat in their sunroom pondering how they came to be in this awkward place. All three cried, especially the daughter, who apologized over and over. The dad (who was the most judgmental of the family) kept focused on the word he'd heard so clearly from God that afternoon — *grace*. He was no longer consumed with replaying the events that led to his daughter's expulsion, or the humiliation of being severely judged by a community of Christians.

Relying on God's grace, he shifted his mental energy from thoughts of revenge and retribution to thoughts of redemption and restoration. His goal now was to help his daughter understand that God does not always spare us from the consequences of our mistakes, but forgives us nonetheless. He explained that there was nothing she could ever do to make her *earthly* father stop loving her and that her *heavenly* father loved her even more!

What happened on the cross covers every sin — including premarital sex.

He shared how God's love was so limitless, so inexhaustible, that he sent his Son into the world for the ultimate act of redemption. He shared how what happened on the cross ushered in the era of grace that covers every sin — including premarital sex.

As he prayed for guidance, the father realized his daughter was probably feeling excluded from God's family. He also knew that if she felt ostracized from God's approval, she would not turn to him for answers. So he reminded her how God cares so deeply about each of his sheep that he would gladly leave 99 in the pen to search for the one who wandered away.

He read aloud from Luke, chapter 15, where Jesus describes what happens when an anxious shepherd locates a missing sheep:

"He joyfully puts it on his shoulders and goes home. Then he calls his friends and neighbors together and says, 'Rejoice with me; I have found my lost sheep.'" [1]

As the father visualized the Good Shepherd, he considered the message the school was sending his young, impressionable daughter. Was it the grace that Jesus practiced? Or the condemnation his opponents specialized in? Was the headmaster concerned about rescuing a sheep that strayed? Or about striking fear into the other students?

Instead of being lovingly pursued like the lost sheep, his daughter was deemed unworthy to associate with the other 99 sheep and thrown out of the pen.

      o   o   o

Expulsion seemed like an ironic punishment. The dad knew Jesus told the Parable of the Lost Sheep to specifically remind religious leaders of his day (and ours) that he came for those who wander away from God, not for those who think they've earned VIP seats in the Kingdom.

It hurt to think about such heartless treatment, but the father hung on to grace like a drowning sailor to a life preserver. Then things got even worse. The girl's former schoolmates called with news that their Bible teacher had used her as an example in his class! When the father questioned the staff, the Bible teacher initially denied everything, despite numerous students confirming the slander. Later, in a phone conversation, he apologized and claimed to understand the importance of grace. But by exploiting the girl in front of her classmates, he failed to extend grace to the one sheep Jesus said was most important.

When the father brought up the Parable of the Lost Sheep, school officials

> **The father hung on to grace like a drowning sailor to a life preserver.**

tap danced around it. When the father asked how they reconciled their actions with the story, they explained that grace meant allowing her to re-apply the following year — if she showed sufficient evidence of redemption. Then they turned and asked the father: "Do you think the school should have had an official response?"

When he replied that a lesser punishment would have been sufficient, they countered with a puzzling statement: "Back in Bible days, a shepherd who recovered a lost sheep would break the legs of the animal so it would not wander away again."

The father was sickened by the imagery. He'd always pictured the shepherd joyfully putting the sheep on his shoulders like a man carrying a beloved child, and then throwing a party once he got home. When he pointed out that their anecdote about animal cruelty was not found in scripture, they mumbled something about historical evidence being their source.

Funny, he thought, *that wasn't the way Jesus told the story.* Their explanation about metaphorically breaking his daughter's legs to teach her a lesson left him uneasy.

Searching for biblical precedent, the father brought up Jesus' teaching about how to treat a believer who sins: *"If your brother sins against you, go and show him his fault, just between the two of you. If he listens to you, you have won your brother over. But if he will not listen, take one or two others along with you ... If he refuses to listen to them, tell it to the church."* [2]

According to Jesus, our first step is to confront a brother privately, face-to-face. Go back multiple times if necessary, and if that fails, then (and only then) go to the authority of the church. In other words, give repeated chances for the person to voluntarily come clean, because the goal of any confrontation and punishment should be *restoration.*

The father asked the officials, "Why did you jump directly to step four of the biblical model for church discipline? Why skip one through three?" After all, the young girl had freely admitted her failure to the authorities. A grace-filled response would have communicated to her, "You are important to God and to us, and we will work to help you follow his perfect plan."

Instead, she was treated like an unrepentant *"pagan."*[3]

When confronted with this contradiction, the headmaster insisted that Jesus' prescription only applied to churches. The father countered that a group of Christians gathering regularly for the purpose of educating believers in their faith *was* a church. But the leaders clung to their technicality.

The father knew that God wants us to bring our sins out into the light and make ourselves accountable to trusted brothers and sisters. When God's light is shining on our area of weakness, it's much harder to continue failing.

The whole idea behind sharing our weaknesses — *"confess your sins to each other"* — is so we can break the bondage of repeated sin. That's the goal of peer-to-peer confession and mutual accountability. But it can only be done in the context of community, not isolation.[4]

The officials responded that this kind of grace was the job of the church and the parents, not the school. But if the *leaders* didn't model Christian principles, how could their students learn to effectively deal with sin? Maybe the staff believed that none of the other kids had any sin. Maybe the school was exactly what it looked like from the outside — a magically perfect place for magically perfect kids.

Not likely.

It's dangerous to think that any kids — believers or not — are immune from sin. It's an impossible standard to maintain, and when harsh penalties are imposed for making bad choices, it's a recipe for guilt. Being shunned, embarrassed and excluded from community produces feelings of inadequacy and worthlessness that could easily result in depression or even suicide.

> **It's dangerous to think that any kids — believers or not — are immune from sin.**

In the end, the headmaster washed his hands, claiming he had no choice. "Board-approved rules" stated that the four major sins called for mandatory expulsion (so smoking is worse than murder?). Everyone who enrolled was aware of what would happen if they sipped a beer or puffed a Marlboro.

The father asked, "Does signing a contract guarantee perfect behavior?" If so, why did statistics show that kids in Christian schools engage in nearly as much drinking, drugs and sexual experimentation as kids in public schools?

Maybe this school had it all figured out. Maybe. But the daughter knew plenty of her classmates were experimenting with all four biggies.

The officials knew it, too. But they also knew the math. If every student who sinned was expelled, tuition revenues would plummet. So they only punished kids who voluntarily came clean about their offenses. In a classic paradox, only those lawbreakers who lied about their conduct could remain enrolled.

For the 99 students who (supposedly) stayed in the sheep pen, that semester's bizarre events taught them two life lessons: First, "If you sin, be sneaky." And second, "If you are confronted, never admit your sin. Don't confess it and don't dare ask for help — the consequences are too severe."

o   o   o

Occasionally, there *are* situations when a person does need to be removed from a situation. When a church leader or a politician is caught in moral failure, it's necessary for them to step down from high-profile positions of authority. Yet even this needs to be done within the context of community. The fallen leader cannot be shunned and sent away to address their problems alone. Even adults need grace and forgiveness from those around them to help them make necessary changes.

How much *more* grace is needed when the person involved is

not a mature leader but a young teenager — new in their faith and susceptible to the temptations of their crazy world? Restoration can only happen with on-going support from friends, family and classmates. Cutting someone off from their community of positive influencers is almost a guarantee of failure.

Unfortunately, the damage done by judgmental believers is often worse than the damage from the sin in the first place. In this case, the headmaster mandated that if the young girl wanted to return the following year, she would have to meet with her counselors periodically to "assess her healing." Her Bible teacher and other school officials promised to check in with the teen periodically to support her.

> **Damage done by judgmental believers can be worse than damage done by sin.**

The father was encouraged. Maybe they did understand grace after all. Perhaps their goal really was the girl's restoration.

But the phone calls and visits never came.

The leaders never followed up on their pledge.

Disappointed and puzzled by their lack of concern, the girl wrote a letter directly to the headmaster, asking for forgiveness and reporting on her spiritual growth. He too promised to call and offer encouragement, but soon forgot.

In one last attempt, the father wrote an open letter asking the school board to review their policy. He hoped there'd be some differing voices on the board who'd take a fresh look at the process. But he suspected the human tendency to gravitate toward nice, tidy, inflexible rules would be hard to overcome.

And he was right. Three months later, the chairman of the board responded by saying no review of the school's policy was necessary. Case closed.

Brazilian novelist Paulo Coelho notes, "It's one thing to feel you are on the right path, but it's another to think that yours is the only path."

The chairman's dismissive letter was a litmus test for the father. Had the board responded in a receptive and thoughtful way, he might have considered sending his daughter back. But setting aside legalism takes courage. It was more than the board could handle, just as Jesus was more than the Pharisees could handle.

o   o   o

Grace is hard to grasp. And sometimes it's messy. It goes against human nature and our desire to have things neatly packaged in a pretty box with a bow on top. Grace is revolutionary and even though the revolution happened 2,000 years ago on Calvary, we still struggle with its implications.

The revolution happened 2,000 years ago, but we still struggle with its implications.

How many "sinners" have heard the hammer of judgment instead of the sweet song of grace? How many have felt pushed away rather than embraced? When punishment is legitimately required, the goal must be to restore the person back to a relationship with God, and only grace can do that.

If keeping rules (or board-approved bylaws) could save anyone, then Jesus died in vain. But we know that the Mosaic Law never saved anyone; it only pointed out and magnified our sin so we'd realize how much we needed a Savior! *"The law was our* (temporary) *guardian until Christ came; it protected us until we could be made right with God through faith."* [5]

With help from God, the parents forgave the school leadership and concentrated on their daughter's healing. Discipline was part of the journey, but affirmations of God's love accompanied every discussion about consequences. Slowly, trust was restored between the parents and the child, and more importantly, between the child and God. As grace was "lived out" in the home, she felt a greater connection to God than ever.

The love she felt was amazing, intoxicating and capable of overpowering the urge to sin. It was indescribable. Undeniable. It was the unfathomable love of a God who cares so deeply that he will do anything to bring us back — including leaving 99 sheep behind to chase us down.

> God will leave 99 sheep behind to chase down one who is lost.

In the movie *The Stoning of Soraya M*, the innocent victim faced her unjust punishment by lamenting, "I'm just an inconvenient wife." To her Christian school, the daughter who slipped was "just an inconvenient student," an embarrassment, a blemish on the school's shiny bright image.

Both women were in the way, and both groups of men found a way to use the "rules" to conveniently dispose of them.

Of all the arguments against legalism, none is more powerful than the sight of religious leaders standing ready to judge — whether they're clenching rocks or rulebooks in their fists.

○   ○   ○

"I like your Christ. I do not like your Christians. Your Christians are nothing like your Christ."

—Mahatma Gandhi[6]

II: GRACE IS NOT...

CHAPTER 8:
Grace Is Not Guilt

The composer was Chopin. The piece was *Opus 53*. The pianist was a nine-year-old Jewish boy in short pants and oversized glasses. After watching dozens of competitors, the crowded hall was mesmerized by the shy newcomer's amazing performance. Fingers flying across the keyboard, the intense boy filled the room with breathtaking music. When he finally stood up and bowed awkwardly, spontaneous applause broke out.

Given his youth and inexperience, the child's performance was a remarkable achievement. A party should have been thrown in his honor. But instead of celebration, the boy faced humiliation from a father who berated his "losing" performance. Making him feel as guilty as possible, the father heaped insults on the talented boy, forcing him to practice extra hours each day and long into the night. The obsessive parent pushed his gifted son so hard that the boy's mind slowly crumbled under the impossible goal of pleasing his father.

Eventually, the guilt drove the budding genius into a mental institution.

As a parent, I cringed when I heard the story of Australian piano prodigy, David Helfgott. A fragile boy, David loved math, chess, and music. His first piano teacher was his own father, a stern man so obsessed with his son's success that he had no tolerance for fun or failure. Later on, a local teacher convinced the reluctant father to let him take over David's musical instruction.

As a teenager, David won the state music championship and was invited to study in America. Afraid of losing control, his father refused to let him to go. Crushed, the teen continued to slave away under his father's roof until he was offered a scholarship to the Royal College of Music in London. Again, David's father tried to block him, but with encouragement from friends he left anyway. He was promptly disowned.

While studying in London, David entered a concerto competition and chose to perform the fiendishly difficult Rachmaninoff's *Third Concerto*. Years earlier, his father had urged him to attempt the dreaded "Rach 3" and he failed to master it. Now he was resurrecting it out of guilt. Haunted by the shame he felt as a child, he worked on the monumental piece to the point of exhaustion and won the prestigious competition.

In the process, he suffered a complete nervous breakdown and was admitted to a psychiatric hospital for shock therapy.

Upon being released, David returned to Australia but was totally rejected by his father. He suffered a relapse and spent 20 more years in an institution. Finally, at the age of 40, he was discharged, and through a bizarre twist of fate stumbled into a piano bar one night and sat down at the keyboard. Rain-soaked, disheveled, and muttering under his breath, he was mocked by the crowd. His garbled, schizophrenic jabbering was almost incoherent, but the patrons were shocked at his astonishing ability to play the piano. One of the owners befriended him and gave him a regular job playing for the customers. After years of therapy following his father's death, he returned to the concert stage and international acclaim.

When David Helfgott's true story was immortalized in the 1996 movie *Shine*, he was invited to play piano onstage at the Oscars and received a thunderous ovation. This movie about overcoming guilt was nominated for seven Academy Awards, with Geoffrey Rush (playing David) winning Best Actor.

Helfgott's psychological collapse is an extreme example,

but guilt is so powerful that even a small amount can cripple us mentally and emotionally. In larger doses it can scar us for life and ultimately drive us away from God.

David's father wanted his son to be world famous. His desire for success wasn't wrong, but he used the wrong motivators — guilt and shame — to try and achieve it. Instead of spurring a person on to do better, guilt usually pushes them in the opposite direction. Why? Because it confirms what we already suspect about ourselves — that we are inadequate, messed-up losers on the brink of disaster. That's not what God thinks of us, but it's the rotten self-image the devil wants us to have.

> **Guilt is so powerful that a small dose can cripple us mentally and emotionally.**

If that sounds a little spooky, bear with me.

Satan is real, and guilt is the main tool he uses to drive a wedge between us and God. When he whispers, "God doesn't love you anymore," we're inclined to believe him because we *already* feel guilty and unworthy. When he says, "You're a lazy under-achiever," we believe it because it reinforces our own guilty pessimism. Guilt is the "evidence" Satan needs to back up the lies he speaks into our lives.

When guilty thoughts fill our mind, it isn't God who is accusing us, it's the enemy. In fact, the word *Satan* in Hebrew actually means "accuser." In Revelation 10, the devil is called *"the accuser of our brothers, who accuses them before our God day and night."* He makes us feel guilty to keep us distracted and emotionally immobilized. He wants us to feel too embarrassed, too ashamed to approach God and restore our fellowship.

God doesn't convict us with guilt, but with the inner witness of his Holy Spirit in our heart. Yes, he absolutely wants life change. Yes, he absolutely wants us to turn away from sin. But he first wants us to know that he loves us unconditionally, despite our shortcomings and failures. When I disappoint God, I know it from within. I don't need the devil or anyone else dumping a bucket of guilt on me. The reason I want to please my God, my wife, my kids and my co-workers is because I *love* them, not because they've made me feel miserable about myself.

In fact, guilt would have the opposite effect.

○   ○   ○

QUESTION: If guilt has no positive transformational power, why do we use it so often as a battering ram on people around us?

ANSWER: Because we have wrong ideas about the nature of God.

When I was a young child, I remember hearing that God was someone that I should fear. You know, as in *"The fear of the Lord is the beginning of wisdom."* [1]

No one told me that "fearing God" really meant being in awe of him, having a deep reverence and respect for him. I took it literally that God was someone to be afraid of. I thought he was out to get me. So did Jim Carey in the movie *Bruce Almighty*: "God is a mean kid sitting on an anthill with a magnifying glass and I'm the ant. He could fix my life, but he'd rather burn off my feelers and watch me squirm!"

For years, I lived in guilt and fear, figuring that God was just waiting for me to screw up so he could punish me. One slip and I'd be the flaming ant being zapped by the angry Big Guy. Unfortunately, there are many Christians and non-Christians who still believe and preach this message of fear.

Religious or not, the majority of people think God is the cause of illness and accidents and calamities. That's why hurricanes and earthquakes are called Acts of God in your insurance policy. In an interview, a race driver talked about the possibility of being killed in a crash, "When it's your time, it's your time. God can get me any way he chooses — crossing the street, driving to work, even a heart attack."

If we think the God who created us is out to get us, no wonder we feel guilty.

My friend and mentor, Craig Mayes, loves to tell about the day he accepted Jesus into his life. He was five years old when the minister of his church came to speak in the children's Sunday School class. He asked the kindergartners a very direct question: "Have you ever been burned by fire or something hot before?" A bunch of little hands went up as the tiny students told one story after another about touching a hot stove or the end of a marshmallow fork. Some had even been burned by actual fire. When all of the horror stories were done,

Most people think God is the cause of illness, accidents and calamities.

the minister looked solemnly at the kids and said, "That pain you felt is what it will feel like in hell if you do not accept Jesus Christ as your Savior." Then he went for the full close on the deal and asked, "Who would like to accept Jesus Christ today?" Craig recalls that as an "exceptionally bright youngster" he raised his hand immediately!

Unfortunately for Craig, the gruesome image haunted him for years until he finally learned that Jesus came to attract us with an offer of radical love, not the fear of eternal punishment: *"Don't you see how wonderfully kind, tolerant, and patient God is with you? Can't you see that his kindness is intended to turn you from your sin?"* [2]

One translation of the same verse evokes a loving parent holding our hand, not an angry God plunging it into fire: *"In kindness he takes us firmly by the hand and leads us into a radical life-change."* [3]

As Craig's experience proved, fear has the ability to produce immediate, short-term results. Unfortunately it usually produces one of two bad outcomes: A nervous life of timidity that hides from reality, or a reckless life of rebellion that seeks fulfillment apart from God. Neither lifestyle is healthy. God's goal is that we have the abundant life that's only found in the freedom of love, not in the slavery of fear: *"For God has not given us the spirit of fear, but of power, and love, and a sound mind."* [4]

Another translation says that instead of *"cowardice and cringing,"* God has given us a *"calm and well-balanced mind."* [5]

○   ○   ○

Few of us know God or the Bible as well as we should, so we don't understand the "depravity" of mankind; that we are fallen creatures doomed to fail and in need of a savior. But our Founding Fathers did, and they built checks and balances into the Constitution to protect us from sinful men seizing power. Today, most people (and voters) don't realize that our human nature is weak and sinful. Instead, secular humanism teaches that mankind is evolving upwards, and that when we finally become fully self-actualized, we'll be able to do anything we put our enlightened minds to!

It's no wonder we think we're strong enough to prevent our own downfall through human willpower. So we grit our teeth and visualize victory. And when mind-over-matter ultimately fails (that's why diets don't work), we beat ourselves up with guilt and shame.

What happens next?

First, guilt makes us try harder. Then, when the extra effort fails, it makes us give up completely. Here's what I mean. Guilt increases our resolve to become a better person, setting our expectations at an unachievable level. When the inevitable failure comes, we hold ourselves in contempt for our inability to control our thoughts or actions. This endless cycle of fear, guilt and disappointment continues with no positive life change. For many, the cycle of failure simply confirms what they were afraid of — that they are utterly incapable of change. This makes them feel even more hopeless. Sadly, people caught in this circular trap of trying, failing and feeling guilty will often continue to live compromised lives that validate their inner badness. They give up. They quit even *trying* to "follow God's rules" and simply default to the world's corrupt standards.

Can you blame them?

God understood that the law he ushered into the world through Moses (remember Charlton Heston and those stone tablets?) was the very thing that would prevent people from having true communion with him. Why? Because no one could ever keep it. Everybody who ever tried has blown it. As we saw earlier, the law was never meant to bridge the gap between God and man. It was a tool to convince us that we needed salvation: *"No one will be declared righteous in his sight by observing the law; rather, through the law we became conscious of sin."* [6]

Our salvation comes by placing our faith in the only being who ever kept the law perfectly — Jesus. His perfect obedience made him the only acceptable substitute to take the punishment we deserved. His righteousness is transferred to us when we admit we can't keep the rules and need his forgiveness: *"But now a righteousness apart from law has been made known ... this righteousness from God comes through faith in Jesus Christ to all who believe ... for all have sinned and fall short of the glory of God, and are justified freely by his grace."* [7]

Until Jesus came and died on the cross, no one could be permanently free from guilt. Whatever they did was only a temporary fix: *"The law always ended up being used as a Band-Aid on sin instead of a deep healing of it."* [8]

Over the centuries the Israelites sacrificed thousands of animals to temporarily cover their sins. Millions of gallons of blood were poured out at the Temple in Jerusalem. Why? Because *"Without the shedding of blood, there is no forgiveness."* [9]

Until Jesus died on the cross, no one could be permanently free from guilt.

Luckily for them, God did not require human blood. Instead of a sinful person dying, an innocent animal could die in his place (remember the term "scapegoat?"). So the people brought their finest cattle, goats and sheep to the Temple. If you couldn't afford large animals, you could offer pigeons or doves instead. But large or small, no sacrifice could erase their sins permanently until the perfect, sin-removing blood of Jesus was shed. As the author of Hebrews writes, *"No matter how many sacrifices were offered year after year, they never added up to a complete solution. If they had, the worshippers would have gone merrily on their way, no longer dragged down by their sins ... The plain fact is that bull and goat blood can't get rid of sin."* [10]

In other words, there is no physical action that can make us acceptable in God's sight. If it could, *"The worshipers would have been cleansed once and for all, and would no longer have felt guilty for their sins."* [11]

No matter how many animals were killed or how much incense was burned or how many coins were tossed in the alms box, the Israelites *still* felt guilty. This was the power and the curse of the law. It kept man in bondage to rules and regulations they would never be able to fully follow. And when they did break one, guilt would come along and whack 'em upside the head!

How hard was it to obey the law?

If you have trouble memorizing the Ten Commandments, consider this: At the heart of *halakhah* (Jewish law) are hundreds of rules that God gave the Israelites in the *Torah* (the first five books of the Bible). These rules were absolutely comprehensive, affecting every aspect of life — what you can and cannot wear, what you can and cannot eat, who you can marry, how to groom yourself, how to conduct business, how to observe holidays, how many steps you can walk on the Sabbath, how to treat your animals, how to deal with mold in the house and spots on your skin and yeast in your cupboards ... and on and on.

No wonder people back in the Old Testament era felt guilty

and unable to please God. And by the time Jesus came along, the religious leaders had added hundreds more of their own rules! Today, rabbis are *still* creating new laws on just about everything. For instance, the latest "Orthodox Jewish Laws of Modesty" dictates that skirts must fall four inches below the knee, sleeves must fall below the elbow and necklines must cover the collarbone. No pants or shorts, no knit fabrics and no solid red garments may be worn. Even the thickness of the material for women's nylons and the maximum acceptable length for earrings are dictated.

Oy vey! That's a lot to worry about.

Fortunately, God never intended us to live a life of constant worry and guilt. When Jesus encountered sin, he didn't use guilt as a tool for change. Instead, he spoke words of love and encouragement. If people (including sincere, committed Christians) don't rely on the power of God's grace, they will stay stuck in their behavioral ruts forever.

Why? Because we cannot change ourselves.

Next time you blow it, remember this — God knew in advance that you would. He's omniscient. He knows everything. Nothing about our failures or sins surprises him: *"For he knows how weak we are; he remembers we are only dust."* God knows us better than we know ourselves: *"He knows us inside and out, keeps in mind that we're made of mud."* [12]

Long before creation, God was fully aware that nerve-racking obedience to written regulations would never bring the peace and freedom he desired for his children. That would only come through the sacrifice of Jesus. And only by understanding the 100 percent total effectiveness of the cross can we begin to understand grace's power to replace guilt with forgiveness.

As a boy in Australia, pianist David Helfgott was deathly afraid of invoking his father's disapproval. Sometimes he felt so guilty for disappointing

Nothing about our failures or sins surprises God. He knows everything.

his dad that he couldn't eat or sleep. But our heavenly Father isn't like that. God is not the overbearing parent who looks over your shoulder as you practice, waiting to slap your hand if you make a mistake. God is more like the proud parent sitting in the front row at your piano recital, bragging about you and grinning ear to ear.

And here's the best part: Whether you play like the next Tchaikovsky or hit more wrong notes than a cat on a keyboard, nothing you do can make God stop applauding.

o   o   o

"Guilt: The gift that keeps on giving."

— Erma Bombeck[13]

CHAPTER 9:
The Shame Game

Backstabber ... double-crosser ... traitor.

Three of the worst insults in the English language. I mean, how many mothers name their sons Judas? And if your last name was Arnold would you ever, ever name your boy Benedict? History's hall of shame is filled with despicable two-faces like...

Brutus — Roman senator who plotted to kill his emperor and closest friend Julius Caesar on the Ides of March.

Julius and Ethyl Rosenberg — Spy duo who sold our nation's top atomic secrets to the Soviets during the Cold War.

Bernie Madoff — Wall Street broker who bilked $65 billion from investors worldwide in an elaborate Ponzi scheme.

Whether it's an athlete injecting steroids or a politician taking bribes, no one likes a con artist. From spouses breaking vows to preachers fleecing flocks, betrayers are universally loathed. Some achy-break our hearts, others empty out our wallets, but they all have the power to hurt us deeply.

And usually the people we trust the most can hurt us the worst.

When medieval poet Dante Alighieri wrote *The Inferno*, he reserved the deepest and darkest level of hell for the sin of betrayal. Set aside for the most malicious sinners, this ninth Circle of Hell is a frigid prison ringed by an icy sea without any light or warmth. Which I'm sure lots of victims would agree is appropriate punishment for those who coldly betrayed them.

Deception is nothing new, starting way back in Genesis when Jacob tricked his brother Esau out of his birthright, and extending all the way to today's Internet identity thieves. But of all the despicable acts of treachery, the betrayal of Jesus Christ by one of his own inner circle is easily the most notorious.

Like the other 11 disciples, Judas Iscariot was personally selected by Jesus, and served alongside him during his entire public ministry. He heard every sermon, saw every miracle and shared every meal with the Master. He was entrusted with the group's moneybag and was close enough to Jesus at the Last Supper to be dipping bread with him from the same cup.

So what drove Judas to commit treason? Money? Jealousy? Self preservation? Some say he saw Jesus' enemies closing in and figured that ratting him out was the best way to save his own skin. Others speculate he was disenchanted when Jesus refused to set himself up as an earthly king, and wanted to bring events to a boiling point that would force him to take charge politically. Whether Judas meant to destroy or promote the Messiah's mission is unknown, but we are certain that — to use spy terminology — he "crossed over."

Hollywood has Judas kill Jesus to wed Mary Magdalene.

At least that's the Bible version. Hollywood's version has Judas kill Jesus so he can wed the hottie Mary Magdalene, father the bloodline of Leonardo Da Vinci, establish 12 secret societies which currently rule the world, and hide the Holy Grail in the Castle Anthrax or under Solomon's Temple, or under the Pope's mattress, whatever, just rest assured that even though the Catholic Church is withholding the scandalous truth, Ron Howard has it all figured out.

Now, can we get back to scripture? Thank you. Just a few days before the Last Supper, Luke tells us that *"Judas went to the chief priests and discussed with them how he might betray Jesus. They were delighted and agreed to give him money. He consented, and watched for an opportunity to hand Jesus over to them when no crowd was present."* [1]

To pull it off, Judas leaves the Last Supper early and tells the authorities that Jesus will be heading up to the deserted Mount of Olives. As planned, he guides the religious leaders and a legion of Roman soldiers to the garden of Gethsemane. There he betrays Jesus with the infamous kiss: *"While he was still speaking a crowd came up, and the man who was called Judas, one of the Twelve, was leading them ... Jesus asked him, 'Judas, are you betraying the Son of Man with a kiss?'"* [2]

The next morning when Judas learns that Christ has been condemned to death, he seems surprised at the severity. Racked with guilt, he changes his mind about the shady business deal. He attempts to return the blood money (about $950) he was paid for handing over Jesus: *"When Judas, who had betrayed him, saw that Jesus was condemned, he was seized with remorse and returned the thirty silver coins to the chief priests and the elders. 'I have sinned,' he said, 'for I have betrayed innocent blood.'"* [3]

The Pharisees laugh in his face.

At that instant, Judas realizes that he's aligned himself with devious men who have no further use for him: *"'What is that to us?' they replied. 'That's your responsibility.'"* After doing their dirty work, he feels tossed aside and utterly alone. Scripture doesn't say, but I'm guessing Judas would have given anything to erase the previous 24 hours and go back to sitting around a campfire with Jesus and his band of brothers. Anything to un-do his awful deed. Anything to escape the crushing sorrow he feels for betraying the most innocent man in the world.

We don't know exactly what caused Judas to sell out his boss. But we do know that his guilt was unbearable. *"Judas threw the money into the temple and left. Then he went away and hanged himself."* [4]

Here's the kicker: Judas wasn't the only disciple to betray Jesus.

Here's the kicker: Judas wasn't the only disciple to betray Jesus.

In Matthew's account, the treason of Judas is placed only a few verses before the treason of Peter. After Jesus was arrested, the temple guards dragged him to the home of the high priest, Caiaphas, for an illegal midnight interrogation. While Jesus is being punched and slapped around by the religious magistrates, Peter is just a few yards away, sitting by a fire in the high priest's courtyard — busily disowning him. Three separate times, Peter vehemently denies even *knowing* Jesus, let alone trying to defend him before the court or rescue him from the guards.

To make it more horrific, Peter's cowardly act took place just one day after he boldly swore to Jesus, *"Even if all fall away on account of you, I never will ... Even if I have to die with you, I will never disown you."*[5]

Do you think Peter felt ashamed? Sick to his stomach? His lies are barely out of his mouth when the friend he has just betrayed walks by! Seeing Jesus led out in chains, beaten and bruised, must have been gut wrenching. But it gets even worse: *"The Lord turned and looked straight at Peter. Then Peter remembered the word the Lord had spoken to him: 'Before the rooster crows today, you will disown me three times.'"*[6]

Three times. Backstabber ... double-crosser ... traitor.

Like Judas, Peter's guilt was unbearable: *"He went outside and wept bitterly."*[7]

Like Judas, Peter's grief was totally overwhelming: *"He went out and cried and cried and cried."*[8]

So there it is. Two disciples. Two acts of betrayal. Both men were wracked with guilt over what they'd done, but each had very different outcomes. Judas committed suicide. Peter went on to be one of the great Christian leaders of all time. Why?

One theory is that the devil possessed Judas and used him as a sort of satanic puppet to do his bidding. On his final trip to

Jerusalem, Jesus declared to his 12 disciples that *"one of you is a devil."* [9] This was not a figure of speech. Jesus was talking about the real live demon that would enter Judas twice (once before he took the bribe from the priests and again during the Last Supper). I submit this same demon also came to Judas after the arrest of Jesus and told him he was so bad that he was beyond forgiveness — so bad that he might as well end his agony through suicide.

And Judas bought the lie.

So that's the difference: Judas listened to Satan. Peter listened to Jesus. After he was raised from the dead, Jesus appeared to Peter and forgave him face-to-face for his betrayal. Three times he asked Peter to declare his love — the same number of times Peter had denied him. Grace replaced guilt, and from that moment on, Peter never again wavered. He spread the gospel around the world, and church history tells us he was crucified upside down for his devotion to Christ.

The lie that Satan told Judas — *that he was beyond forgiveness* — is the same lie he's still using today. As you read this, millions of people are suffering under truckloads of guilt, but they avoid seeking God's help because they think that what they've done is beyond forgiveness.

Two traitors. One listened to Satan. One listened to Jesus.

That hopeless "beyond forgiveness" state of mind perfectly described a good friend of mine named Joe...

○   ○   ○

For most of his adult life, Joe felt profoundly guilty for dozens of real and imaginary shortcomings. It was like he walked around with a cloud of shame hanging over his head blocking out the sun. What made Joe's case so unusual was that the guilt pangs haunting him were self-imposed — he held himself in complete and utter contempt.

How is that possible? Who books their own guilt trip?

As we saw with David Helfgott, guilt is often inflicted on us from an outside source — like a harsh parent, a vindictive friend, or a judgmental authority figure. But sometimes the worst guilt of all comes from the *inside* — a little voice in our head telling us we're no good, that we're washed-up losers. This discouraging inner monologue works 24/7 to convince us we're to blame for everything bad in our own lives and probably in those around us, too.

A voice in our head tells us we're no good; that even God has given up on us.

If we listen long enough, the voice of guilt will persuade us we're *sooo* bad that even God has given up on us.

That was Joe's favorite in-brain radio station — the "all-guilt-all-the-time" format. Yet his inner anguish was in stark contrast to his outer demeanor. Each week he would cheerfully lead a group of men, including myself, in a fascinating Bible study. His knowledge of scripture was amazing. Here's the weird part: Joe knew every verse on the subject of grace, but refused to accept it for himself. He could teach on forgiveness for hours but was incapable of receiving it.

After we'd become friends, Joe told me he felt like God came to bring healing and redemption to everyone on the planet *except him*. I'm not joking. For some reason, he simply could not break out of the crippling cycle of guilt that caused him to ruin every key relationship in his life.

Joe's downward spiral began with a tragedy. At a family picnic, his young niece was discovered floating face down in a lake. She had slipped off while Joe was in charge of watching her, and he blamed himself for the accident. While she survived the near drowning, she was mentally impaired. It was more than Joe could bear. He embezzled funds from his company to provide for his niece's family. And when his crime was discovered, he decided — like Judas — that only suicide could end his pain. Then Jesus showed up. Literally. Seconds before taking his life, Joe had a heavenly intervention.

By a miracle of grace, Joe was physically alive and even more convinced that Jesus was real, but the tortured thoughts came back.

> **Seconds before taking his life, Joe had a heavenly intervention.**

Years after his attempted suicide, Joe was still incapable of experiencing forgiveness. Even though he knew scripture, he was caught in an endless loop of negative behavior that kept replaying. Just when it seemed like Joe was applying God's truth to his life and things were looking brighter, destructive habits would resurface and plunge him back into despair.

Sadly, his wife and kids suffered from his emotional roller coaster.

The final straw for Joe's wife, Kappy, was discovering that he had secretly provided alcohol to her daughter and friends at a weekend gathering in their home after she'd gone to bed. Joe had never felt accepted by her kids or respected as their stepfather. And no wonder — his parenting style was harsh and abrasive. Driven by his own feelings of guilt, he continually shoved scripture and Bible teachings in their face, pointing out their shortcomings instead of celebrating their gifts. Failing in his role as their father, he tried instead to be their friend, and that included being their bartender. His stepdaughter's party pals thought he was "fun" and he went to extremes to win their approval, hoping it would rub off on his own kids.

When Kappy confronted Joe about the underage drinking, he apologized to her but hid it from his men's group. He hoped the couple could work it out on their own. But Kappy was at the end of her rope. She could no longer take the destructive cycle of this man who professed to be following Jesus but didn't walk the talk. Fed up with broken promises, she asked him to leave their home. Kappy believed the separation was necessary for her children's well being. She also secretly hoped it would lead to her husband's reconciliation with God.

Months of counseling followed for Joe, first alone and then with his wife. Sadly, the sessions didn't help. Meetings with the entire family brought out deep-seated fears from the children, who confided they no longer trusted him.

After so much hurt and hypocrisy, the situation seemed hopeless.

Kappy was distraught. She had endured ten years of marital chaos, financial strain and emotional pain. But this final quagmire was the most confusing of all. On one hand, she believed God desired her to remain married and work things out. On the other hand, the awful weariness of life with Joe was sapping her strength. She prayed to God, seeking his direction and apologizing for her part in the breakdown of their marriage. Eventually, she concluded she could no longer live the life God intended for her if she stayed with Joe. Whether it was God's peace or just sheer exhaustion that gave her the will to pull the plug, she'll never know.

Either way, it was time to go.

When she told Joe about her decision, he reluctantly agreed to a separation. When he asked for another chance, she replied, "How many times can you expect me to repeat the same vicious cycle?" She was understandably reluctant to be vulnerable again. But this time she sensed something different in Joe's response. Instead of promising outward changes, he spoke of an inward transformation he felt taking place. He confessed that it was his disobedience that had brought their marriage to the brink of dissolution.

In her heart, Kappy desperately wanted to believe him, but she had heard it all before. This time she needed more than words.

Although she prayed daily for Joe's permanent transformation, she felt divorce would be the final outcome.

After eight months of living apart, Kappy filed the papers.

In her mind, she had already moved on, and began to make plans for her new life with the kids. At first, Joe had stayed with a friend. But by now he was living alone in his parent's empty house. Deeply discouraged, he finally came clean with his men's group. We prayed for him continually but privately doubted there was any chance to save his marriage.

You might be asking: *Why the pessimism? Can't God do everything?*

Yes, but generally speaking, God does not relieve us of the natural consequences we create for ourselves by disobeying. Our group assumed Joe would suffer life-long repercussions for his actions. So instead of praying for Joe and Kappy to get back together, we started praying for Joe's surrender, for that complete bottom-of-the-barrel hoist-the-white-flag experience God uses to get people's full attention. Joe did not need to think about family or friends or attorneys or legalities. He needed to focus on just *one* thing — God's desire to be the all-sufficient center of his life.

It's what we should have been praying for all along.

While Joe was off living by himself, his computer consulting business faltered. Revenues slipped dramatically. Although it provided spurts of income, it was no longer enough to support him, let alone his family. Then, in one of those wonderful "God moments," Joe received an invitation to take his consulting skills on the road for a national company. There were just two problems: First, accepting the position would mean geographic separation from his wife (who he still hoped to reconcile with). Second, it meant the small group Bible study he had led for so many years would come to an abrupt end.

In a blink, the two things Joe thought he needed most were being removed by God. And slowly but surely, his pride was being chipped away. *"You're blessed when you're at the end of your rope. With less of you there is more of God and his rule."* [10]

For the first time, he began to recognize feelings of guilt as a spiritual attack from the enemy, not the punishment of God. And when feelings of failure crept up, he began looking to the future instead of the past. Most of all, he began to see God as the source of his self-worth. *"You're blessed when you feel you've lost what is most dear to you. Only then can you be embraced by the One most dear to you."* [11]

Then something amazing accelerated the healing process.

Driving home from Chicago on a late summer day, Joe began to think about all that he had lost. He had no money, no place to live, no wife, no family and no small group. It seemed like everything important to him had been stripped away, piece by piece. But instead of allowing guilt and depression to shape his thoughts, he set his mind on Jesus. And then, right there on I-94, the still, small voice of God penetrated his thoughts. He distinctly remembers God asking him, *"Joe, am I enough for you?"*

> **Everything important to him had been stripped away, piece by piece.**

It was a question he had pondered before, but never from this new perspective of being totally broken. It was as if God was saying, *"Joe, if I never restore your marriage, never reconcile you to your stepchildren, never restore your financial position or give you a place to live, would you still love me and follow me?"*

And for the first time in his life, Joe surrendered it all to God: "Yes, Lord. You are more than enough for me. I thank you for your love and grace."

When Joe returned home, he called me immediately to tell me about his miracle on the freeway. It was a moment I'll never forget. The Joe I heard on the other end of the line was not the same Joe who had left days earlier. Suddenly, our talk was not focused on the *results* — like saving a marriage or restoring a family — but on the *process*, on experiencing God's grace in a profound way. I could tell his attention had shifted from following his inner monologue to following God's voice, like a compass needle snapping around to true north.

Hearing Joe, I believed he had finally declared unconditional surrender.

When he tried to convey this "newness" to Kappy, her skepticism kicked in. Understandably. She'd heard this line before and had fallen for it too many times. By now, there was a ton of painful baggage, and the thought of going through the inevitable disappointment all over again was overwhelming. Instead of welcoming him back into the family, she rained on his parade: "I'm too afraid to believe you. It sounds too good to be true. I am still moving ahead with the divorce proceedings."

Talk about a buzz kill! But this time around, Joe did not collapse and throw a pity party. Instead, he tried to understand his wife's position and — maybe for the first time — genuinely cared more about her happiness than his own. And although things looked grim, he still wanted to fight for his marriage. Against all odds, he felt a small glimmer of hope.

With the divorce papers en route, Joe realized that technically he had several weeks before he was legally required to sign them. He decided to hold out until the last possible moment. The guys in Joe's life (including me) let him know that it was unlikely anything would change. Likewise, Kappy's friends viewed Joe's sudden transformation with great skepticism and urged her not to get duped again.

In a last ditch attempt, Joe asked Kappy if they could meet with a local couple who mentored other couples through an organization called Abide. Devoted to helping families in crisis, founders Mike and Robyn had named their ministry in honor of Jesus' words: *"If a man abides (remains) in me and I in him, he will bear much fruit; apart from me you can do nothing."* [12]

Kappy reluctantly (very reluctantly) agreed to go, but had

little or no hope it would do any good. She fully expected to be judged by the Christian mentors for her decision to divorce. Before going, she prayed for strength and the courage of her conviction to move on with her life. She also prayed a dangerous prayer — asking God to show up at this meeting.

And show up he did.

She fully expected to be judged for her decision to divorce.

When Mike and Robyn affirmed her hurt feelings and desperate heart, Kappy felt like she was actually being heard for the first time in her marriage. And when they asked her to allow more time for God to do his work, she agreed. Why? Kappy swears she heard God whisper, *"I am not asking you to trust Joe. He is not trustworthy. I am asking you to trust me."*

With that heavenly admonition, she consented to the time extension to see if God would confirm the reality of Joe's transformation. But she was unprepared for the work God would do in *her*. Brick by brick, he slowly began tearing down the stony wall around Kappy's heart. The barrier had taken ten years of marriage to build, and each brick had a name like pain, fear, bitterness, betrayal, resentment and anger.

In her quiet time, Kappy heard God asking her to "yield" to him. This seemed odd, because she thought she had already been following his lead through the entire divorce process. And then she heard God ask the same question he had asked Joe: *"Do you trust me? Regardless of the outcome?"*

○   ○   ○

In late September, Kappy heard about a special marriage retreat coming up. She wasn't quite sure why, but she invited Joe. Everything in her flesh screamed "This will never work." But she felt a nudge from God to give it one last try. "At least we'll learn how to communicate. Could be helpful after the divorce," she thought. When Joe eagerly agreed to go, she warned him to lower his expectations. She literally told him, "It would take a miracle to repair the damage that has been done."

Thankfully, God is still in the miracle business.

On the first night of the retreat, Kappy's unapproachable demeanor and closed-off body language communicated she did not want to be there. Her resigned expression clearly read: "Big waste of time. My marriage is hopeless."

At the first session, participants were asked to introduce themselves. When it was their turn, Kappy stood up, "Hi. We're the crisis couple."

But God's grace is capable of softening a hardened heart, and as the weekend went on, her attitude changed from "absolutely not" to "maybe."

Kappy knew that most of the issues in their marriage were Joe's to own, but she also knew that when it comes to relationships, no one is completely blameless. The speaker explained that if couples like Joe and Kappy continued to look at each other's shortcomings, they would never redevelop closeness. But if they kept their gaze locked on God, they would individually grow closer to him, and as a result, grow closer to each other. For the first time in years, Kappy caught a new vision of their life together and the wonderful man Joe could be if he truly followed Christ. And slowly, a small spark of love for Joe began to reignite in her heart.

A small spark of love began to reignite in her heart.

Early that Sunday morning, Kappy felt God ask if she was ready to follow him wherever he was taking her. She felt equal parts excitement and fear. Her brain shouted, *No! You can't go through this again*. But in her heart she felt "the peace that passes all understanding." To the amazement of everyone at the retreat — especially Joe — she publically announced she was dropping the divorce proceedings!

They returned from the marriage weekend fully committed to working things out.

○   ○   ○

Sometimes I wish God operated like the magic genie in Aladdin's lamp. Then he would grant our wishes instantly. But God does not perform quickie fixes for any relationship — including broken marriages. Instead, he works through a process, a step-by-step plan designed to bring lasting healing. For Joe and Kappy, it wasn't easy. And yes, they stumbled along the way. But they committed to keep moving forward, honoring Jesus by doing it his way. Prioritizing their *vertical* relationship with God automatically helped their *horizontal* relationship with each other.

Eventually, the whole family got re-involved in counseling sessions where each member could safely hear and be heard. With God's help, love and mutual respect slowly replaced animosity and distrust in relationships that had once looked hopeless.

Are there still times of failure? Sure, that's true in all relationships, especially marriage. In fact, somebody has said "Marriage isn't about perfection but about daily forgiveness." And that's Joe and Kappy's mantra, too. Instead of retaliating after a fight, they ask God (and each other) for forgiveness. Instead of calling it quits, they ask God for patience and perspective. And instead of letting pride or ego derail their recovery, they focus on how they can use what they've learned to help others. In fact, they joyfully mentor other struggling couples with the humble vision, "We want our mess to be our message."

Marriage isn't about perfection but about daily forgiveness.

Six months after the pivotal marriage retreat, I had the privilege of being part of a real-life miracle — I was asked to speak at a joyous ceremony where Kappy and Joe renewed their wedding vows in front of family and friends!

9. THE SHAME GAME

Looking at the reunited couple, I shared the story of Joe's fateful encounter with Jesus on the road from Chicago. I told the crowd that the question God asked Joe was not meant just for him. It is something all believers will hear (if we listen) at some point in our walk with Christ: *"Am I enough for you?"*

If your answer is "yes," strap in for the ride of your life, and get ready to move from the mundane to the miraculous. Joe and Kappy have, and their story of redemption is a powerful testimony of God's grace triumphing over man's guilt.

○ ○ ○

No matter what we've done that makes us feel guilty, the grace and forgiveness of God is always available. Just like it was available to Joe the Bad Husband, Peter the Denier ... and yes, even to Judas the Betrayer, if only he would have asked.

Every one of us has done something stupid or embarrassing. We've all done something mean or ugly or even genuinely evil that we regret. When that happens, remember that Peter also faltered big and fell hard. One minute he's jumping out of the boat and walking on water, the next minute he's panicking and sinking. One minute he's bragging about how he would follow Jesus to the bitter end, the next minute he's betraying him three times.

> **We've all done something mean or ugly or evil that we regret.**

No question that Peter's behavior was pretty hit-or-miss — and pretty much *exactly* like the rest of us.

Which makes me wonder why God picked messy, imperfect people like you and me to fulfill the Great Commission. Think about it. Instead of using magnificent, awe-inspiring angels to spread the good news of redemption, he chose ordinary human beings — people who would doubt him and disobey him on a daily basis. People who could eat, sleep and work with God-in-the-flesh for three years and then panic and scatter like scared sheep. People who would sell him out for a bag of cash.

But don't be too rough on Peter. Or even Judas.

If we're truthful, we've all disowned God in our own lives, and probably for a lot less than 30 pieces of silver. Maybe we conveniently pretended to not know Jesus at a job interview, or a family gathering, or at a bar or movie or wherever there's a chance to be put on the spot. Selling out

Selling out Jesus is easier and more common than we think.

Jesus is easier and more common than we think, and the guilt it produces can be devastating. But when you do slip and fall, don't ever believe any voice that says *you're so bad you're beyond forgiveness.*

When you're bombarded by a thousand negative voices shouting and whispering "You stink, you're a loser, you blew it," the only voice you need to key in on is the one that says: *"My grace is sufficient for you, for my power is made perfect in weakness."* [13]

God's grace *is sufficient* to forgive and redeem anyone and everyone who will accept it, and since that offer is extended to backstabbers, double-crossers and traitors, it most certainly includes a nice person like you.

Or like Joe.

After ten years of being a rotten husband, Joe didn't *deserve* another chance. And after screwing up his family, Joe couldn't *earn* another chance. But that's what grace is — *a free gift that we don't deserve and could never earn.* When Kappy gave Joe a touch of grace by agreeing to see the marriage mentors, she didn't expect much, but wonderful things started happening in unseen realms. When she extended a little *more* grace by inviting him to the marriage weekend, she still didn't expect much, but God's love was working behind the scenes to change everything.

Notice that Kappy didn't forgive Joe all at once in some huge, heroic act of mercy. What she did was just open the door a tiny crack ... and grace did the rest. Any amount of grace — no matter how small — can produce huge, unexpected, long-range results. So don't be discouraged waiting for a big miracle to happen on the spot. Think of grace as a tiny acorn that can produce a towering oak tree, and just keep on planting seeds.

A seed could be doing a small act of unexpected kindness. A seed could be forgiving someone who's hurt you. A seed could be returning an insult with a compliment. Or it could be helping someone feel accepted instead of rejected.

Lots of people see God the way Joe did — as an angry schoolmaster. If you ask them, God exists mainly to make us feel inadequate, unworthy, and miserable.

Voltaire said, "God created man in his own image and likeness, and then we returned the favor." He's right! Many of us have created our own version of God — complete with human weaknesses and negative character traits. We've invented a false deity in our own image who rules his subjects with guilt and fear. When people picture God that way, their guilt builds up over the years until even thinking about him makes them uncomfortable.

No wonder they pretend he doesn't exist.

If that's you, know this: The God we follow is the God of grace, not the God of guilt. He is the God of relationships, not the God of rules.

In the courtroom of life, Jesus isn't our prosecutor, he's our defense attorney: *God did not go to all the trouble of sending his Son merely to point an accusing finger, telling the world how bad it was. He came to help, to put the world right again. Anyone who trusts in him is acquitted.*[14]

So let's start acting like it.

○　　○　　○

"Guilt: Punishing yourself before God doesn't."

— Alan Cohen[15]

II: GRACE IS NOT...

CHAPTER 10:
Grace Is Not Self-Righteousness

Tears rolled down their cheeks as members of the "Little Rock Nine" watched Barack Obama being sworn in as President. Back in 1957, these former classmates could only dream that a person of color would one day be president. As students, they were jeered at, spit on and threatened by angry white mobs. In 2008, they each received personal invitations from president-elect Obama to attend his historic inauguration.

Five decades before their tearful reunion in Washington, these African Americans had been chosen to attend Arkansas' largest all-white high school because of their excellent grades. The night before school was to start, Governor Orval Faubus called out the National Guard to surround Little Rock Central High to prevent any black students from entering. When the first of the nine arrived at school, she faced a crowd of over 1,000 angry protesters chanting, screaming and threatening to riot. Images of Elizabeth Eckford courageously walking through a chanting mob ("Two, four, six, eight, we ain't gonna integrate") brought international attention to the crisis. Two weeks later, President Eisenhower sent 1,200 soldiers to Arkansas to escort all nine black students to class. Throughout the school year the Little Rock Nine endured constant verbal and physical harassment.

Their enrollment was the first test of the Supreme Court's *Brown vs. Board of Education* decision, ordering integration of public schools. The heroism of these civil rights pioneers is an inspirational reminder of the enormous progress America has made in race relations. There's still work to be done, but try to imagine the reaction of Governor Faubus (if he were alive today) to the ascension of African Americans like Supreme Court Justice Clarence Thomas, Secretaries of State Colin Powell and Condoleezza Rice, not to mention President Barack Obama!

Racism in any form is evil and ugly. But it's not unique to our country. And it's certainly nothing new. For centuries, the Israelites considered their race superior to not only their enemies but even their peaceful neighbors. One group they particularly despised was the Samaritans. In fact, the Jews hated these "half-breeds" so much they would travel miles out of their way to avoid setting foot on their land. Both nations were descendants of Jacob, but a rift developed during the Babylonian captivity when the Samaritan Jews stayed behind and intermarried with the heathen nations. To make it worse, the Samaritans practiced an alternative form of Judaism, rejecting the Jerusalem Temple and building their own center of worship on Mt. Gerizim in Samaria. This racial hatred grew with each generation, until by the time of Jesus, the term "Samaritan" was a curse word.

When the Jewish leaders verbally attacked Jesus, they could think of no worse insult than using this racial slur: *"Aren't we right in saying that you are a Samaritan and demon-possessed?"* [1]

Racism ran deep, even among Jesus' handpicked team.

The racism ran deep, even among Jesus' handpicked team. Luke describes the disciple's over-the-top reaction when a Samaritan village didn't roll out the red carpet for the Twelve: *"Lord, do you want us to call fire down from heaven to destroy them?"* [2]

After working alongside the loving, merciful, compassionate Jesus for three years, James and John had no qualms about incinerating a whole town full of innocent Samaritans!

This racial animosity set the scene for a dramatic conversation recorded in John 4 between Jesus and a woman who got more than she bargained for on her daily visit to the village well...

Jews going from Galilee to Jerusalem took a huge detour to avoid traveling through Samaria. But on one occasion, Jesus deliberately took a short-cut over the mountains, straight through Samaria. After walking half a day, he stopped to rest beside an old well which had been dug by Jacob hundreds of years before at the foot of Mount Gerizim. Hot and tired, Jesus sent his disciples on ahead to buy food in a nearby village. When he looked down into the well he could see water a hundred feet below. But he had no rope or bucket to hoist up a drink.

Just at that moment a Samaritan woman walked up with a water jar on her head and a rope in her hand. Thirsty from his journey, Jesus asked her for a drink. The woman saw from his looks and clothes that he was a Jew, "No offense, sir, but no Jew has ever spoken to me before. In fact, they'd spit in my face if they had the chance. So why are you asking *me* for a drink?"

She knew Jews looked down on her kind, and she was ready for trouble. But Jesus treated her with total respect. He knew she'd been married five times and was currently shacking up with yet another man, but he did not condemn her. He knew she was living in open adultery, but spoke only of God's grace and the living water he came to bring. He affirmed her worth, and by telling her the truth about who he was — the Messiah — encouraged her to turn from her life of sin.

No guilt, no judgment. Just grace. The result? *"Many of the Samaritans from that town believed in him because of the woman's testimony."* [3]

Based only on what this outcast woman told them, the entire village rushed back and asked Jesus to come to their town and teach them. He went with them, and taught there for two days. And many of the people became believers!

Now imagine the same story, but with a high-ranking Pharisee encountering the woman instead of Jesus...

Thirsty, the immaculately dressed Pharisee looked down his nose at the promiscuous Samaritan woman and hissed with disgust. Asking her to step away from him, he shouted to the people around, "Is there anyone here besides this skanky Samaritan who can give me a cup of water? God knows I shouldn't accept a drink from any of you, let alone this filthy scum. I might catch something. Why can't you people be more like me?" The woman lowered her head in shame and slipped away. She pulled up her veil to hide the tears that ran down her dusty cheeks. Rejected by yet another religious leader, scorned again for her immorality, she was more convinced than ever of her worthlessness.

Pharisees appoint themselves as the unelected morality police.

After a tongue lashing like that, she would have gone right back to her life of sin. And an entire village would have missed hearing that God loves them.

The two previous stories could be summed up in one sentence: *Jesus extended grace, the Pharisee extended judgment.* And although my alternate version is hypothetical, we've all met self-righteous people just like him. The reason they feel qualified to judge others (and not themselves) has always been the same — they feel morally superior. In their mind, they are doing such a good job at keeping God's rules that he is impressed with them and disappointed with the rest of us. Which is why they appoint themselves as the unelected morality police.

Wait, what? Isn't being righteous a good thing? Glad you asked. The answer is yes and no. There are two totally different kinds of righteousness: *God-righteousness* and *self-righteousness*. To begin, let's look at the good kind, the kind that comes from God...

○   ○   ○

Only God is totally and completely righteous in every way. It is God's nature to be perfectly holy, truthful, faithful and just. Everything he thinks or says or does is exactly the "right thing" to think or say or do. It cannot be otherwise. This is mind-boggling, but true. His will is 100 percent righteous and so are his actions. Always. God's righteousness is infinite, eternal and unchangeable.

God is totally righteous because he is totally without sin. But when it comes to people, *"there is none righteous, not even one."* There's never been a totally sinless human being. If you're like me, you might be darn near perfect (except that I just sinned by lying) but close only counts in horseshoes and hand grenades. Scripture says *"all have sinned and fallen short of God's glory."* [4]

In the most lop-sided trade in the universe, God exchanged my sins for his righteousness.

Because of sin, man cannot be righteous. At least not on his own. The only way a sinful man could be considered righteous by a holy God is if that God conferred his own righteousness upon that man. And that's exactly what happened! When Jesus took my place and died on the cross, God exchanged *my* sins for *his* righteousness. In the most lop-sided trade in the universe, he got punished for my sins and I got credited for his righteousness: *"God has declared him who had no sin to be sin for us, so that in him we might become the righteousness of God."* [5]

Because he was totally sinless, Jesus was legally eligible to pay the penalty for all my sins — past, present and future. This transaction means God could legally declare me innocent. Not guilty. Righteous. Thanks to what Jesus did, I am now in "right standing" before God.

This next statement is so outrageous that I blush to write it down: I am fully loved, cherished and accepted by God, without question, without time limit. And all he asks for in return is my trust in Christ.

As Lee Iacocca (the man credited with saving Chrysler from bankruptcy) once said, "If you can find a better deal, take it."

This righteousness that was "transferred to my account" is available free to anyone and everyone who believes and receives. It can't be worked for and it can't be earned. It's a gift: *"For it is by grace you have been saved, through faith — and this not from yourselves, it is the gift of God — not by works, so that no one can boast."* [6]

Mother Teresa and Joe Six-Pack must come to God exactly the same way — by grace alone.

Everyone from Mother Teresa to Joe Six-Pack comes into right relationship with God exactly the same way — by grace alone. This God-righteousness is not attainable by performing good works in Calcutta or Kalamazoo: *"Saving is all his idea, and all his work. All we do is trust him enough to let him do it. It's God's gift from start to finish."* [7]

Jesus did nothing to deserve the Roman whip or the crown of thorns or the nails in his hands. If you saw Mel Gibson's *The Passion of the Christ* you got a small idea of the torture he endured. But remember, he was not a victim, he was a volunteer. He voluntarily left heaven to take the punishment we deserved: *"Christ died for the ungodly."* And although we did nothing to warrant his love, Jesus died for us anyway: *"God demonstrates his own love for us in this: While we were still sinners, Christ died for us."* [8]

Because of this "great exchange," God is able to treat us *as if we have never sinned.* The instant we ask him for forgiveness, our slate is wiped clean. Most people, even longtime Christians, can't grasp that. It sounds too good to be true — a life without guilt, a life of believing that God is for you and not against you. But it *is* true. He wants to treat every one of us like we have never sinned. But he can't, unless we let him.

> **You can be freed from the penalty of sin forever. Right now.**

If you have never told God, "I need you in my life," I invite you to do it now: **"God, I know I've made mistakes. I'm sorry for the wrong things I've done. I want to be forgiven. I want to have a relationship with you. I want you to be my heavenly Father. I want to go to heaven when I die. I believe that you sent your Son, Jesus, to earth. I believe he lived a sinless life, died on the cross for me, and rose from the dead three days later. Come into my heart, Jesus. Be my Lord and Savior. Make me a new creation. Thank you for washing my sins away. Jesus, in your name I pray. Amen."**

If you prayed something like that from your heart, either just now or sometime in the past, *you have the righteousness of God.* You are freed from the penalty of sin forever.

If you've joined the millions who've decided to follow Jesus, congrats, I'll see you in heaven someday. But know this — whenever and wherever you came to Christ, it was because God himself was tugging on your heart to do so. He's the *initiator* of grace, we are the responder. He reaches out to us, not us to him. Grace was all his idea from start to finish. We can't take any credit for our own salvation. Singer and author, Michael Card, understood this at an early age. When he was just eight, adults asked him if he had "asked Jesus into his heart." He replied, "No, Jesus asked *me* into *His* heart." Card recalls, "I realized the impetus really came from Him and that He was inviting me."[9]

You may not look different on the outside or feel different on the inside, but your faith in God has made you righteous: *"For in the gospel, a righteousness from God is revealed, a righteousness that is by faith from first to last."*[10] In this easily overlooked passage in Romans, Paul condenses the secret of salvation into a single phrase that Martin Luther called his "gateway to heaven."

As an Augustinian monk, Luther was tortured with doubts about his salvation. He described his conduct as "impeccable and irreproachable" but still felt separated from God by his guilt: "I stood before God as a sinner troubled in conscience." His anguish pushed him away from God, "I hated and murmured against him." To ease his guilt, he tried confessions, penances, and abstinences. In 1510, he even tried a pilgrimage to Rome where he crawled up Pilate's Stairs on his hands and knees. It was the custom of pilgrims to climb this shrine one step at a time, saying prayers and kissing the marble where the blood of Jesus supposedly fell (the Pope promised an indulgence to all who endured the climb). But halfway up Luther remembered the words of the prophet Habakkuk, *"The just will live by faith."*[11] The story goes that when he recalled this verse he stopped climbing, turned around and went straight back to Germany.

Later, while meditating on scripture, the feisty monk had the game-changing revelation that would rock the establishment church to the core. Luther's insight into the first chapter of Romans replaced a religion based on dead works with a relationship based on living grace. When he analyzed the phrase *"righteousness from God,"* the father of the Reformation said: "I felt myself to be reborn and to have gone through open doors into paradise. The whole of scripture took on a new meaning ... this passage of Paul became to me a gateway to heaven."[12]

Unfortunately, not everyone is like Luther — they're too proud to accept God's free gift and try to earn their salvation by working for it. Both the Old and New Testament say that righteousness comes from God alone. But human nature drives us to rely on our own efforts instead of grace. In a nutshell, that human effort is the bad kind of righteousness — *self-righteousness.* And it's a lie. A lie that goes all the way back to the Garden...

o   o   o

True, godly righteousness means desiring to live by *God's* standards of right and wrong, submitting to *God's* leadership. But ever since Adam and Eve, man has tried to set his own standard of righteousness — to be morally independent of God. Maybe Satan was humming Sinatra's "I Did It My Way" just before he was cast out of heaven. I can't say for sure. But this prideful determination to "do it my way" was definitely Lucifer's downfall: *"How you have fallen from heaven ... you have been cast down to the earth ...You said in your heart, I will ascend to heaven; I will raise my throne above the stars of God ... I will make myself like the Most High."* [13]

This same Lucifer who led a failed mutiny against God later told Adam and Eve they too could be like the Most High, calling their own shots: *"When you eat of it your eyes will be opened, and you will be like God, knowing good and evil."* [14]

They fell for it, literally, and we've lived in a fallen world ever since.

As we follow the offspring of the First Couple down through history, we see the absolute futility of "self redemption."

BEFORE the law was given, man became so utterly depraved that God sent the Flood to wipe them out: *"The Lord saw how great man's wickedness on the earth had become, and that every inclination of the thoughts of his heart was only evil all the time. The Lord was grieved that he had made man on the earth."* [15] And that's when God commissioned Noah to build the Ark. After 40 days of rain, mankind had a chance for a fresh start. But Noah's clan of eight survivors soon repopulated the earth with degenerate outlaws more wicked than their drowned ancestors.

AFTER the law was given, all attempts to obey it failed. Some kept it better than others, but nobody obeyed it completely. From the high priest to the town drunk, nobody got a perfect score. But of the two, the wino in the gutter was probably better off. Why? Because he knows he needs help! When a self-righteous person blows it, they don't ask God for forgiveness, they rationalize it away: "I'm not as bad as so-and-so. At least I don't do such-and-such."

Since they won't admit they need a savior, they grade themselves on a curve, using a moral scorecard they create themselves: *"Those who think they can do it on their own end up obsessed with measuring their own moral muscle but never get around to exercising it in real life."* [16]

Instead of asking for mercy, a self-righteous person will simply try harder, pray longer, sing louder, whatever. But despite their hard work, all they can do is clean up their outside appearance. Sin isn't like dirt on our skin, it's dirt on our heart, and we have no way to deal with it on our own. So instead of looking inward at their own sin, they look outward at *yours.*

Christians are best known for telling people how to look, think, behave and vote.

And boy, do they let you know it when you fall short!

Judging from today's news coverage, believers seem best known for being self-righteous — for telling other people how to look and think and behave and vote. The average guy on the street now thinks Christians hate gays, minorities, feminists, environmentalists, tattoo artists, rappers, immigrants, you name it.

But slamming people is not what Jesus was known for. In fact, he saved his criticisms for the self-righteous "saints" of his society, not the "sinners."

No wonder the religious types wanted to get rid of him.

If you see a religious person pumping up his ego instead of giving credit to Jesus, you can bet he's certifiably self-righteous. Paul says we should never boast *"except in the cross of our Lord Jesus Christ."* [17] Hype and spin and self-promotion may be the world's way to the top, but Jesus said we shouldn't do our good deeds to be noticed by others. Shakespeare said the whole world is a stage, but God is not impressed by our theatrics: *"Be especially careful when you are trying to be good so that you don't make a performance out of it. It might be good theater, but the God who made you won't be applauding."* [18]

o   o   o

Whenever I warn people about the risks of legalism and judging others, one question always comes up: *Are we supposed to just ignore sin or let our friends engage in risky behavior?* Again, the answer is yes and no. Introducing people to Jesus is our job. Changing their lives is his job. When a person gets in right relation with God, the Holy Spirit will deal with them about sin issues. If they're *not* in relation with God, you can't expect them to obey his rules anyway. They won't *want* to and they won't be *able* to. When a believer tells a non-believer that their behavior doesn't meet God's standards, it's like speaking a foreign language.

> **Introducing people to Jesus is our job. Changing their lives is his job.**

Think of it this way. If you're a parent, you've got rules around your house regarding chores, bedtime, homework and so on. But are the *neighbor kids* obligated to obey *your* family's rules? Same for people who aren't part of God's family. Our job is to lovingly proclaim God's kingdom, not to condemn non-Christians for living like ... well, like *we* used to!

Of course, there are times when we need to step in and speak out, but beware of acting superior (because we're not). Our advice shouldn't have even a hint of pride or smugness or "I told you so." Wait for appropriate times and ways to warn others about destructive behaviors. But make sure you're motivated only by love. Anything else comes off like we're "holier than thou," and nothing stinks up a room faster than that.

So there's a big, big difference between being "God-righteous" and "self-righteous." God-righteous people extend *grace*. Self-righteous people extend *judgment*. Here's how each type might react to the exact same news...

SELF-RIGHTEOUS. "15 years old and pregnant. Just what this country needs — another unwed mother to feed. I'm not surprised, the way she dresses. Looks like a hooker half the time. And all those tattoos. Nice job, trailer trash."

GOD-RIGHTEOUS. "Do we still have our old crib in the garage? Let's give her our stroller, too. I'm thrilled she's keeping the baby. Let's ask her parents if we can host a baby shower. Can't wait to invite her to my new mother's group."

Here's another situation...

SELF-RIGHTEOUS. "I heard Frank just got canned. Probably caught him goofing off. Or stealing. Lots of companies are getting rid of slackers. Anyway, I told him this was going to happen. Should've got more training like I did."

GOD-RIGHTEOUS. "So sorry to hear Frank got laid off. Must be devastating. I'll ask around to see if we have any openings. Maybe I can help him whip up a new resume. I'll ask if he needs some cash to tide them over."

Have you ever met Self-Righteous Guy from these examples? Did he brag about his own accomplishments? Was he cold-hearted? Chances are you were completely turned off. Guys like him talk a good game, but have no love for hurting people. Unlike him, Jesus pursued messed-up, marginalized people with radical, underserved love. And so should we.

Did you notice Self-Righteous Guy always compares himself favorably to people he looks down on? This public display of moral superiority is why Jesus condemned the Pharisees. In Luke's gospel, Jesus revealed what God thinks of spiritual ego trippers. His private audience for this parable contained *"some who were confident of their own righteousness."*

You can almost feel the showdown coming.

Imagine how awkward it was for them to hear: *"Two men went up to the temple to pray ... the Pharisee stood up and prayed about himself: 'God, I thank you that I am not like other men — robbers, evildoers, adulterers ... I fast twice a week and give a tenth of all I get.' But the tax collector stood at a distance. He would not even look up to heaven, but beat his breast, and said, 'God, have mercy on me, a sinner.'"*

In this scenario, we have the highest and the lowest strata of society both talking to God. The results? *"I tell you that this man* (the tax collector), *rather than the other* (the Pharisee), *went home justified before God. For everyone who exalts himself will be humbled, and he who humbles himself will be exalted."* [19]

> **Jesus pursued messed-up, marginalized people with radical, underserved love. So should we.**

Sometimes it's not so easy to spot the self-righteous person because they seem to be doing all the right things. But Jesus knows, and he's far more concerned about our motives than our actual acts: *"Be careful not to do your 'acts of righteousness' before men, to be seen by them. If you do, you will have no reward from your Father in heaven ... when you give to the needy, do not let your left hand know what your right hand is doing, so that your giving may be in secret. Then your Father, who sees what is done in secret, will reward you."* [20]

The Pharisees boasted openly about their "rightness" with God, using themselves as society's standard of perfection. In the process, they pushed people away from God with their hypocrisy. True righteousness is a gift from God, but when we use it to criticize somebody else, we turn a blessing into a curse.

○   ○   ○

In his Sermon on the Mount, Jesus said we were blessed if we *"hungered and thirsted for righteousness."* That means we should have a deep yearning for personal holiness (right living), a desire to do what pleases God (obedience), and a burn in our heart to help others (compassion). So definitely pursue righteousness, but make sure you're after *God's* righteousness and not a version you create on your own. *"Seek first his kingdom and his righteousness."* [21]

The Pharisees knew the law backwards and forwards, and because of that felt they were right with God. But they weren't. No matter how good we are, we cannot live up to the standard of God (perfect obedience) or the character of God (perfect holiness). Jesus warned anyone who thought they could, *"Unless your righteousness surpasses that of the Pharisees and the teachers of the law, you will certainly not enter the kingdom of heaven."* [22]

To "surpass" the strict obedience of the Pharisees meant you would have to be literally perfect — never slipping up even once. James writes, *"For whoever keeps the whole law and yet stumbles at just one point is guilty of breaking all of it."* [23]

If the law is your umpire, it's "One strike and you're out!" Here's what I mean: Suppose a man is super-spiritual and somehow manages to live without committing a single sin for 37 years. The whole religious community looks up to him. Then one day, he's walking to church, praying out loud as he goes. Suddenly, he hears a sound and when he looks up a pigeon poops on his forehead. He curses! *Ooops.* Under law, that one sin would erase his entire lifetime of good deeds and obedience. He goes from innocent to guilty in one big splat.

You can imagine how hard this person would try to hide his slip-up from the religious community. And that's how self-righteous people operate. They cover up their black marks, while holding up their gold stars. They look down on anyone who fails to live up to their moral standings. But they're like the guy who cusses out the pigeon. They know they've fallen short but *refuse to admit it.*

The religious leaders hid their secret sins behind positions of power and influence. But Jesus pointed out their shortcomings. He knew the darkness in their hearts. And he knew exposing it would lead to his death. Disregarding his own safety, he made the Pharisees his mortal enemies by making their hypocrisy public: *"Woe to you, teachers of the law and Pharisees, you hypocrites! ... On the outside you appear to people as righteous but on the inside you are full of hypocrisy and wickedness."* [24]

Ironically, the Pharisees did not see themselves as God's enemy, but as his chosen defenders. So they lived a phony religious life, pretending they had no need for forgiveness. No wonder Jesus called them "snakes" and "vipers."

But they studied day and night. What did they miss?

The Pharisees had one giant blind spot: They failed to grasp that redemption comes *before* righteousness. You cannot reverse the order. And you cannot redeem

> You cannot redeem yourself any more than you can give birth to yourself.

yourself any more than you can give birth to yourself. *"Not by works of righteousness which we have done, but according to his mercy he saved us."* [25]

Anyone who thinks they can become righteous by sweat equity doesn't understand true Christianity at all. Paul said *"For if righteousness could be gained through the law, Christ died for nothing."* [26]

That pivotal verse begs the question: *Should we try to keep the law?*

The law still provides good standards for personal behavior and an orderly society. It protects private property, marriage, public safety and health standards. But it's not binding on us today in the same sense. When Jesus died on the cross, he put an "end" to Old Testament law: *"Christ is the end of the law so that there may be righteousness for everyone who believes."* [27]

The word "end" in this verse can mean "termination," but more likely in this context, it means "fulfillment." Because Jesus fulfilled the law perfectly, we are freed from its condemnation and guilt. But we should still follow its moral and ethical guidelines — out of love for the one who wrote it! In a letter to the Galatians, Paul says we are now under the law of Christ, not the Law of Moses.[28]

What *is* that new law? The Royal Combo!

It sounds like a burger with fries, but this tasty Combo is actually the two-part admonition of Jesus: *"Love the Lord your God with all your heart and with all your soul and with all your mind ... and to love your neighbor as yourself."*[29]

If we fulfill this double-barreled commandment, we will automatically be obeying all the rules that God requires: *"All the Law and the Prophets hang on these two commands."*[30]

Think about it — if you love God, you won't carve an idol or worship a false god or use his name in vain, right? And if you love your neighbor, you won't steal from him, or murder him, or sleep with his spouse, or lie about him in court! As Christ-followers, we obey because we are grateful — not because we are trying to earn Brownie points with God.

As author Max Lucado said, "The law can show us where we do wrong, but it can't make us eager to do right. Grace can."[31] We're free to serve Jesus out of gratitude and love, *"This is love for God: to obey his commands."*[32]

That's the difference between *religion* and *relationship*.

Someone once called religion "man trying to make himself right before God." It's a pretty good definition, because every world religion *except* Christianity claims that salvation is attained by human effort — that by being good and working hard and performing religious rituals we can become our own redeemer.

If anyone could have "self-redeemed," it would have been Paul — the strictest Pharisee of all. He even tortured fellow Jews who broke away to follow Christ. But after his conversion, he told those same believers to live free, like privileged children, not slaves. He knew firsthand how people feverishly work to win God's favor: *"The Jews are impressively energetic regarding God — but they are doing everything backwards. They don't seem to realize that this salvation is God's business."* [33]

○   ○   ○

God's grace is amazing. And because of it, many of us have kicked bad habits, overcome addictions and turned our lives around. But experiencing transformational life change carries a two-pronged temptation — to begin believing that we are special and that we can tell others how to live.

This is how *God-righteous* people sometimes become *self-righteous* people. They forget it was grace alone that changed them. Christian leaders who gain recognition for their talent or accomplishments can begin to think they're drawing crowds or selling books or appearing on *Oprah* because of what *they do* rather than what God *has done.*

The Book of Proverbs warns *"pride comes before a fall."* And it can happen where you least expect it. One internationally known television preacher made pornography his favorite target. Night after night, he preached fire and brimstone against sexual sin, dabbing his brow and jabbing his finger at anyone who had a problem with lust. Then one day he was caught with a prostitute in his car, committing adultery amidst stacks of porn magazines. He confessed to having been addicted for years. His life and ministry were ruined — not so much by his sin, but by his hypocrisy and refusal to get help.

More recently a national religious leader known as an advocate for family values was caught with his longtime homosexual lover who also supplied him

There's a little Pharisee in all of us. It's called the "Me Monster."

with illegal drugs. On the outside this happily married pastor looked fine and gave great sermons, but on the inside he was leading a double life. Worst of all, he had made a great living by loudly criticizing other people for their sins.

Unfortunately, there's a little of that same Pharisaical pride in all of us. We've all overlooked our own mistakes in the rush to judge someone else. Comedian Brian Regan calls it "The Me Monster." It's what convinces us we're better and more important than anyone else. It's why we extend grace to ourselves and judgment to others. It's daily proof that we're in it for us, that "it's all about me" — and if we don't admit it, we don't understand what it means to be human.

○   ○   ○

God's gifts are never given to puff us up. They're given to bless others. If we distance ourselves from people we consider "unrighteous," we are missing it. If we feel superior to those who look, speak, dress, believe or behave different than us, we've got it backwards.

This toxic self-righteousness is what creates racial hatred. It fueled racism at Little Rock High School in 1957 and it fueled racism back in ancient Palestine.

In Luke 10, a severely beaten Jew is lying half dead on the roadside. A high-ranking religious official who leads worship at the temple spots him. He looks at the bleeding man but crosses the road to avoid him. Next, a Levite walks up. He is also a religious dignitary, but walks by and ignores the suffering man. Lastly, a Samaritan — from the race the Jews hated — sees the man. He stops and helps the injured victim.

Of course, this unlikely hero has "bad theology" and a "bad pedigree." But God is not impressed by what impresses us. He is not swayed by family trees, educational degrees, financial success, political power, celebrity status, prestigious awards, or religious affiliation.

He is only impressed by (are your ready?) ... surrender.

When somebody surrenders and says, *"Not what I will, but*

what you will" heaven rejoices.[34] When somebody says, *"Here am I, send me"* the angels toss their halos in the air and throw a party. [35]

God isn't impressed if we go to church every day. Or if we donate enough money to build a hospital named after us. God is impressed when one of his children demonstrates his character by extending grace. Which is what the Samaritan did when he stopped to bandage the wounds of his sworn enemy.

When Jesus made the racial outcast the star of his parable, it blew the minds of Jerusalem's "ethnically pure" leaders. But it was more than irony that Jesus was after. He carefully cast the characters in the Good Samaritan to emphasize his point: The high and mighty of this world have always been too self-absorbed to recognize their need for a savior. So God picked the losers (like you and me and the half-breed hero) instead. *"God chose the foolish things of the world to shame the wise; God chose the weak things of the world to shame the strong. He chose the lowly things of this world and the despised things."*[36]

Even though he wasn't a religious leader, the Samaritan was the most God-like of the three men, reaching across racial and economic barriers to save a life. The battered man on the side of the road didn't *deserve* the Samaritan's help. And he was certainly in no shape to *earn* it.

But that's what grace is — a wonderful gift we don't deserve and could never earn: *"He took our sin-dead lives and made us alive in Christ. He did this all on his own, with no help from us!"*[37]

The *self*-righteous man brags about himself and struts around like a king. The *God*-righteous man remembers how the real King wrapped a servant's towel around his holy waist and washed his disciple's smelly feet.

And that is grace in action.

o   o   o

"Jesus Christ didn't come into this world to make bad people good. He came to make dead people live."

— Ravi Zacharias[38]

II: GRACE IS NOT...

CHAPTER 11:
Does God Hate Mr. Rogers?

The small country church was packed with mourners consoling the family of a young Marine killed by a roadside bomb in Iraq. Seated on the front pew, the boy's parents held hands and fought back tears as their pastor spoke to the crowd. When the eulogy concluded, guests filed past the flag-draped coffin as a military honor guard stood silently at attention. In a moment the soldiers would carefully fold the American flag 13 times into a tight triangle and hand it to the grieving parents as a symbol of respect and gratitude for their sacrifice.

Inside the church, the only sounds were the somber chords of the old Wurlitzer and the hushed whispers of condolence.

Outside the church, all hell was breaking loose.

Standing directly across the street, a small mob of noisy protesters held up signs reading "God Hates Fags" and "America Is Doomed." Chanting anti-gay epithets, the protesters marched around this military funeral with a message so vicious and out of place that it made the national news. At first, their choice of targets didn't make sense. This was a funeral for a fallen hero. He was not a homosexual. Nor was anyone openly gay in his regiment. But the protesters insisted that God was killing soldiers in Iraq as judgment against America for tolerating gays. To their twisted minds, it made perfect sense to disrupt this most personal and solemn ceremony to get their message of hate into the mainstream media.

Two things made this horrific intrusion even more disturbing. First, it wasn't an isolated incident. This same sick spectacle has been repeated by this group at 200 other military funerals. Second, the protesters claim to be "Christians," acting on orders from God. If non-Christians ever need more evidence to dismiss believers as hate mongers and bigots, this group is Exhibit A.

Based in Kansas, the group calls itself an "independent Baptist church" (attendance is estimated at fewer than 50, many are family members).They first got the media's attention by disrupting the funeral of a gay college student brutally murdered in 1998. Although this marked their first time in the national spotlight, they had already been picketing the funerals of AIDS victims since 1991. Among other targets, they protested at memorial services for 13 West Virginia coal miners killed in 2006, claiming the disaster was God's revenge against America.

Condemning people to hell is the group's specialty. At the funeral for another soldier killed in Iraq, their spokesperson told a television reporter that the dead soldier was "already burning in hell." Even Billy Graham isn't safe. The group pickets Graham's crusades, claiming the evangelist will burn in hell for failing to endorse their "God Hates Fags" doctrine.

Condemning people to hell is the hate group's specialty.

It's hard to determine who the group hates most. According to their website, Jews (they call them "Christ Killers"), Catholics (they call Pope Benedict the "Godfather of Pedophiles"), and members of every world religion are headed for hell. Even the innocuous Amish are bound for perdition. Members of the group have protested at celebrity funerals ranging from Fred Rogers (the PBS star of *Mr. Roger's Neighborhood*) to Jerry Falwell (founder of the Moral Majority). Although they seem to hate everyone except themselves, the group despises gays above all other "sinners" and believes homosexuality should be punishable by death. They maintain that gays *cannot* repent and that every tragedy in the world is linked to the "unpardonable sin" of homosexuality.

Claiming to speak for God, they matter-of-factly proclaim that he is punishing this nation and using terrorism as his weapon of choice.

The damage done by this religious fringe group is way out of proportion to their size. Christians (and sane people everywhere) are appalled at the church's tactics. Their self-righteous message has prompted Christian leaders of every denomination to denounce the group. But they continue with their signs and bullhorns, publically judging others in the name of a God they don't seem all that familiar with. Jesus would have never tolerated such a hateful response, not even to the Pharisees who plotted his death.

> **Some have twisted the Great Commission into the Great Condemnation.**

It's virtually inconceivable that anyone claiming to follow the teachings of Jesus could twist the Great Commission — the spreading of the gospel — into a mission of condemnation. In fact, our role as Christ-followers is the total opposite: *"For God did not send his Son into the world to condemn the world, but to save the world through him."* [1]

Wait a minute — didn't God condemn entire cities?

Yes, back in the Old Testament, God severely judged people who were involved in gross immorality like child sacrifice and idolatry. In Genesis, we read how the citizens of Sodom and Gomorrah tried to turn a heavenly visit by angels into a gang rape. Street crime and sexual violence were rampant, but God mercifully agreed to spare the twin cities if Abraham could find just ten righteous men living there. Unfortunately, there were none to be found and God's patience ran out: *"Then the Lord rained down burning sulfur."* [2]

But condemnation was never God's first response.

Throughout the Bible, we see that even in the face of utter depravity, God was merciful to any individual or any nation who would listen and repent. That's why he called upon Jonah to go and preach to the wicked city of Nineveh. You probably recall how Jonah stubbornly refused to go, ran in the opposite direction and wound up in the belly of a whale. But do you know *why* he was so reluctant to go? Because Jonah felt that his people were morally superior to the Ninevites! He believed that anyone outside of his circle should suffer God's wrath. Sound familiar?

Blinded by pride and self-righteousness, Jonah (like the anti-gay pastor) believed the Jews deserved God's mercy but non-Jews did not. This grumbling, disobedient prophet was perfectly willing to let a city of 120,000 men, women and children perish because he didn't like their behavior. Again, sound familiar?

When a human being picks who should receive grace and who should receive judgment, it's proof they're clueless about the nature of God. The truth is that *none* of us deserve grace; we *all* deserve judgment! Jonah (and many people today) didn't understand that grace — by definition — goes to the *undeserving*.

Jonah was ticked off that God would show compassion to an enemy of Israel, but he reluctantly warned them to repent. Amazingly, the Ninevites heeded his warnings, turned to God and were spared from judgment. Not because they *deserved* deliverance — they were big into witchcraft, plundering and torture — but because God is a God of mercy. And that's what the gang from Kansas doesn't get. Labeling people who God loves as "fags" and "whores" is denying them his mercy, lying to them about his character, and pushing them away from anything to do with true Christianity.

o   o   o

The destruction of Sodom and Gomorrah occurred under the Old Covenant — a temporary contract God made with mankind employing laws and regulations at its core instead of grace. God had predetermined this system of laws would be useful for maintaining an orderly society, but would not have the ability to transform men's hearts. It started with the Ten Commandments that Moses brought down from Mt. Sinai and ended with the death of Jesus on the cross.

With the death, burial and resurrection of Jesus, God ushered in a New Covenant. When Jesus uttered his last words *"It is finished,"* he was referring to the Old Covenant with its impossible-to-keep system of laws. This New Covenant was about love, not law. When asked which commandment was the greatest, Jesus answered without hesitation that we should love God and love others.

Did God get rid of the law? Are the Big Ten obsolete?

No way. In fact, nine of them are repeated in the New Testament. (The one that's missing is observing the Sabbath. As believers saved by grace, we enjoy not just a *day* of rest, but a *lifetime* of rest. We no longer work to earn God's favor, but rest in what he's done on our behalf.) We know that Jesus kept the law perfectly, or he wouldn't have been qualified as the sinless sacrifice. Talking about those laws he followed so flawlessly, Jesus said: *"I have not come to abolish them, but to fulfill them."* [3] Another translation says, *"I'm not here to demolish but to complete."* [4]

The Sermon on the Mount can be viewed as a living commentary on the Ten Commandments, with Jesus as the true interpreter of what the Mosaic Law really meant. He re-emphasized its moral teachings, but went beyond the letter of the law (keeping it outwardly) to the intent behind the law (keeping it inwardly). When Jesus condemned superficial

> **Nine of the Ten Commandments are repeated in the New Testament.**

"good works" like public prayer, giving alms and fasting, it was because they were being done for show, to impress others. We should definitely keep doing those things, *but from the heart.*

So the laws of God are still vitally important, but now we can obey them out of love instead of fear. Gratitude instead of obligation.

Here's more great news: When we submit to the lordship of Jesus, the Spirit of God comes to live inside of us, and he gives us the supernatural ability we need to live a pure, obedient, holy life: *"You will receive power when the Holy Spirit comes on you."*[5]

Our good works cannot save us. But God saves us to do good works.

This ability or power is often called "enabling grace."

So there's saving grace and enabling grace. Sorry if that sounds complicated. Here's the 4-1-1: After grace *saves* us, it *enables* us to become whatever God calls us to be. It empowers us to do the work he's chosen for us. In that sense, grace and power are almost synonymous.

Let's recap this dynamic duo.

SAVING GRACE is your get-out-of-jail-free card. When it comes to breaking God's laws, we're all guilty. But saving grace declares us innocent. How? The only way we can be pronounced "not guilty" is if an innocent person steps in and takes the blame for us — *saving* us from punishment. That person is Jesus.

But there is more to grace than forgiveness.

ENABLING GRACE is the power God uses to work his will in our lives. It allows ordinary people to do extraordinary things beyond their natural abilities: *"The things which are impossible with men are possible with God."*[6]

As we've seen, our good works cannot save us. But God saves us to do good works! We are to expand his kingdom and proclaim his kingdom until he returns to claim it. The natural byproduct of a person saved by grace is a productive life of good works and cheerful obedience. God gives us enabling grace so that we can obey him and serve him. *"Let us have grace, whereby we may serve God."*[7]

Little is known about Jesus' boyhood. But Luke's gospel notes that as an adolescent, Jesus grew in grace and favor. His observation describes a young Jesus — probably under 12 years old — who had not yet celebrated *bar mitzvah* to take his adult role in the religious community. *"The child grew and became strong in spirit, filled with wisdom; and the grace of God was upon Him."* [8] This grace was the enabling grace of God, revealed as Jesus began to exhibit his distinctive personality and potential to contribute good things to his village.

The Apostle Paul was the original workaholic. He planted churches, trained leaders, evangelized Asia, and wrote epistles like a teenager with unlimited texting. He may have accomplished more for God than any single man in history. But he always knew where his ability came from: *"It was God giving me the work to do, God giving me the energy to do it."* [9]

Paul worked hard, but the impact of his work was multiplied far beyond human capabilities by the grace of Jesus working through him. Thanks to enabling grace, it doesn't matter if we are weak or poor or insignificant — when God wants us to do something for him, he supplies everything we need for the task. In fact, the weaker we are, the stronger he is! God told Paul, *"My grace is sufficient for you, for my power is made perfect in weakness."* [10]

The Apostle Paul was the original workaholic.

When God calls us to do a task, he supplies the ideas, the energy, the resources, even the finances to accomplish it: *"God is able to make all grace abound to you, so that in all things at all times, having all that you need, you will abound in every good work."* [11]

Singer-songwriter Michael Card credits his considerable success to God's enabling grace — even though his original reason for becoming a musician (to attract girls) was "nothing remotely spiritual." Card says that's the beauty of grace, "God even uses our mixed motives. God uses those things, thank goodness, because it's all we've got. He takes our foolishness and our fragileness and does incredible stuff with them."[12]

As freedom-loving Americans, we were raised to be self-reliant. That can be a virtue. But as believers we need to re-think that and become *God-reliant*. Otherwise when a task seems beyond our natural abilities, we'll be tempted to give up and quit. We'll think, "I'm weak in that area, I can't do that, I'll just screw it up." But if we rely on God's enabling grace, we can put our trust in *his* abilities and say, "I might be weak but God is all-powerful and he lives in me."

That's how Paul prevailed against all odds. After suffering enormous hardships, persecution and disappointments he could confidently say, *"I can do all things through Christ who strengthens me."*[13]

Okay, so grace *"builds you up."*[14] But how do we get it? By asking! *"Let us therefore come boldly unto the throne of grace, that we may obtain mercy, and find grace to help in time of need."*[15]

Don't be embarrassed to ask for grace. Don't think your request will annoy God. One translation says we are to come and ask *"with confidence."*[16]

○   ○   ○

Under the New Covenant, judgment has been superseded by grace. And since God does not judge *us*, how dare we judge others? Why should we parade around with vicious signs condemning people? Wouldn't it be better to treat all people with love and respect? To surprise them with random acts of compassion?

The answer is a resounding love-your-enemies "yes." In fact, someone way smarter than me has said that compassion is the new apologetics.

Sounds good, but what the heck is "apologetics?"

For centuries, Christian thinkers have defended the true faith against heresies and opposing beliefs through a systematic use of reason called *apologetics*. This intellectual branch of theology attempts to prove the truth of our doctrines by rational argument. That's the good part.

The not so good part is when this formal logic is used to coerce non-Christians to become believers. Debating can be fun. And it can be intellectually stimulating. But it seldom converts anyone. When the Apostle Paul — undisputed genius of the first century — debated the Greek philosophers at Mars Hill in Athens, only a few were swayed.[17] Smart people can argue both sides of an issue till they're blue in the face. But no one, not even a hardcore atheist, can argue with compassion-based generosity and serving.

Instead of trotting out 57 scientific and philosophical reasons why God exists, why not just *prove* he exists by showing his love in action? Why not let the world see that Jesus is alive by feeding them and clothing them and giving them a cup of cold water in his name?[18] Why not let them see Jesus in us as we rehab houses, or deliver meals or visit the sick? Instead of picketing against homosexuals, what if we developed real friendships and caring relationships with them?

This radical, pursuing love of Jesus is at the very core of the New Testament. Didn't Jesus say he would leave the 99 sheep for one who was lost? Didn't he say all of heaven rejoices when one sinner repents? Then how can some people still misinterpret his clear message of love and viciously attack "sinners?"

Here's my theory: In Jesus' day, the religious leaders assumed that suffering people were sick or poor or lame because of some detestable act that they or their parents committed. They assumed (like many of us) that awful things (like AIDs or herpes or hepatitis) happen to people because they are sinners. But Jesus never did a lifestyle check when **Jesus resisted assigning blame, and so should we.** someone asked for help. He just healed them. In fact, when the disciples asked him who was to blame for a man's blindness, Jesus replied, *"Neither this man or his parents sinned, but this happened so that the work of God might be displayed in his life."* [19]

Jesus resisted assigning blame, and so should we.

As Rick Warren of Saddleback Church points out, the Good Samaritan did not ask how the injured man ended up in the ditch. He did not ask about his denomination, his political party or his sexual orientation. He simply saw a man in need, and cared for him out of compassion.

o   o   o

Watching the Kansas-based church spout off at somebody's funeral is a classic example of modern-day Pharisees blind to their *own* sins (hatred, racism, homophobia, anti-Semitism, bigotry, etc.) but eager to point out flaws in others. The Royal Commandment of loving God and loving others leaves no room for condemning people for their lifestyle or judging them for their choices.

Could Jesus possibly hate young soldiers because the military they're part of has a policy allowing homosexuals within their ranks? Of course not. Could Jesus hate a church that allows sinners to attend their services? Of course not — he preached love and forgiveness to criminals, prostitutes and crooked tax collectors.

WARNING: This next section might rub you the wrong way. Ready?

Grace is absolutely universal and if it applies to *anyone* it applies to *everyone* — straight, gay, lesbian, bisexual, whatever. The invitation for salvation and forgiveness is addressed to *"whoever believes."* Does God hate the Catholic priests who preyed on innocent young children? Does God hate the pastor who leads the protesters from Kansas? No, he does not. His heart aches for them. He abhors their behavior, but he loves them unconditionally.

Throughout its existence, organized religion has had an unfortunate tendency to become legalistic, judgmental and condemning. These periods of self-righteous fervor have been some of the darkest blots in church history. Over the centuries, misguided zealots have done great injustices — even killing — in the name of God. The bloody Crusades of the twelfth century still block efforts to create harmony and trust between Christianity and Islam today.

Grace is absolutely universal and if it applies to *anyone* it applies to *everyone*.

How would the world be different if our spiritual ancestors had found a way to love their Muslim neighbors instead of fighting them?

But quarreling among *ourselves* is even worse. What if medieval Catholics and Protestants had let their mutual love of Jesus cover their doctrinal differences? What if they had displayed unity to the pagan world instead of burning each other at the stake? What if forgiveness and grace had replaced fear and suspicion at the fifteenth-century Spanish Inquisition? Or in the streets of twentieth-century Belfast?

Christian author Paul Billheimer calls this disunity "Satan's master strategy." He lays the blame for our ineffectiveness on our doctrinal squabbling: "The sin of disunity probably has caused more souls to be lost than all other sins combined."[20]

Sadly, many historic opportunities for unity are lost forever. But here's one that's not: What if the 38,000 Christian denominations on earth today got united behind Jesus and worked together to expand his kingdom? It's hard to imagine, and frankly, it doesn't look promising. Yet Jesus commanded it nonetheless, knowing that love was the only solution for bridging our differences, *"By this all men will know that you are my disciples, if you love one another."*[21]

○   ○   ○

We don't have to look at history to see evidence of toxic

religion. It's alive and well right under our noses. I recently heard about an assistant pastor who was dating a young lady in his church. The two had fallen in love and were seriously considering marriage. However, like many young couples, they failed to set appropriate intimacy boundaries. This led to an evening when they both let down their guard and gave into sexual temptation. When the clergyman confessed it to his superior, he was told to end the relationship immediately and have no further contact with the woman. When she repeatedly tried to talk with him, he refused to return her calls or emails. When she confronted him after church, he turned and ran the other way. Confused and hurt, she desperately wanted to discuss their slip-up and learn from it. But instead of extending grace, he totally rejected her.

Toxic religion is alive and well right under our noses.

Then one Sunday, the assistant pastor was selected to preach his first sermon. He chose to speak on the subject of temptation. He opened with a variety of anecdotes, then began a "true story" about sexual temptation. The young woman in the audience cringed. Looking directly at her, he declared that Satan uses other people in our lives to deceive us, and we need to eliminate those tempters from our life. The girl couldn't believe her ears. She blushed, sensing that everyone in the room knew exactly who he was talking about. He explained that his female temptress was "of the devil" and that he himself had no part in their mutual sin. He concluded by saying that once he realized his girlfriend was doing Satan's work, he cut her off completely.

Imagine being that young woman.

Satan *is* the great deceiver, but we are all held accountable to God for our own individual actions. To deflect blame onto someone else is to deny reality. That day, the young pastor ignored his own sin to judge a woman who had been a loyal, loving friend. His self-righteous attack trampled on her self respect. Thankfully, she had a strong group of supportive friends who saw through the garbage he was spewing.

This kind of hypocrisy reminds me of a friend who once described the church she grew up in with a single word. She called it the "fine" church. Whenever anyone asked how someone else was doing, the reply was always "fine."

How's your marriage doing? Fine. *Is everything good with your job?* Fine. *How are those wonderful kids of yours?* Fine.

Everybody was "fine" all the time, and nobody pressed deeper to find out otherwise. It bothered her because a church community is the one place we should expect to find authentic, honest relationships. Under the protective "umbrella of grace," it's the one place where we should feel safe enough to lower our guard.

To come clean.

To take off the mask.

If people can't be real at church, where *can* they be? But some churches promote phoniness as part of their culture. They brush failure and sin and hurt underneath the carpet or out the back door so no one will see it.

Everything's fine here. We're just an incredible group of super-blessed Christians, living super-godly lives.

Phooey.

We all know the truth. Everything isn't always fine. And when inevitably somebody in the "fine" church isn't so fine, it rocks the boat. It spoils the illusion. It freaks people out. And consequently, hurting people don't experience the grace and acceptance they need. Instead, they are spoken to in whispers and hushed tones for fear of embarrassment. They're told to deal with their pain privately, to keep it between themselves and God. *Wrong.* God puts people in our lives to share our burdens and to help us get through our pain.

If you go to a "fine" church, here's the real deal: If you look

> **God puts people in our lives to share our burdens and to help us through our pain.**

below the surface, everything is not fine, and never will be, as long as imperfect humans like you and me make up the membership of Christ's Body. That's why we need his grace on a minute-by-minute basis. So let's stop playing games and admit it.

If the revolution of love that Jesus ushered in on the cross is missing from your church, *something is wrong*. If you leave your church service feeling beat up, guilty or depressed, *something is wrong*. If you constantly hear a message of judgment and despair instead of grace and hope, then *something is definitely wrong*.

○   ○   ○

Grace was the heart of Jesus' message and the reason he came. Any local church or denomination that doesn't understand this has somehow drifted off course over the years.

In the centuries following the embryonic early church, organized Christendom shifted back to religious legalism. Then, around 1517, a priest named Martin Luther rediscovered the power of grace while reading Paul's writings in Romans. As we saw in chapter 10, Luther reasoned that justification by faith alone was the heart of the gospel — that a sinful person could have right legal standing before a holy God based solely on the work of Jesus imputed to them.

To put it simply, Luther said that salvation by grace was based on *faith in Christ plus nothing*.

But in the pre-Reformation church, clergy had added so many fabricated obligations to this formula that grace was all but forgotten. Unable to read scripture, illiterate churchgoers were taught they should perform rituals and go on pilgrimages and buy indulgences and touch holy relics and even punish themselves physically — all without ever having real assurance of salvation.

After secluding himself in an all-male Augustinian monastery, Luther discovered that even while cloistered away from the temptations of the world, sin was still alive and well in his heart. To resist it, he devoted himself to rigorous prayers and relentless study, but he still felt unclean before God. The more he tried to live a holy life, the more he was convinced of his own unworthiness. The harder he worked to control his thoughts, the more impure his thoughts became. Finally, he concluded (like the Apostle Paul) that his only hope to escape damnation was not human effort but total reliance on the grace of God.

Over the centuries since Luther, the pendulum has swung back and forth between grace and works, but within the last 25 years, a new breed of church has brought grace back to the forefront. Across the world, there has been an increasing focus on preaching God's message of love and grace. This "grace awakening" relies more on developing a deep relationship with God and less on performance-based religion. As a result, these new faith communities are growing exponentially while many older mainline denominations are losing people and closing their doors.

> **Luther declared salvation by grace was based on faith in Christ plus nothing.**

These emerging churches are growing, not because they're "watering down the gospel" (as some would say), but because they understand that the true heart of the gospel is grace. They know that church isn't about people pretending to be perfect, but about a God who is passionately looking for broken, messed up, undeserving people. When any church — regardless of worship style or format — preaches grace like the original apostles did, the Lord will add *"to their numbers daily those who were being saved."* [22]

If you visit one of these grace-based churches (I highly recommend it), you'll likely find some prostitutes, alcoholics, drug dealers, porn addicts, gamblers, adulterers, swindlers, deadbeats and criminals. The very crowd Jesus would have invited over for dinner to your house. You won't find a lot of the "fine" crowd, because these churches encourage attenders to ask tough questions, wrestle with relevant issues and challenge each other in accountability relationships. And in the security of smaller groups that meet offsite, people are even more free to be open and authentic with each other.

This freedom to fail, this transparent "culture of grace," comes from the top down when church leaders admit they have feet of clay, that their struggles to follow God are the same as ours. In this culture, life transformation can take place. In this culture, the Holy Spirit turns people who think God is irrelevant into fully devoted followers of Christ. Surrounded by grace, seekers come to know God and to love him, which in turn leads to their desire to be right with him.

Church isn't about pretending to be perfect. It's about God passionately looking for messed up, broken people.

This isn't *self*-righteousness. This is the *God*-righteousness that turns people into ex-prostitutes, ex-alcoholics, ex-drug dealers, ex-porn addicts, ex-gamblers, ex-adulterers, ex-swindlers, ex-dead beats and ex-criminals. *"If anyone is in Christ, he is a new creation; the old has gone, the new has come! All this is from God, who reconciled us to himself through Christ and gave us the ministry of reconciliation."* [23]

Did you notice that our ministry is *reconciliation*? Not judgment, condemnation, or bullying. Not cursing, arguing, or protesting. The word reconciliation means "reestablishing a relationship, bringing two parties back together." Our job is to tell people that God is not angry with them, that he doesn't hate them, and that he wants to reestablish a relationship that was broken off by sin.

The Kansas-based funeral crashers travel with an arsenal of weird, angry protest signs. Most are shocking. Some are unprintable. But their single most misleading sign reads "God Is Angry Every Day." Presumably not at them of course, but at you and me and everyone who fails to meet their self-righteous standard of morality. The ironic truth is that God *is* angry. But he isn't angry at gay men or the entertainment industry or the U.S. military. He's angry at self-righteous religious people who grossly misrepresent him to the world of precious sinners he loved enough to die for. He's angry at what *Time* columnist Nancy Gibbs calls "the vaudeville of gaudy righteousness."[24]

> **Our ministry is reconciliation. Not judgment, condemnation, or bullying.**

But what about *us*? We may not carry picket signs, but we may carry traces of self-righteousness. We may not shout vulgarities, but we may whisper hurtful things about certain people who God sees as being of inestimable value.

Before we condemn the lunatics who disrupt sacred ceremonies with their media circus, let's admit that we all need to examine our own hearts: *Am I too quick to judge others? Is there anyone I refuse to forgive? Have I written anyone off as too sinful to pray for? Do I take secret joy in the hardship of others? Have I ever withheld compassion because of someone's lifestyle?*

If you answered "yes" to any of these questions, congratulations, you're human! And humans are the only beings in the universe that God Almighty loved enough to send his only Son to rescue and restore.

○   ○   ○

"I am not what I ought to be, I am not what I want to be, I am not what I hope to be in another world; but still I am not what I once used to be, and by the grace of God I am what I am."

— John Newton[25]

II: GRACE IS NOT…

CHAPTER 12:
Grace Is Not Condemnation

After spending 16 years on death row, Stephen Moody was ready to die.

"I understand the consequence of my crime," Moody told reporters from inside his visiting cage. "I made the decision to put myself here. I don't blame my situation on anybody but myself."

Sentenced to death for murdering an alleged drug dealer, Moody was executed in Huntsville, Texas on Wednesday, October 11, 2009. Strapped to the death chamber gurney, he briefly addressed his victim's family through a window. Then, after consoling his friends and relatives, he nodded, "Warden, pull the trigger."

The lethal drugs began flowing into his veins at 6:20 p.m. and he was pronounced dead by a doctor just eight minutes later.

Back in 1991, Moody and a friend had followed a man to his Houston home, broke in and demanded money and drugs. When the crippled homeowner kneeled down and begged for his life, Moody aimed a sawed-off shotgun at his chest. Then, for reasons unknown, he fired his weapon at point blank range. Moody took about $1,200 from the man's pocket and fled.

A career criminal, Moody readily admitted his guilt, "You pay for what you do. It was just supposed to be a robbery. But when you go into a place with a loaded gun, you put yourself in that situation."

Unlike many condemned prisoners, Moody had asked that

no last-minute appeals be filed to block his execution. As a team of lawyers and candle-holding protesters clamored to delay his lethal injection, Moody declined, "I don't want life without parole. I'd rather be dead."

The national debate over capital punishment continues to rage, but one thing is certain: Nobody involved in Moody's execution — regardless of their politics — enjoyed the experience.

Even though he was declared guilty, and even though he confessed to the crime, condemning him to death was traumatic for everyone involved. It was hard on the jury and hard on the judge. It was hard on the guards who strapped him to the steel cart with five leather belts and two steel shackles. It was hard on the technicians who inserted intravenous needles into each of his arms. And it was hard on the warden who flipped the switch on the infusion pump that sent a high-tech cocktail of poison into Moody's bloodstream.

With the prison chaplain standing at Moody's feet, the lethal recipe was administered in three stages: First, a powerful sedative rendered Moody unconscious in less than a minute. Second, a muscle relaxant ceased all muscle movement except his heart. And finally, potassium chloride stopped his heart from beating.

Medical science has tried to make modern execution as painless and humane as possible. Then why was this entire 16-year process so agonizing to watch and participate in? Because no rational, law-abiding person takes pleasure in condemning a fellow human being to death.

They demanded the most gruesome, painful death imaginable.

Unless, of course, that person happened to be a Pharisee.

These guys had absolutely no qualms about condemning Jesus to death — and they didn't wait 16 years to make it happen! The Pharisees sitting on the Jewish Sanhedrin (the highest court in Israel) bypassed due process and rushed

Jesus through an illegal nighttime trial, then turned him over to the Romans for a speedy execution. And instead of a painless euthanizing, they demanded the most gruesome, painful death imaginable — crucifixion.

The Romans were highly proficient at torture and death, but even they were surprised by the Pharisee's bloodlust. At first, Pontius Pilate — never known to be soft on crime — refused to execute such an obviously innocent man on such obviously trumped-up charges. But when he tried to set Jesus free in exchange for Barabbas, the Pharisees incited the fickle crowd into a roaring frenzy. To force Pilate's hand, they used his reluctance to kill the man called "King of the Jews" to question his loyalty to Caesar. Fearing a riot and maybe the loss of his job, Pilate finally gave the orders to execute. To disassociate himself from the over-eager Pharisees, he publically washed his hands of the matter.

Who were these Pharisees who could condemn so easily and without remorse? They were Israel's top-ranking religious leaders. They fanatically enforced community standards for morality and orthodoxy, patrolling Jerusalem like Taliban clerics looking for infractions.

Maybe you're wondering: *If Pharisees were so vindictive and mean-spirited, how did they ever expect to please God?*

By practicing what author Tim Keller calls "self salvation." In his book *The Reason for God*, he writes, "The devil, if anything, prefers Pharisees — men and women who try to save themselves." Scrupulously following the law, they hoped to separate themselves from ordinary men — the word *Pharisee* means "separatist" — and rise above the rest of society. In their minds, God would have no choice but to fling open heaven's pearly gates for them!

They saw their exalted social and political status not as a gift, but as a merit badge earned by flaunting impeccable doctrine and imposing moral absolutism. Wielding their religious superiority like a weapon, they ruled through fear, backed up by their secret police and elite temple guards.

Maybe you're wondering: *Of all people, why would the "religious" leaders be so rotten?*

I've often wondered how Pharisees could read and dissect and memorize scripture but not see their own shortcomings. How could they study prophecies about the promised Messiah but completely miss him when he walked among them? How could the religious people be the ones who conspire to destroy Jesus? Physicist Steven Weinberg has a theory: "With or without religion, you would have good people doing good things and evil people doing evil things. But for good people to do evil things, that takes religion."[1]

The beloved English writer, C.S. Lewis, echoed the irony, "Of all bad men, religious bad men are the worst."

Jesus saw through their religious facade like a walking X-ray machine. He saw the spiritual damage they were inflicting, and exposed them in an extended attack recorded in Matthew's gospel.

> **Jesus saw through their religious facade like a walking X-ray machine.**

First, he exposed their hypocrisy. With a phrase we still use today to chide hypocrites, he declared, *"They do not practice what they preach."*

Next, he exposed their vanity. Dressed in impressive robes, they paraded around like the rock stars of their day. Jesus described their fashion show: *"Everything they do is done for men to see: They make their phylacteries wide and the tassels on their garments long."*

Phylacteries were miniature leather boxes that contained scripture verses. The Pharisees strapped one on their wrist and one on their forehead. They looked the part, but they had long ago lost the meaning of the words the boxes contained. Their garments were fringed with ornate tassels. God had commanded his people to put fringe on their robes to help them remember the Ten Commandments. But the Pharisees used them to impress the common people by drawing attention to themselves instead: *"They love the place of honor at the banquets and the most important seats in the synagogues, they love to be greeted in the marketplaces and to have men call them Rabbi."* [2]

Finally, he exposed their discrimination. These pompous leaders all but slammed the door to God's kingdom by blocking people who were genuinely seeking him: *"Woe to you, teachers of the law and Pharisees, you hypocrites! You shut the kingdom of heaven in men's faces. You yourselves do not enter, nor will you let those enter who are trying to."* [3]

From all over Israel, Jewish farmers, shepherds and tradesmen came to the temple in Jerusalem to hear the good news of God, but the Pharisees burdened them with mountains of protocol, regulations and temple fees. They also shut the door on the Gentiles who came to investigate

> **Religious "insiders" try to slam the door of God's kingdom to all "outsiders."**

God. Many non-Jews admired the Jewish moral standards and were drawn to monotheism. Unfortunately, the Pharisees didn't teach them about the glorious hope of Israel, but forced them to convert to Judaism with its crushing burden of impossible-to-obey regulations: *"You travel over land and sea to win a single convert, and when he becomes one, you make him twice as much a son of hell as you are."* [4]

○   ○   ○

So what happened? Why the bizarre fixations?

At one time, Pharisees were the chosen leaders of God's chosen people. But like their counterparts today, they became obsessed with rules and rituals at the expense of virtues like forgiveness and compassion: *"Woe to you, teachers of the law and Pharisees, you hypocrites! You give a tenth of your spices ... But you have neglected the more important matters of the law — justice, mercy and faithfulness."* [5]

With their encyclopedic knowledge of scripture, they should have been the most faithful of all God's people. But instead, their hearts became filled with greed and political intrigue. They lived to promote themselves; sensitive to public opinion but insensitive to God's will.

Jesus addressed this incongruity with a strange word picture: *"You blind guides! You strain out a gnat but swallow a camel."*[6]

Let me explain. The Pharisees were fastidious about keeping strict dietary regulations. Before taking a drink, they poured their water through a strainer to make sure that no tiny gnats — known as an unclean insect — were in the cup. These hypocrites made absolutely sure that what they drank was pure, but missed huge impurities in their hearts like hate, pride and hypocrisy.

So what is hypocrisy?

Easy. It's the guy who orders a triple bacon burger with a diet Coke. It's the guy who acts busy in front of the boss but goofs off the rest of the time. It's the guy who complains about government but doesn't register to vote. It's the guy who praises you to your face but slams you behind your back.

Hypocrisy is the guy who orders a triple bacon burger with a diet Coke.

Know anyone like that? Got a mirror? All of us act hypocritically at one time or another, usually without even thinking about it.

Abraham Lincoln defined a hypocrite as *"the man who murdered both his parents then pleaded for mercy on the grounds that he was an orphan."*

Outwardly, the hypocrite Pharisees were squeaky clean. But inwardly they were a different story. Mean. Jealous. Corrupt. Being God in the flesh, Jesus knew their true hearts and fearlessly called them out for it: *"You hypocrites! You clean the outside of the cup and dish, but inside they are full of greed and self-indulgence."*[7]

Jesus compared them to nicely decorated crypts. Pretty

monuments on the outside, but full of rotting flesh inside. An ornate mausoleum might be impressive to look at, but if you broke the seal and opened the door, the stench of death would make you vomit. Same for the Pharisees. To the man on the street they smelled like religious perfume, but to Jesus, they smelled like spiritual decay: *"You are like whitewashed tombs, which look beautiful on the outside but on the inside are full of dead men's bones and everything unclean. In the same way, on the outside you appear to people as righteous but on the inside you are full of hypocrisy and wickedness."*[8]

That kind of talk is not going to win you points among the religious rulers, then or now. But Jesus didn't stop with metaphors. In case the Pharisees missed his point (they didn't) he spelled out his disgust with them: *"You snakes! You brood of vipers! How will you escape being condemned to hell?"*[9]

Jesus continually stood up for victims of injustice.

The Pharisees used their power and position not to bless and inspire, but to suppress and control. In stark contrast, Jesus continually stood up for victims of injustice and wrongful condemnation. We saw this clearly in the story of the adulterous woman back in chapter 5. The Pharisees used her misfortune to back Jesus into a corner, to try and force him into some inconsistency between his teachings and those of Moses.

They had reason for optimism. By this time in Judaism, the original "Law of Moses" had grown to include centuries of oral traditions invented by rabbis. This complex hybrid of God's law and man's meddling was how the religious hierarchy kept control over the people. In this case, however, Jesus turns the tables on them...

o o o

One day as Jesus was teaching in the temple courts, the Pharisees brought a "woman caught in adultery" before him and said, *"In the law, Moses commanded us to stone such women. Now what do you say?"*

Jesus knew their trick. If he suggested stoning her he would be in conflict with the Romans who banned the Jews from carrying out death sentences. If he suggested *not* stoning her he would be in conflict with the Mosaic Law. Instead, Jesus responded with a third alternative that has confounded moralists ever since: *"Jesus bent down and started to write on the ground with his finger."*

We don't know what he was writing.[10] It's possible he was jotting down the Ten Commandments. Or maybe it was the individual secret sins of her accusers. Or maybe he was writing out God's new plan, how he would soon be the sacrificial lamb that would die as the final sin offering for all mankind.

When the Pharisees didn't disperse, he stood up and delivered the words that still resonate through history: *"If any of you is without sin, let him be the first to throw a stone."*

Then he bent over and quietly resumed writing. The silence was deafening. We can only imagine the sound of the stones as they dropped to the ground, one by one. It started with the oldest men first, perhaps convicted by a lifetime of sin. Eventually even the younger, bolder Pharisees gave in. Whether they left because they were afraid of being exposed or because he had touched their guilty consciences, we'll never know.

Soon, there was no one left with the woman except Jesus. He looked at her and asked, *"Woman where are they? Has no one condemned you?"*

She replied, *"No one, sir."*

"Then neither do I condemn you," Jesus declared. *"Go now and leave your life of sin."*[11]

Let's peel back one more layer of this familiar story. This event was the perfect opportunity for Jesus to reveal the heart of the Father once and for all. If he *was* the God of judgment and condemnation (as many think) Jesus could have proved it by zapping this nasty sinner in the public square. After all, Jesus said,

"If you've seen me, you've seen the Father." But instead of an angry judge, we see a merciful savior lifting this humiliated woman up from the dirt. Instead of branding her with a scarlet letter "A" on her forehead, he brushes off the dust with words of affirmation and then admonishes her to take a better path from that point forward.

It would have been a lot easier (and sadly, more popular) just to stone her, to remove the stain of her ugly life from the religious community. But it was time for a new direction, a New Covenant with God's people, and Jesus demonstrated that he was the one who would deliver it.

Are sins like adultery and lust still wrong under this New Covenant?

> **Instead of an angry judge, we see a merciful savior rescuing a humiliated woman.**

Of course. Jesus didn't do away with the law, he fulfilled it.[12] Please notice he clearly told the adulterous woman, *"Go now and leave your life of sin."* He didn't condemn, but he also didn't condone.

Instead, he extended grace.

○   ○   ○

In our court system, judges are trained, tested, and deemed *qualified* by the state to deliver guilty verdicts to defendants. But when those of us who are *not qualified* (primarily because we're not God) condemn somebody, the negative consequences can last for eternity. Here's why: If a judge condemns someone in a courtroom, they can still find God's grace behind bars. But when we condemn someone in everyday life, they might turn away from God forever. By condemning them, we affirm the lies of the enemy: *"You are guilty and deserve a life of pain ... You might as well keep on sinning ... God wants nothing to do with people like you."*

Harsh words are even more destructive when they declare someone guilty for circumstances beyond their control. When someone important to us — parent, teacher, spouse or boss — repeatedly tells us that we're no good, that we don't have what it takes, what are the chances we'll succeed? What are the chances we'll have a happy, productive life?

Not good.

According to the Prison Fellowship Ministry, the one thing that most prisoners have in common is that they were told by a

When we condemn someone, they might turn away from God forever.

parent or authority figure they would end up in jail someday. Nobody told them they could be successful or accomplish great things. Instead, they were told they would fail. They were verbally condemned at a young age, and the unfair prediction of "guilty" often came true later in life.

Maybe that's why convicted killer Stephen Moody spent more years *in* prison than out. Maybe that's why most of his adult life was spent waiting for a day of execution. I don't know his spiritual condition when the doctor's needle entered his arm, but reports indicated he at least had contact with the prison chaplain.

Who goes to heaven and who doesn't is God's business. But one thing is certain. If anyone — from an adulterous woman to a career criminal — turns to Christ, we can be sure that Jesus will never, ever toss a stone. *"Don't pick on people, jump on their failures, and criticize their faults — unless, of course, you want the same treatment. Don't condemn those who are down; that hardness can boomerang."* [13]

And because Jesus doesn't condemn anyone, neither should we.

○ ○ ○

"No sinners are as intolerant as those that have just turned saints."
— Charles Colton [14]

CHAPTER 13:
Crime and Punishment

Police divers all share the same nightmare: When you believe the water is as murky as it can possibly get, suddenly it becomes even blacker.

In the icy waters off Prince Edwards Island, a team of recovery divers groped along the bottom of a fishing harbor in zero visibility. Trained for black water diving, the lead diver could not see his powerful dive light six inches in front of his facemask. Stirred around by swirling currents, the muddy bottom was littered with lobster traps, fishing nets and entangling lines that could snag a diver and hold him until his main tanks and backup reserve ran dry. On the surface, an anxious crew in the police boat studied trails of air bubbles and tracked each diver's movements via tether lines securely tied around their waist. A series of tugs on the rope was their only form of communication — *left, right, up, down, stand by, I'm entangled but I'm okay, I'm not okay and need immediate assistance.*

Adding to the hazards, the outgoing tide tried to suck the weary divers east into the frigid Atlantic. Inch by inch, the RCMP team crawled along the bottom in half-hour shifts, until numbing cold drove them up for relief. Each time they surfaced, the crowd lining the docks grew larger. Warmed by hot coffee, they went down again and again. Feeling their way blindly across the debris field that clogged the harbor floor, each diver both hoped for and dreaded finding the object of their search.

○   ○   ○

Jimi's father died in a motorcycle accident when he was just eleven months old. As a young widow, Jimi's mother hooked up with one dysfunctional boyfriend after another. A depressing series of always drunk, sometimes dangerous men paraded through Jimi's childhood. Many of them were openly abusive to his mom and his siblings. Fortunately, his grandmother recognized the difficult situation and intervened by taking custody of Jimi's two older brothers.

A series of drunk, dangerous men paraded through Jimi's childhood.

Finally, after years of making bad choices, the troubled mother began getting her life back together, and for a while Jimi and his younger brother, Carl, lived with her in relative peace.

By 1976, Jimi's mom had a new boyfriend named Billy. Life was good with Billy in the house and the bad days seemed over. That August, he invited the mom and her two youngest sons to come with him to Canada's Prince Edward Island, along the eastern seaboard. The grandmother pleaded with her daughter not to take the boys. She said they were welcome at her house. But Jimi and his brother actually looked forward to spending this vacation with their mother. Through dozens of abusive relationships, Jimi had watched his mom suffer heartbreak from each lover that passed through. But this new boyfriend seemed different. Nicer. Surely a trip with him would be a welcome oasis from the chaos he'd grown up with.

When they arrived on the northern island outpost, they headed over to Billy's parent's house. They had lived on the island most of their lives, and owned a local restaurant. The little town was a fishing village, and tuna was the prize catch. The harbor was buzzing with activity as captains and crews set out to sea in search of the big bluefin tuna. It was the busiest time of the year and the last opportunity for fishermen to earn enough money to survive the winter. So while the boys stayed with Billy's parents, they seldom saw them. The hardworking duo toiled in their deli from before sunrise to well after sundown.

The first night in Canada, Jimi's mom told the boys that she and Billy would be going on an all-day fishing trip the next morning. She explained that their charter left at 8:00 a.m. and the boys would come to the harbor with her in the morning. She told nine-year-old Jimi that he would be in charge of watching seven-year-old Carl. They could hang out at the harbor, she said, and check in with the older couple every so often to make sure everything was all right.

The prospect of spending a carefree summer day in a beautiful seaside town was so exciting that Jimi could hardly sleep that night.

Early the next morning, the two boys and their mother walked into the town along the sea. The smell of the salty air and the cry of gulls overhead was like magic to Jimi. She took them down by the harbor and showed them row after row of

Jimi dreamed of being the captain of his own boat.

colorful boats. The boys especially liked watching the captains and crews of the fishing boats getting ready for their day at sea. They had never seen such large boats in person or such stout, bearded men before. The rugged crewmen seemed as strong as the sturdy boats they worked on, not only in their stature, but in their tough banter. Watching the men laugh and joke with each other, Jimi dreamed of being a fisherman someday, maybe even the captain of his own boat.

Jimi's daydream was interrupted by the shout of a familiar voice. Billy, already on the charter boat, hollered "Time to fish!" The mom quickly gave final instructions to her two boys. She put Jimi in charge, reminding him he was responsible for his little brother. She told them to stay within sight of the docks, and encouraged them to watch for fishermen returning with their prize catch. Then she took off down the wharf, hopped onto the boat and into the arms of Billy. With a wave, she headed off for a day designed to help her forget about life back home.

Jimi and Carl wandered throughout the harbor docks, tossing bread to the gulls and checking out the different boats. Sailboats, skiffs, dinghies and fishing trawlers bobbed up and down at their dockside berths. It was a whole new world for Jimi, and he liked the bustling activity of this ocean community. There was something peaceful and purposeful about this place, and it was a welcome contrast to his turbulent life. Using his vivid imagination, Jimi dreamed about what life could be like here. Maybe he could come back and work on a fishing boat when he got older. Adventure on the high seas seemed far more exciting than school or work. He liked the idea of having people look up to him as a leader, and he loved the sound of "Captain Jimi."

> **Adventure on the high seas seemed far more exciting than school or work.**

Glancing down one of the docks, Jimi noticed a bearded man in a turtleneck shirt and knit cap sitting on the deck of his fishing boat. The other boats had long since left harbor, and it looked like he was not going out that day. Jimi asked if they could come onboard and check out his boat. The bearded man said he was too busy at the time, but they could come back later and he would gladly let them onboard. Something sly in the man's voice scared Jimi. Without knowing exactly why, he put his arm around his little brother and quickly turned away. Frightened for the first time since arriving, he sensed something was wrong. But soon the warm sun and the growing hunger in his stomach helped him forget the strange man. Skipping and whistling, the boys headed for the restaurant.

After a hearty breakfast of eggs and Canadian bacon, they wandered back out to the harbor and onto the docks. By now the sun was high in the sky and they no longer needed their sweatshirts. Exploring the docks, they spotted an area where crab traps were piled high atop one another. The towering stacks were like a city with narrow avenues running through rows of buildings. It was just the place for two young boys to find adventure. They climbed and scrambled up and down and over the cityscape for hours. Laughing and teasing, they found it easy to lose one another in the maze. To get the best view, Jimi climbed to the top of Trap Mountain and surveyed the harbor from his new vantage point.

Perched as high as the crow's nest on a schooner, he once again dreamed of being a sea captain. Closing his eyes, he could see himself holding the large wheel of his own fishing boat. Nets bulging with fish were being hauled in and the crew nodded up in admiration at their savvy skipper.

Suddenly, the harsh glint of sunlight on waves snapped him back to reality. Hungry for lunch, he looked around for his brother. He was nowhere to be found. Thinking it was another game of hide-and-seek, Jimi climbed down from his tower and looked through the stacked traps. When he couldn't find him there, he started walking up and down the docks. No doubt, Carl was admiring the moored boats or pretending to be a pirate.

Twenty minutes later, Jimi still hadn't found little Carl. He walked out onto one deserted pier after another, until he finally spotted a white-bearded fisherman sitting in the captain's chair of a charter boat. Jimi asked the man if he had seen his brother, and the man nodded that he had indeed seen him just a few moments earlier. He added that the small boy was hanging out on the next pier over. Jimi looked across the water and to his dismay realized it was the same pier where the strange man in the knit cap had invited them onto his boat. He quickly ran to the crowded restaurant and told them he had lost his brother.

The police were called and a frantic search began for the missing boy.

A frantic search began for the missing boy.

Jimi did his nine-year-old best to tell the officers about the strange man in the knit cap on the boat, but they didn't seem interested. After what seemed an eternity, the fishing boat carrying Jimi's mom and Billy chugged in from their excursion. Seeing the large number of people standing at water's edge and the uniformed police moving through the crowd, they knew something was wrong. When Jimi saw his mom on the gangplank, he ran up to her and breathlessly told her that Carl was missing.

She let out a shriek and ran to the police to find out what they knew. She stayed at the harbor all night as the search-and-rescue team combed the area for the little boy. Jimi was sent back to the house for an awful night of waiting for news.

The next morning, Jimi's mom sent Billy back to his parent's home to get her son Jimi. She said she wanted him to be with her. She told him she had lost one son and did not want to lose another. Unfortunately, her words would turn out to be prophetic.

Jimi can only recall fragments of conversation and fleeting images from the harbor that morning, but he clearly remembers the police divers. They swam methodically back and forth, covering every inch of the harbor. This went on for hours. Then one of them went down, came back up and asked for a red flag buoy to be placed in the water. To Jimi's horror, it was right next to the boat owned by the strange man in the knit cap. As the crowd converged on the area, an ambulance pulled up close to the dock and a stretcher was brought out. On the gurney lay a long black bag with a full-length zipper.

As the crowd converged, an ambulance pulled up to the dock.

For a moment the harbor was totally, eerily silent.

Then a diver's head broke the surface. The crowd gasped as the diver slowly lifted a limp body from beneath the water. Although it had only been in the harbor for 18 hours, the tiny corpse was badly deformed from the seawater and the ravenous crabs that had fed on it overnight. Jimi's mom collapsed to the ground in shock as the familiar blue jeans and tee-shirt confirmed it was her little boy. When she staggered upright, she looked at Jimi and totally lost control. She smacked him hard across the face and started screaming at the top of her lungs. He doesn't remember what she said, but remembers being terribly scared and confused. He began sobbing, unsure if he was grieving for his brother or for himself. Concerned rescue workers tried to console both of them, but the mother was hysterical and pushed them away.

Jimi can't recall exact details about that afternoon. Much of that frantic scene is still a blur, as if a defense mechanism in the brain knows we can only deal with so much emotional pain and shuts down our memory bank.

So he's not sure of all that transpired that day. But he *definitely* remembers what happened that evening.

The family sat quietly in the darkened living room. For hours, hardly a word was spoken. Then without warning or explanation, Jimi's mom grabbed him, dragged him out to the car, and shoved him in the passenger seat. The tires squealed as she raced out of the driveway. Jimi had no idea where they were going, but he was scared. Gripping the steering wheel with white knuckles, Jimi's mom looked at him with fiery red eyes and shouted, "You did this! You killed your brother! I told you to watch him and now look what you have done!"

Jimi buried his face in his hands and cried until his shirt was wet. But the pain he felt over losing his brother paled in comparison to the hurt he now felt over being held responsible for the death. Till that moment, he hadn't blamed himself or even considered that the tragedy might have been his fault. It was too horrible to think about.

But it must be true, he thought. *My mother told me so.*

Just then, Jimi's mother pulled the sedan up to a dark building outside of town. It was the county morgue. She yanked him out of the car, marched him inside and asked the assistant to see the body of her son. She said she wanted to positively identify him. Jimi couldn't believe what happened next. The assistant pulled out the metal drawer, slid out the stainless steel slab and drew back the covers. Jimi's mom groaned and covered her mouth, tears streaming down her face. But it was not sorrow she felt. It was anger, and in her anger, she did the unthinkable. She grabbed Jimi's head and pushed it into her youngest son's bloated chest. "Look at him," she growled. "I want you to look closely at what you did! I want you to remember this forever."

And forever he would.

The next day, Jimi's grandmother arranged to fly him back home. When he told his grandmother his side of the story, she announced he would be living with her from now on. His mother did not put up a fight.

Grandma introduced Jimi to God by taking him to church with her every Sunday. At age 15, he remembers asking Jesus into his heart. For a while, things seemed much better. Shortly after graduation from high school, Jimi joined the Navy. He was released early from his tour of duty after several attempts by his mother to take her own life. He went back to school and earned a two-year degree. Jimi remembers how proud his grandmother was when he graduated from the Corrections Academy. He soon got a job as a corrections officer. Sadly, his grandmother died shortly after he was hired.

Jimi went into a tailspin. The only loving, stable person in his life was gone. With her went the security and normalcy he longed for. Grandma had done much to redeem the little boy's life, but the damage committed before she rescued him ate away at his soul.

He seemed doomed to fulfill his mother's dire prediction.

Jimi doesn't remember much more about his early life. Recollections of his childhood after Carl's death are shadowed

162

by pain. What he *does* remember is that his life began to conform to what his mother told him that terrible August day: He was irresponsible. He was guilty. He was a bad son, a bad brother, a bad person.

And he was on track to fulfill her prediction.

○   ○   ○

I first met Jim after a seminar I teach called "24/7 with Jesus." The workshop is a full day of looking at ways to experience Christ more fully. Following my lecture, Jim came up and introduced himself. He said many of the stories I told had touched his heart. He said he too had a painful story, but was now living in the grace of Jesus Christ. He wondered if I would have lunch with him.

I agreed, but I was not prepared for what I was about to hear.

As Jim shared his life story, I wondered how this intelligent man had gone so far astray. While working in corrections, he had dreams of moving up to become a police officer. One of his jobs involved a "work-leave" program, where prisoners are allowed to work for wages, but have to pay rent. When some money went missing, Jim was accused of stealing it — even though a voluntary polygraph test cleared him. Smooth-talking veteran officers persuaded Jim to resign, a move they suggested would help him find work in another county.

> **I was not prepared for what I was about to hear.**

Wallowing in self pity, Jim hit the bottle pretty hard and was caught driving intoxicated. This DUI arrest ended his chances of being rehired as a corrections officer and dashed his dreams of ever becoming a cop.

For several years, Jim bounced around in different jobs, but partying and living the fast life prevented him from succeeding at much. Finally, he was offered a job as a loan officer for a mortgage company. He seemed to excel in this and the business climate of the late Nineties was very good for the mortgage industry. Soon he had a new job offer from an even better company and moved up the ladder. To help a friend get a job, he pulled some strings with his former employer. He loaned this friend some money to get through a tough time, but when his friend was suspected of embezzling, Jim was brought into the investigation. Many of the home loans had been originated in Jim's name and taken over by his friend to close. When investigators saw checks written to Jim to pay back his personal loan, they figured he was in on the scheme.

Again, Jim took a voluntary polygraph test that showed he had no knowledge of what his friend was doing. But investigators told him a jury would never buy it. They warned that even accepting stolen money is a crime. Eventually, he pled down to a lesser charge. But this reduced charge still carried a prison sentence, and the former corrections officer was now behind bars.

During his 18 months in Jackson Prison, Jim remembers distinctly hearing the voice of God whispering to him, "You belong to me." He heard it but he did not believe it. Somehow, his instinct was to run away from God instead of toward him. He figured he was innately bad, and that his ex-con stigma would stick with him forever.

Just three months after being released, Jim violated his parole by leaving the state and served another six months in prison. The seeds of failure his mother had planted in him were coming to full bloom. Hurt by his past, he deceived others, lied about his life, and without really trying, became the bad person she had predicted.

Released from prison, he knew it would be difficult to find a job. So he started his own auto detailing company. At first the business soared, and Jim seemed to have good management instincts. But a serious back injury kept him from doing consistent work. He soon drifted back to the dark side, and somehow became involved with the same drug dealers he once guarded in jail. With a scarred psyche and a prison record, he figured this was the crowd he belonged with. Unlike everyone else, they accepted him without condemnation. Soon he was running a booming business detailing the luxury cars of well-known drug dealers.

A steady flow of Bentleys, BMWs and Escalades lined his shop. Life was good. Cash flow was good. Then it happened.

> **Bentleys, BMWs and Escalades lined his shop. Life was good. Cash flow was good.**

On a humid July afternoon, Detroit police contacted Jim. They were told that he often detailed the car of a drug dealer who was wanted for murder. They asked Jim to help them nail the guy. At first Jim wanted nothing to do with the sting. But after further thought, he decided it might help restore his reputation. A persistent (and sometimes threatening) police force finally convinced him. When the murder suspect showed up to have his car detailed, Jim secretly contacted the police. When the dealer came back to pick up his gleaming ride, the cops were there with guns drawn.

For sticking his neck out, Jim expected respect and admiration from the local police. Instead, he was labeled a bad character who hung out with other bad characters. And now he had the deadly label of "police informant" on the street.

Understandably, his customer base dried up overnight. His sudden loss of clientele and his ongoing back troubles forced him to shut down the business. Disability insurance kept him in physical therapy for his spinal injury. It also kept him financially afloat. But an unlucky evening at a Detroit casino would send him back to prison faster than you can say "snake eyes." At the craps table he met a beautiful prostitute who said she was stranded and needed a ride home. Always the gentleman, Jim agreed to give her a lift. But when her pimp followed them at a high rate of speed, Jim realized he might be in real danger. At the

He was found guilty of larceny and sent back to prison.

next stoplight, he forced the young lady from his car, accidentally speeding off with her purse. Charges were filed and he was found guilty of larceny and sent back to prison.

It seemed like Jim had a crime problem, but the truth was, he had a *hearing* problem. For years he failed to listen to the Holy Spirit whispering, "You belong to me." Instead of yielding to God, he stubbornly insisted on following his own brilliant plans. The results? Bad food, iron bars and an orange jump suit with a number stenciled on it.

Upon his third release from prison, things began to look a little brighter. He met a remarkable young lady named Beth Ann. Beth had grown up in a strong Christian home, and despite Jim's troubled past, she felt drawn to help him. They started to date and soon fell in love. Less than two months later, they were engaged and married shortly thereafter. For the first time since being a teenager, Jim was attending church regularly and trying to straighten out his behavior.

At Beth's church, Jim began to hear things he had never heard before: *"No matter what you have done, Jesus forgives you. He loves you and desires that you know him in a real and personal way. But in the end, the action step is yours. You must make a decision to follow him. He will not violate your free will. So the question is, will you choose death going your own way, or life through Jesus Christ?"*

It didn't take long for Jim to understand that his way had only led to failure, and he vowed to live a clean and upright life with God's help.

Things seemed great, but old habits die hard. When Jim slipped back into questionable activities, he covered them up from his wife. When Beth Ann learned he had not been honest with her, she felt betrayed. She wondered if she ever really knew the man she had married so quickly.

She asked him to leave.

Jim went to live with an aunt and uncle he had met only a few months before. He was thankful for a place to sleep, but heartbroken about being separated from his wife. Looking at his battered suitcase, he concluded his life was a complete and utter failure. Feeling condemned and miserable, he decided to kill himself.

But instead of pulling the trigger, he fell to his knees and for the second time in his life asked Jesus to take over and manage his life.

Somehow — only by the grace of God — Beth Ann found strength to pray for Jim and for their marriage to be saved. After seeking counseling together, a miracle occurred and Beth Ann fell in love with Jim all over again. He knew in his heart that she was a gift from God. At the same time, God brought Christian men into Jim's life to help mentor him in his new walk with Christ.

> **Instead of pulling the trigger, he fell to his knees.**

I felt honored to be one of those men.

Despite his new relationship with Christ, Jim's past still haunted him. Despite "going straight," his situation was slipping from bad to worse. The murderer Jim helped arrest was convicted and sent to prison, but the killer had plenty of friends out on the street. Still able to communicate with his gang, the angry drug dealer ordered threats on the squealer's life. Jim and Beth Ann often returned home to find strange-looking men ominously hanging out in their parking lot. One morning they awoke to find a large dead animal on their porch. Another evening they caught the wife and son of the convicted murderer posting flyers around their apartment complex. Under a photo of Jim, a headline read: "Do you know that a convicted criminal lives here?"

It was all Jim could do to restrain himself physically, but thankfully he once again heard the whisper to "do things God's way." This time he listened. Instead of retaliating against the duo, he prayed for them before asking them to leave.

○   ○   ○

I first met Jim in the midst of this post-prison turmoil. He admitted to not being "totally forthright" with his new wife about his troubled past. He had told her the major stuff, but things didn't always add up. A man-to-man with a local pastor convinced Jim he needed to tell Beth Ann everything. He divulged the truth — the whole truth and nothing but — about every mistake he'd made.

Beth Ann's first reaction was to flee. She had never known Jim's full history, and wondered if life could ever be normal with him. But something told her that if God wanted their marriage to happen, it was for a *reason*. She knew she could not do it alone, so she prayed for a "restoration team" of strong Christian men to enter Jim's life.

I think God put me on that team because he knew nothing would shock me. I also had a deep interest in why people's *past* can prevent them from having a close relationship with God in the *present*. As I listened to Jim's story, I suspected he was a prisoner to the most powerful event in his life — the death of his little brother.

God put me on that team because he knew nothing would shock me.

Witnessing a tragedy at his young age would have been difficult enough. But his mother's condemning words planted a lie deep in his mind. Year after year, a voice in his head chanted: *"Guilty, guilty, guilty. You can never be forgiven. Not even by God."*

With a vivid memory of the county morgue and his mom's hateful words echoing through his mind, Jim virtually had "Loser" tattooed on his heart. With so much guilt on tap, Satan always had something to use against Jim.

Whenever Jim started making progress and moving beyond the tragedy, the enemy was right there, bringing Carl's drowning to the forefront of his mind. No matter how hard he tried to forget, Jim was prisoner to thoughts that made him feel worthless and hopeless.

I explained to Jim that his surrender to Jesus could prevent *new* lies from dominating his mind. But unless he dealt with the *old* lies, he would never experience the abundant life God designed for him.

Call it perfect timing, God's will, or mere coincidence, but I had just read a book by Greg Boyd that helped me understand what Jim was dealing with. According to *Seeing is Believing*, we all think in images, multisensory representations capable of taking us back to powerful events in our lives. Many of these pictures represent good events, times when we learned positive truths about the nature of God and life. But some of the pictures in the "image gallery" of our past represent distortions and outright lies. For Jim, his brother's death was the first of many negative images that confirmed his lack of worth as a human being.

> **Call it perfect timing, God's will, or mere coincidence.**

To break that cycle, he would have to go back to the pivotal event in his life and ask Jesus to replace the lie with the truth.

In his book, Greg Boyd shares an event that happened when he was only three years old. His mother had died young, and his strict grandmother was raising him. On the night before Christmas, she called her grandchildren over to get a single "early present" before the big day. One by one, each child peeked into their stocking and pulled out something that was precious to them. Being the youngest, Greg went last. But when he looked into his stocking, it was empty! He desperately searched around with his hand, but found nothing. When he looked at his grandmother with bewilderment, she explained that bad boys like him did not deserve a gift.

This well-meaning elderly woman mistook the toddler's high energy for being an intentionally troublesome child. And she used that Christmas Eve to teach him a lesson. She had hoped it would be an incentive to change his behavior. Instead, it planted a hurtful lie deep in his young mind. And for much of Greg's life, his reaction to her condemnation confirmed her verdict. Throughout his formative years, he acted out in rebelliousness and even refused to follow God.

Eventually, after earning two PhDs from Harvard and Yale, Boyd's desire for biblical truth led him to seek answers about himself. As he recalled the events of his youth, he zeroed in on the nightmare before Christmas.

Admitting that his holiday trauma pales in comparison to horrors other children endure, Boyd nevertheless knew it was a lie he had accepted as true. He describes going back to the event mentally and picturing himself there in the room as an adult. In his mind, he is holding the tiny hand of toddler Greggy and the strong hand of Jesus. Each trip back, he asked Jesus to replace the false image with one that represented truth: "What was true about me, the little Greggy, at that time?"

Looking back to his childhood, he zeroed in on the nightmare before Christmas.

After months of doing this exercise, his prayer was finally answered.

Deep in the recesses of his memory, Jesus asked Greg to look in the Christmas stocking again. This time, there was a bright red airplane inside, something he always wanted as a child but never got. His eyes grew wide with excitement as he pulled the gift from the sock. He had forgotten how much he'd wanted that toy!

In one powerful moment, Jesus showed Greg that the Father would give him anything his heart desired if it lined up with God's will — including healing this crippling memory. By seeking truth, Greg was finally able to remove a negative picture from his mind's gallery. An image that held him captive for years was gone, and the enemy had one less tool at his disposal.

I told Jim he needed to do the same thing. He agreed to read Boyd's book and seek the healing he needed. He would start with the most powerful image, and then work forward through other lies.

Jesus offers forgiveness for the mistakes of our past — whether they were intentional or not. For some of us, feeling "forgiven" begins the moment we turn our life over to Christ. For others, it happens slowly, as we chip away at negative images. When the last lie is taken down off the wall and thrown away, Jesus can fully occupy our thought life and replace hurtful memories with truth. What truth am I talking about? The truth that *we are, and always have been, deeply loved by God.*

If you're enslaved to your past, hanging on to guilt and shame, ask Jesus for grace to move beyond it.

The more baggage we have, the harder it is to empty our gallery of guilt and shame, but it can be done. If you're willing to start with the first misrepresentation you were subjected to, real healing can occur. Dealing with the impact this "first lie" had on your life, and then tackling the other fakes and forgeries hanging in the gallery is the key to freedom: *"Then you will know truth, and the truth will set you free."* [1]

But be ready for a few setbacks. As somebody said, "The truth will set you free, but first it will piss you off."

Both Jim and Greg had to go backward before they could go forward. They had to reach into their childhood to dismantle the original lies that held them back. Some lies are hidden in our subconscious (like Greg's) and some are well known to us (like Jim's). Either way, if you find yourself living in slavery to something in your past, ask Jesus for grace to move beyond it.

The Apostle Peter was an imperfect man, an impulsive man famous for folding under pressure. He even denied knowing Jesus. So if anyone knew the power of God's love and forgiveness, it was him. His advice encourages all of us who are still toting around some funky baggage: *"Love covers over a multitude of sins."* [2]

That's true not only for the one who sins, but for the one

who was sinned *against*. Replace Satan's lies with God's truth, and you will cover the effect of sin with love, forever blanketing a false image with the power of grace.

○   ○   ○

"Lying to ourselves is more deeply ingrained than lying to others."

— Fyodor Dostoevsky[3]

III: GRACE IS…

III: GRACE IS...

CHAPTER 14:
Grace Is Mercy

As a kid growing up in the snowy Midwest, I remember getting up early to watch the Tournament of Roses Parade on our black and white television. According to my parents, I'd be stationed in front of our Zenith every New Year's Day, balancing a bowl of Cheerios in my lap. Dressed in footie pajamas, I couldn't wait to see if the latest flowery creations could top the floats of the preceding year.

Thirty years later, I found myself in downtown Pasadena, scouting out a chunk of sidewalk and staking my claim to a prime position for the early morning festivities of January 1. After decades of watching the extravaganza on TV, I finally took my family to Southern California to get up close and personal with America's oldest and most famous parade.

We weren't alone. Police estimate that nearly one million people attend the Rose Parade. Plus another 40-million Americans watch the live broadcast.

Originally called the Battle of Flowers, the first festival was held in 1890, and consisted of local citizens decorating their horse-drawn buggies with flowers. The parade *we* saw boasted 60 elaborate floats, extravagantly decorated to illustrate that year's "Hollywood" theme. Interspersed among the floats were 22 marching bands and 18 equestrian units, topped off by a celebrity Grand Marshal and the Rose Queen with her court.

Today's high-tech floats have come a long way since the

Tournament's early days. Float building is a multi-million dollar business, and construction crews work year round. When sheer jaw-dropping beauty isn't enough, computerized animation dazzles onlookers lining the 5.5-mile parade route. We personally witnessed a guitar-playing dinosaur, a huge talking robot, and King Kong stomping through a jungle, all controlled by computers. But despite the new technology, the event has remained true to its floral beginnings — every inch of every float must be covered with real flowers.

No plastic flowers, no exceptions.

Prepping for my trip west, I learned that each float starts with a bare framework of steel and chicken wire. Since only natural organic materials are allowed, designers supplement flowers with leaves, seeds and bark. Thousands of volunteers swarm over the floats in the days after Christmas, their hands and clothes covered with glue and petals. The most delicate flowers are added last, individually placed in tiny vials of water and set into the float one by one.

The floats are adorned with more than *18-million flowers* from all over the world — roses, carnations, even exotic orchids. Usually, the flowers are used intact to cover a section of the float. But sometimes the petals are plucked off and mashed in a blender to become "flower paint." When one float needed a yellow hue, volunteers painstakingly glued individual popcorn seeds in thousands of perfect rows — thick side up, pointy side down. No wonder the parade takes over 80,000 hours of combined manpower to pull off!

Attending the parade was a dream come true. Our family had always enjoyed it on TV, but the stunning colors and intricate workmanship can only be fully appreciated in person. For two-and-a-half magical hours, we marveled at the marching bands, costumed horses and breathtaking displays.

The event was spectacular and the morning was totally enjoyable — until the crowds down the block began booing and heckling something. We couldn't see what was making them angry, but the taunts grew louder. Then we saw it. Marching behind the last float was a group of uninvited Christians. They held large signs reading "Repent or Burn in Hell" and "Turn from Your Sinful Ways!" As they marched up Colorado Boulevard, the crowd jeered and hissed. In stark contrast to the beauty of the roses and carnations that morning, the marcher's message choked out the crowd's joy as surely as weeds choke out a flower garden.

> **Marching behind the last float was a group of uninvited Christians.**

My usually noisy children sat speechless on the sidewalk in stunned disbelief. When the booing subsided, I asked them what they thought about the marchers. They said they were embarrassed. I told them that I was, too. Angry, sad, mortified — I couldn't pin it down, but my cheeks were blushing as red as the roses in the Queen's bouquet.

Confused, I tried to sort out my emotions: *Was I embarrassed because of my belief in Christ? Was I ashamed of the Jesus who died for my sake?*

Hell, no! I was embarrassed that other Christians could get it so wrong. That they could utterly misrepresent a loving God to millions of people who deserved an accurate portrayal. I remember thinking that if the marchers had built a float instead of carrying signs, their Hollywood theme would have been "101 Damnations."

I don't know what was in their hearts that morning. But by their *actions*, they were saying, "We are morally superior beings. We've got life all figured out. God is obviously pleased with us and really ticked off at you."

I'm sure that beneath their signs and slogans, the Christian marchers were decent people with good motives. But to the crowds they came off as self-righteous, pious and quite frankly, obnoxious. Their judgmental tone ("Turn or Burn!") was in stark contrast to the mercy Jesus exhorts us to show all people: *"Blessed are the merciful, for they will be shown mercy."* [1]

Found in the famous Sermon on the Mount, this declaration of mercy is especially significant because it's in what some call the "inaugural address" of King Jesus. Here for the first time, he explains what was expected of anyone choosing to follow him. And here he identifies *mercy* as one of the essential beatitudes — or "attitudes to be in."

So what is mercy? Is it different from grace?

Put it this way — if Mercy and Grace were people, they'd be sisters. Not identical twins, but sisters. They're almost always found together and if you find one by herself, you can bet the other must be nearby.

Let's look at their similar — but different — meanings.

MERCY is defined as: *Compassion or kindness extended to someone, help shown to victims of misfortune.*

GRACE is defined as: *Divine favor unmerited by man, kindly treatment on the part of a superior.*

An easier way to remember the difference between the two "sisters" is: *Grace is getting something we* don't *deserve (like salvation) and mercy is not getting something we* do *deserve (like judgment).*

How important is mercy? Appearing over 250 times in the Bible, it's the core of Christianity, and it's shaped Western culture for the good. Because of the Bible's influence, most people today see mercy as a virtue. But most ancient civilizations did not. Have you seen the movie *Gladiator*? Or *Spartacus*? The Romans despised mercy and saw it as weakness. The followers of Caesar embraced four cardinal virtues: wisdom, justice, temperance, and courage — but *not* mercy.

> **The Romans and Greeks despised mercy. They saw it as weakness.**

Even the enlightened Greeks disdained mercy. The philosopher Aristotle called it a "troublesome emotion."

But before we condemn the ancients, we should admit to our own lack of mercy. Although we don't howl for blood and declare "thumbs down" like an emperor in the Coliseum, we *do* tend to insulate ourselves from the suffering of others. Worse yet, we sometimes enjoy it. At least vicariously. That's why movies about revenge and vengeance are so exciting (and marketable) compared to "boring" tales of mercy and forgiveness.

Consider the 2009 movie *Taken*, starring Liam Neeson. When his character beats the stuffing out of Euro-trash villains who kidnap his daughter, I cheered wildly. And I wasn't alone. That's why there's a huge (and always profitable) genre of revenge movies like *Braveheart* and *Kill Bill*. Even alien robots dish it out in *Transformers 2*.

Think about Stallone in *Rambo*, Bronson in *Death Wish*, or Schwarzenegger in *Commando*. We openly (or grudgingly) admire the sheer badass attitude of these iconic heroes who show no mercy. But why?

To understand how we can remain so insulated from suffering, I looked deeper into the word *mercy*. In modern everyday English, it usually means "pity or sympathy."

But in the language Jesus spoke (Aramaic) it's deeper than just feeling sorry for someone in trouble. It means literally going through what that person is going through. It means identifying so strongly with them that you feel with their feelings and see with their eyes. This is more than having a flash of pity when

Real mercy means literally experiencing what another person is going through.

you see a bum in the gutter or a neighbor in the hospital or a dad in the unemployment line; it means actually *experiencing* it.

It's what Native Americans called walking a mile in the other man's moccasins, and it means to *experience things together with another person*.

179

If you're thinking that sounds tough to do, you're right. The mercy and forgiveness that Jesus taught are not humanly possible. They can only happen when the Holy Spirit lives in your heart and empowers you with God's own love for others. Mercy toward anyone (let alone your enemy!) can only occur when we realize how merciful God has been to *us*.

We can't forgive others until we first appreciate that God has forgiven us.

If the Pasadena marchers had really understood God's mercy toward *them*, they might have showed it to *others*. Instead of "Repent!" their signs might have read "God Loves You and So Do We!" Instead of judging people, they might have passed out bottles of water or volunteered to work in the first aid booth. And people would have been drawn to the merciful Jesus they saw in them.

○   ○   ○

Starting way back in the second book of the Bible, we see that mercy is at the core of God's character. In a brief but very revealing "autobiography," he describes himself as: *"A God of mercy and grace, endlessly patient — so much love, so deeply true — loyal in love for a thousand generations, forgiving iniquity, rebellion, and sin."* [2]

Continuously for 40 years, Moses cried out for mercy on behalf of guilty Israel, asking God to forgive and preserve the stubborn, disobedient Jews as they wandered around the wilderness. Isaiah, Elijah, Jeremiah — in fact every Old Testament prophet — appealed to God's self-described mercy and praised him for his unfailing compassion.

When David extols the eternal qualities of God, grace and mercy are at the top of his list. According to the psalmist, God is *"abundant in mercy to all those who call upon him."* His mercy is *"above the heavens"* and *"endures forever."* He is *"slow to anger and great in mercy."* [3]

Want to be successful?

Forget Dr. Phil. According to the wisest man who ever lived, being merciful is the secret to success in life. In one translation, Solomon says we should wear mercy and truth *"like a necklace."* Another version says, *"Tie them around your neck as a reminder. Write them deep within your heart. Then you will find favor with both God and people."*[4]

That's worth a whole bookstore of self-improvement advice. And in one succinct verse near the end of the Old Testament, God boils down everything he expects of us: *"And what does the Lord require of you? To act justly and to love mercy and to walk humbly with your God."*[5]

> **Forget Dr. Phil. Solomon says being merciful is the secret to success in life.**

400 years later, when the New Testament was written, mercy is still the central theme. In fact, the man who wrote much of it, the Apostle Paul, describes God as *"the Father of mercies and God of all comfort."*[6]

But this mercy isn't to be hoarded up for our own use. Paul goes on to say that God comforts us in our troubles *"so that we can comfort those in any trouble with the comfort we ourselves have received."*[7]

Did you catch that? Mercy is given to us so we can use it to help *others* suffering similar afflictions. Mercy — by definition — is always focused outwards.

o   o   o

Great humanitarians have dedicated their lives to feeding the hungry and protecting the weak. That is noble and we should do that. But do you know what the *greatest* human act of mercy is? Sharing God's gift of grace with people who don't know him! God made us his "ambassadors" representing him on the earth. And part of our diplomatic duties is to attract people to Christ — by acting like him.

Paul didn't ask the early church to march around with angry slogans or spoil the Roman festivals with inflammatory signs. Instead, he prayed that early Christians would live *"a life Jesus would be proud of ... making Jesus Christ attractive to all, getting everyone involved in the glory and praise of God."*[8]

Paul didn't ask the early church to march around with angry slogans.

God wants to use you and me to draw people to himself — like the coolest, most attractive float in the Rose Parade: *"God leads us from place to place in one perpetual victory parade. Through us, he brings knowledge of Christ. Everywhere we go, people breathe in the exquisite fragrance. Because of Christ, we give off a sweet scent rising to God."*[9]

That's the parade we're supposed to be in, the one that attracts — not repels — people to Jesus. The one that smells like 18-million flowers going by, not the one that stinks like hypocrisy and judgment.

When people think of Christ-followers, they should think of mercy, compassion and generosity — not hatred, harshness and finger pointing. They should think of servants carrying food and blankets, not protesters carrying signs and bullhorns.

Jesus said we are to be the "salt of the earth." Part of what salt does is to cleanse and preserve. But it should also make people thirsty — craving the living water we've found in Jesus.

There's a story about two old timers: The first geezer says, "It's windy." Second geezer says, "No, it's Thursday." To which the first guy replies, "I'm thirsty, too. Let's get a beer." If we're not making people thirsty for God, it's probably because we're not sharing his mercy and grace.

Jesus also said we are the "light of the world." In a world as dark as the one we live in (check out today's newspaper), even a small light really stands out. When I visited Mammoth Cave, the guide extinguished all the lights in a huge underground cavern. After waiting a moment for our eyes to adjust to absolute blackness, he lit a single match. In the absence of all other lights, this small flame illuminated every wall and crevice of the room. Likewise, a small act of mercy and grace will attract an inordinate amount of attention: *"Let your light shine before men, that they may see your good deeds and praise your Father in heaven."* [10]

○   ○   ○

Hertz may be number one in rental cars, but God is number one in the mercy business. Jesus' own family understood this. When Mary was pregnant with him, she visited her cousin Elizabeth, the mother of John the Baptist. There, she boldly proclaimed God's mercy in the *Magnificat* (the Song of Mary): *"His mercy extends to those who fear him from generation to generation ... He has helped his servant Israel, remembering to be merciful."* [11]

In a world as dark as ours, even a small light really stands out.

And James, the brother of Jesus, agreed that *"the Lord is full of compassion and is merciful."* [12]

So what's our response?

Simple. If God is full of mercy, *then we should be, too.* Of all people on earth, believers should be the most merciful.

Sounds logical. Makes sense.

But in real life, it's tough for religious people to extend mercy. It's weird, it's backwards, but those who've been forgiven themselves often find it hardest to forgive others. If we're brutally honest, some of us still feel that certain people are just too evil to be forgiven or don't deserve a second chance. For whatever reasons, we're tempted to think that particular individuals or groups are somehow beyond God's mercy.

Wrong.

Mercy is available to everyone. Even to groups of people

who make us feel uncomfortable. You know, "those" people. Those with certain backgrounds or lifestyles or orientations or politics.

Luckily, God's grace and mercy is for all people of all colors, shapes and sizes. Unlike us, God wants *all* men to be saved. So his mercy is not limited. And since he has given us — his ambassadors — the job of proclaiming that mercy, we must not be limited, either: *"He wants not only us but everyone saved ... everyone to get to know the truth we've learned."* [13]

Who's responsible for this risky, illogical open-door policy? That come-as-you-are whosoever guy Jesus, *"who offered himself in exchange for everyone held captive by sin, to set them all free."* [14]

What about psycho killers and child molesters and the nefarious villains of history?

Whoa. Did he say "everyone?"

What about psycho killers and child molesters and the nefarious villains of history? It might make your skin crawl, but God's abundant mercy means forgiveness for wicked, sinful people like you and me and Attila the Hun, too. If God's mercy can only forgive up to a point and then runs out of power, we're in deep trouble. Fortunately, God's divine mercy is infinitely wide and his saving grace is infinitely deep. And though Pharisees and fundamentalists grind their teeth when they hear it, *there is no one who is beyond God's saving power.*

A teacher I knew once described the scale of human righteousness with a visual aid. He pulled out ten playing cards and held them up. He said one of the cards represented Mother Teresa. Another card represented Adolph Hitler. Then he asked, "If Hitler's life was a 'one' and Mother Teresa's was a 'ten', where would we fall in that scale?" Most people responded by saying "somewhere in the middle."

Then he stacked the ten cards on the floor, and asked us to imagine a stack of cards so tall that it went all the way up through the ceiling into the outer atmosphere. "That," he said, "is how far away from God we all are."

In other words, God does not distinguish between the dictator and the saint. He only judges us by whether we accept Jesus as the Lord of our lives or we don't.

But remember this — becoming a Christ-follower does not mean we are any *better* than anyone else. Don't be "that guy" at the dinner table or water cooler and brag about your salvation like it's a status symbol. Being a Christian only means we've recognized our weakness, repented of our failings and realized our need for God's forgiveness. And when we humbly do that, we receive God's inexhaustible, inexpressible grace — no matter where we fall in life's deck of cards.

So God's mercy is universally available. But it's not automatic. We can't work for salvation, but we do have to *ask* for it. Because grace is a gift, we can't earn it. But we must *request* it. We must realize our need for God's mercy and then ask for it. And the Bible guarantees that if we ask, God will answer: *"Everyone who calls on the name of the Lord will be saved."* [15]

> **Following Jesus doesn't mean we're better than anyone else. Only that we realize our weakness.**

When it comes to mercy, we must first recognize we need it, then ask God for it, and then — here is where we usually drop the ball — *proclaim it to others.*

How can we keep such good news to ourselves?

I'm not a theologian, but I *do* know that God's mercy rescued a total jerk like me. And I need to let others know it, too. While we were still "dead men walking," God took the initiative to rescue us. But he didn't whisk us up to heaven the minute we were born again. Why not? Because as his ambassadors, we must live among the people who are far from our King. We are a living billboard of hope — proof that God can intervene; that if he can do it for *us* he can do it for *anyone*.

If you believe in God, never forget that the non-believers you meet are just as valuable and precious to him as we are. The only difference is that someone told us about mercy and grace.

Now it's our turn. Evangelism is just one beggar telling another beggar where the free bread is being handed out.

To communicate God's mercy to the world around us, we need to live it out daily. Including how we speak. Too often Christian conversations are framed in terms of "us and them." But Jesus wants us to demolish walls, not build them. Instead of labeling people, let's get to know them relationally. Instead of being known as the attackers, let's be the peacemakers. Instead of being called the condemners, let's be the forgivers.

This switch in attitude will be an irresistible attraction.

○   ○   ○

In a sermon recorded in Luke, Christ was talking to his disciples about merciful behavior in terms that seem to contradict logic, let alone human nature: *"Love your enemies, do good to those who hate you, bless those who curse you, pray for those who mistreat you. If someone strikes you on one cheek, turn to him the other also."*[16]

These instructions were as shocking then as they are now. And theologians have argued about them for centuries. But in the very next verse, Jesus reinforces his indisputable command: *"Be merciful, just as your Father is merciful."*[17]

No doubt his brother James was in the audience that day. Years later, James talked about this unconventional mercy and identified its true source and purpose: *"But the wisdom from above is first pure, then peaceable, gentle, reasonable, full of mercy and good fruits, unwavering, without hypocrisy."*[18]

By linking mercy with good fruits, James is saying that unless we put mercy into action by applying it through good works, we are inconsistent and maybe even hypocritical. In today's lingo he could have said "Put your mercy where your mouth is."

o   o   o

One day on a hillside near Capernaum, Jesus sat down and began to teach. Large crowds had followed him out to this sunny site on the northern coast of the Sea of Galilee. Perhaps he picked this natural amphitheater because the slope amplified his voice so everyone within 200 yards could easily hear him.

> **James was saying, "Put your mercy where your mouth is."**

As Jesus looked out at the throngs of people, he specifically noticed that many Pharisees had also joined the crowd.

Ironically, this group memorized the tiniest details of scripture but missed the huge over-arching concepts like mercy and justice. They didn't understand the law's true purpose — to teach people what sin was and to point toward a coming Messiah who would fulfill it. And when the Promised One finally came, the Pharisees were too blind to see him. So instead of drawing people closer to God, they pushed them farther away.

Little did they know that Christ's message that day would help overturn the wrong thinking their clique perpetuated.

In one brief speech, Jesus turned everything the religious hierarchy believed in upside down: *"Blessed are the poor in spirit ... blessed are the meek ... blessed are those who thirst for righteousness."*[20]

Notice he did not say "those who *are* righteous" but "those who *thirst* for righteousness." The Pharisees weren't thirsty. They thought they'd already attained righteousness by their good works. Jesus was speaking directly to their hypocrisy, but it was going right over their heads. Then he uttered a cause-and-effect premise so simple it could not possibly be misunderstood: *"Blessed are the merciful, for they will be shown mercy."*[21]

Mercy is a tough word if you're a Pharisee. Why? Because being merciful means we love and accept people just as they are, wherever they're at in their spiritual journey. We don't try to change them or scold them or convince them how wrong their beliefs are. Unlike the religious zealots, we let God do the convicting, the changing and the transforming.

Our nature is to "fix people" after we judge them.

Easier said than done.

Our nature is to "fix people" after we judge them. And often our judgment is based on a distorted view. Only God can see the full picture. So only God has the right to judge. The French have a saying, "To know all is to forgive all." If we could look inside a person we'd see they're a lot like us — flawed and broken and hurting. The old cliché "There but for the grace of God go I" is wonderfully, profoundly true. If we knew the full background of people we wouldn't judge them. Instead, we'd invoke the Golden Rule: *"Do to others what you would have them do to you."* [22]

And what I want done to *me* is mercy!

God made us alive in Christ, not just for our eternal salvation, but for our daily lives here on earth. Yet how many of us feel truly "alive" most days? Maybe we feel spiritually sluggish and emotionally drained — like we're "running on empty" — because our priorities are screwed up. If we extended mercy to others the way God extended it to us, we would waste a lot less valuable time and mental energy being critical of people and their choices.

As we saw in chapter 6, Jesus is clear on our priorities: *"Why do you look at the speck of sawdust in your brother's eye and pay no attention to the plank in your own eye?"* [23]

Notice Jesus did *not* say, "Ignore the speck in your brother's eye." He is just saying to judge ourselves first, before we counsel others. He still expects us to help others grow in their maturity and faith. But understanding our own imperfect nature — that we're all works in progress — will make us humble and give us the perspective we need to teach others lovingly, not judgmentally.

o   o   o

Commands like *"Be merciful"* and *"Do good works"* are easier said than done. Human nature gets in the way. Big time. But with Christ living in us, we can start to reflect the merciful nature of God in what we do and say. That's why Jesus could confidently challenge scared, self-centered humans to *"Love your enemies"* — because he knew God the Father also loved *his* enemies: *"God is kind to the ungrateful and wicked. Be merciful, just as your Father is merciful."* [24]

Unlike the vengeful, petty gods of the Greeks and Romans, mercy is the response of the One True God to his enemies. All of them. Including us. This pre-emptive, unconditional mercy was the response of our Savior to people who spit in his face. And it was the response of the Good Samaritan to the injured Jew

Jesus didn't say, "Ignore the speck in your brother's eye." He just said, "You first."

who despised him. And it should be our response to the pain and suffering we find anywhere in the world, regardless of race, religion, gender or politics.

But what about the marchers carrying the "Repent" signs? Was that a good idea?

Good and bad. Mostly bad. As we saw in chapter 5, repentance simply means "to turn around and change directions." So we *do* need to repent. But to badger or bully people to repent of their sins *before* they hear who God is — in a way that makes sense to them — is backwards. It simply won't work. Which is why Jesus came to earth — to personally reveal the merciful character and compassionate nature of God to a hurting world.

A world the religious community was busy ignoring...

o   o   o

One day, Jesus was having dinner at Matthew's house. At this party, *"many tax collectors and 'sinners' came and ate with him.*"[25] Seeing Jesus hanging out with this motley crew made the Pharisees furious. Why were they so grossed out by the guest list? Because they believed God's grace only extended to the chosen few who were keeping the Mosaic Law. Anyone else was to be shunned and ostracized.

Jesus attracted hookers, beggars, lepers and all the riff-raff the religious community shut out.

The irony of the dinner party (and the entire Gospel) was that the self-righteous leaders didn't realize their need for mercy, but the "tax collectors and sinners" did! Which is why Jesus attracted hookers and beggars and lepers and Roman soldiers and all the riff-raff the religious community shut out. They *knew* they needed help and that Jesus was their only hope. Those who didn't recognize themselves as sinners didn't ask God for forgiveness.

It's still true today.

When Jesus quoted Hosea 6:6 to the religious scholars, *"I desire mercy, not sacrifice,"* he was chiding them for majoring on the minors — for spending their time on religious rituals instead of helping the hungry, hurting, and oppressed around them. What about us? All the church meetings we attend and all the candles we light and all the repetitious prayers we mumble do not come close to equaling a single act of mercy and kindness. Gandhi said, "To give pleasure to a single heart by a single act is better than a thousand heads bowing in prayer."

If we're followers of Jesus, our eyes have been opened, and we have no excuse. We should wake up every morning eager to go out looking for opportunities to do good on his behalf. God doesn't want me to just focus on him one hour a week in a church service. He wants me to be living and working for him the other 167 hours a week: *"For we are God's workmanship, created in Christ Jesus to do good works, which God prepared in advance for us to do."*[26]

Around the globe, people are suffering from poverty and political oppression. I've seen it first hand in third-world countries in both hemispheres. But however drastic their *physical* needs are, their most important need is *spiritual* — to be restored to a right relationship with God. Today, billions of living souls are trapped in a legalistic, performance-based quest for God that will leave them frustrated and disillusioned. It's our job (and our joy) to tell them about forgiveness and freedom — that God's mercy is just a prayer away.

○   ○   ○

"When I'm having my portrait painted I don't want justice, I want mercy."

— Billy Hughes[27]

III: GRACE IS...

CHAPTER 15:
Breaking the Cycle

It's official. Detroit is a *helluva* tough place to live.

Motown clinched the title of "poorest large city in America" back in 2005 when the Census Bureau showed 34 percent of Detroiters lived below the poverty level. Since then, Detroit's unemployment rate climbed to 30 percent in 2009, the highest since Michigan started keeping records. Unofficially, experts estimate actual joblessness at a staggering 50 percent.

With that kind of poverty, you might guess that lots of Detroiters get mugged, car jacked and burglarized. And you'd be right. But is the Motor City crime rate high enough to snag top honors?

You bet your Glock it is.

In 2009, Forbes Magazine named Detroit "America's most dangerous city," with a staggering rate of 1,220 violent crimes committed per 100,000 people. To create their list, Forbes used violent crime statistics from the FBI's latest report, focusing on murder, manslaughter, rape, robbery and aggravated assault. No wonder ABC set its latest crime show *Detroit 1-8-7* in the downtrodden city.[1]

But it wasn't always that way.

At one time, Detroit was America's fourth-largest city, with the highest per capita income in the country. Detroit's population boom began when Henry Ford astonished the world in 1914 by offering an unprecedented wage of $5 a day. Farmers left their plows and headed north in droves. By 1920 the city had swelled to 990,000. The automotive capital of the world reached its peak in 1950, with 1.8 million hardworking residents.

Today, it's less than half that size.

Why? Starting in the late 1950s, Detroit was swept by a wave of "white flight," as the Caucasian population dropped by 23 percent. The riots of 1967 spurred another massive migration to the suburbs. Five days of rioting left 43 dead, 7,000 arrested, and just about everybody else either angry or terrified or both. To make things tougher, Detroit began a steep economic decline in the 1960s as manufacturing jobs were first outsourced to Mexico and China. During the 1970s, court-ordered busing pushed even more families out. During the 1980s, thousands of voters packed up and left as the city's first black mayor, Coleman Young, exacerbated racial tensions. Many have criticized the outspoken five-term Mayor Young for his polarizing style that pitted city against suburbs in a losing battle.

> **Detroit was America's fourth-largest city, with the highest per capita income.**

As the middle class left town, federal aid programs filled the vacuum with a welfare culture of dependency that rewarded unemployed men for not working and unmarried women for having babies. Sadly, the well-intentioned benefits fast-tracked the demise of intact families. Today, 75 to 80 percent of all Detroit childbirths are to unwed mothers. The combination of drugs, gangs, and crime continues to drive residents to safer neighborhoods in the suburbs north of Eight Mile Road. Those left behind endure a school system that graduates only 25 percent of its students, the lowest among the nation's 50 largest cities.

As Detroiters fled, tens of thousands of homes were left empty. In just four decades, the Motor City went from having the highest rate of home ownership in the nation to the highest rate of home foreclosures.

Foreign competitors battered the Big Three. Factories closed, and the urban landscape was littered with abandoned buildings on a scale never before seen in America. Hundreds of immense factories that were once "the arsenal of democracy" are now empty shells, vandalized by gangs and rented by Hollywood producers as movie sets for apocalyptic flicks like *RoboCop*, *Matrix*, *The Island*, and *Red Dawn*.

The Wall Street Journal explains why Tinsel Town loves Motown: "Want to blow up a building or burn it down? Detroit is happy to help. Wayne County officials, sitting on countless empty homes and factories, ask only that producers pay for demolition and clean-up." [2]

The statistics are sobering. The outlook is bleak.

But I haven't given up on Detroit. Nor am I bashing the city. In fact, I'm a huge supporter. However, my optimism isn't based on politics or urban planning or a government bailout. It's based on knowing that courageous Detroit residents like my friends Jamail and Nicole are personally committed to making a difference in spite of overwhelming odds...

> I haven't given up on Detroit. In fact, I'm a huge supporter.

○   ○   ○

Gunfire echoed through the Brightmoor neighborhood of northwest Detroit like a string of giant firecrackers. Then squealing tires as the shooter's car peeled away. Soon the sirens would wail and overworked police would arrive to push away the onlookers gathering to gawk at the sprawled body of another teenage victim. Through his open window, Jamail could hear the squad cars and EMT ambulance rushing through the streets.

As he lay awake on that steamy August night, Jamail was having second thoughts about his recent move back into the inner city home of his childhood. After all, just a block away from where his wife Nicole and their two young daughters lay peacefully sleeping, another young boy was shot and killed while sitting on a park bench.

The shooting victim had been a good kid when he was younger, but like most boys in this neighborhood, he had no adult male in his home. As he grew, the

Why did someone pump a bullet into this bright, ambitious boy?

older boys who roamed the area became his surrogate father. Unfortunately, they'd also grown up with no responsible men to model a way of life that didn't involve street crime and gangs. Emulating his older idols, the boy turned to drug trafficking as a way to make money, mostly to put food on the table for his brothers and sisters. Their heroin-addicted mother was hardly ever around, and when she did show up she was too high to notice the rats and cockroaches or that the water had been turned off by the city or that the copper pipes had been stripped out by looters and sold for scrap. To be a breadwinner at age 12 was just business as usual in this neighborhood that Jamail knew all too well.

As the neighbors buzzed about the latest killing, questions haunted Jamail: *Why did someone pump a bullet into this bright, ambitious boy?* Maybe he was robbed by a crackhead customer. Or maybe he'd wandered into another gang's turf. Maybe he was killed to reduce competition or to send a warning to a rival. Most likely, he was gunned down to even a vendetta in some long-running gang feud. Whatever the reason, his homicide was so commonplace it didn't merit a mention in the next day's news.

o   o   o

When Jamail graduated with his MBA, it marked the end of a very long journey and the beginning of the sweet life he had dreamed about since boyhood. With his degree in hand, he finally had his one-way ticket out of the "hood" and onto easy street. Between classes, he had pursued a career in real estate, and was successful at buying and fixing-up homes on the side and flipping them for a nice profit. Life was looking up. Way up. But a desire soon crept in that money couldn't satisfy. He had made the leap out of poverty and into the American dream, but he could not escape the legacy of his life in Brightmoor. Something powerful tugged at his heart to help others still trapped in the poverty cycle.

Like the teenager shot on the park bench, Jamail also grew up in a fatherless home dependent on welfare. Between government checks, his mother traded sex for drugs, producing four different babies from four different men. Not surprisingly, none of the men were active in their children's lives. Jamail's "dad" had died from drug-related complications, and his mom was strung out on heroin most of the time.

Jamail was born in Missouri, and his earliest memories are from the slums of St. Louis. It was there his mom decided to clean up her act. One day she simply walked in off the streets and made a dramatic announcement to the puzzled kids — they were packing up and moving to Ft. Worth, Texas. One of Jamail's sisters had a birth father living there, and he gave them all permission to move in. Although Jamail's mom was determined to start a new life, her latest boyfriend was a gambler and a drug dealer — not exactly the positive influence she needed to stay off smack. While he did try to provide for the children, it was just a matter of time before things started spinning out of control again. Not long after their move to Texas, mom was back into her heroin addiction.

After a while she stopped hiding her habit. Dirty needles and matchbooks littered the floor. Shooting up in front of the kids, the mom grew weaker and sicker from the drugs. Jamail can clearly recall her emaciated body passed out with a syringe still hanging from her arm. When the veins in her arms collapsed, she began shooting smack into her ankles and thighs until every appendage was scarred and bruised from needle punctures.

Jamail tried his best to distract his sisters. But living in a house full of drug paraphernalia and vomit and junkies crashing in the hallways set a depressing tone.

Then one day, without warning, Jamail's mother walked out on her boyfriend and four children and did not come back.

The man was able to make contact with an "Aunt Bernice" in Detroit, and soon the kids were sent off to live with her. Bernice took the kids to church every Sunday, and even though Jamail was only eight years old, he already knew the hope and promise of Jesus in his life. Back in St. Louis, a beat-up church bus used to cruise around his impoverished neighborhood, taking raggedy children of all ages to Sunday School. Jamail hopped on one day with a friend, and committed his life to Christ at the age of five. From that day on, he believed God would someday use him and his hard-knock life experiences to influence others.

> **Jamail's mom walked out on her four kids and did not come back.**

Eventually, Jamail's mom resurfaced in St. Louis and contacted Bernice in Detroit. She asked her to send the children back to her. Aunt Bernice knew it was a terrible idea, but had no choice. Reluctantly, she loaded them on a Greyhound bus and waved goodbye. With the children back in their mom's custody, the coveted welfare checks resumed and the mother used them to feed her heroin addiction. For three grueling years, Jamail and his sisters "squatted" in an abandoned house in the inner city. Living like beggars, they often went for weeks without knowing where their mother was, surviving on garbage and handouts, living without fresh food, clean clothes or proper shelter.

In Jamail's own words it was a living hell: "I know what it's like to be a child looking into an empty cupboard and wondering if I would eat that day. I know what it's like not to have heat in the winter time, and to live without electricity or running water. I know what it's like to care for toddler siblings for days at a time, wondering if my mother would ever come home again. And I know what it feels like to see a parent handcuffed and taken away by police for drugs or child abuse or neglect. I know what it feels like to be abandoned by my mother, put into foster homes and farmed out to relatives."

For his first 12 years, Jamail experienced neglect and poverty that few of us can imagine. But one day, he experienced God's grace in a powerful way. It started out like any other day in the condemned house with broken windows and kicked-in doors. As usual, mom was gone and the wind whistled through holes in the walls. Then out of nowhere, his mother came home, handed Jamail her welfare money and told him not to give it to her under any circumstances. She decided to end her drug addiction once and for all — cold turkey — and by the power of God, she did. A week later, she bought five one-way bus tickets to Detroit. Arriving without a single possession, the destitute family moved in to live with Aunt Bernice.

Jamail remembers this as the turning point in his life. Like a character in a Dickens' novel, he had survived a dozen years of darkness and despair, and was now moving toward a hopeful future.

In an amazing act of grace, Aunt Bernice gave the prodigal mother something she didn't deserve and could never earn—she took the repeat offender's entire family into her home. Besides free room and board, Jamail's aunt gave them another priceless gift — she took the **His mom decided to end her drug addiction. Cold turkey.** family to church with her every Sunday, and encouraged them to read the Bible. As Jamail witnessed this kind of grace and mercy in action, he got a clear vision for his life. He was determined from that point on that he would make something of himself and break his family's cycle of poverty. He pursued a college prep degree at Detroit's renowned Cass Technical High School, obtained his B.S. from Grand Valley State, a Masters degree from Central University and ultimately his MBA from Walsh College.

Having traveled so far up the socio-economic ladder made Jamail a huge success story among the people in his neighborhood. They were proud he had made it out of their world, the dead-end world of poor decisions and bad breaks. They were proud he had broken the patterns that kids learn in a place with few men to emulate except pimps and dealers, and nothing much to look forward to except chronic unemployment, prison or violent death.

As he pursued his corporate ambitions, Jamail made good on his promise to help those less fortunate by mentoring inner-city teens with backgrounds similar to his. One night while tutoring at-risk kids, he met a beautiful young woman named Nicole who also had a heart for urban youth. And when Jamail learned that Nicole had also grown up in the Brightmoor area, he knew God was knitting their hearts together for a purpose greater than romance. After their marriage, they sensed God asking them to leave their lucrative business careers and start a Detroit-based mission for youth. In 1998 they started a fledgling ministry called City Mission with seven students and seven volunteer tutors.

For two years, the couple faithfully drove in from the suburbs and worked with kids from some of the toughest streets in Detroit. Things were going well. The classes grew larger and the volunteer base swelled. But something was missing. At the close of each night, they'd give out hugs, wave goodbye to the students and drive back to their nice home in their nice neighborhood. After working so hard for so long, they felt they had earned the right to live in safety and security. But God was tugging at their hearts to leave their comfort zone and follow him on a journey with an uncertain outcome and no roadmap.

God was urging them to trade their comfort zone for the combat zone.

Unlike Abraham, their journey wasn't to the Promised Land, but back to the very place they both had struggled to break out of years before. A place the police described as a crime-infested combat zone. A place where no successful person in his right mind would voluntarily choose to live.

While others were heading north *out* of Detroit, God was asking this young family to head south and represent him to the city's forgotten youth. It didn't make sense to most people. But Jamail and Nicole realized that if they wanted to see meaningful, sustainable change in their old community, it would have to be from the inside. So they sold their comfortable suburban home, packed up their possessions and moved back into Brightmoor. It was radical. It was risky.

It was a crazy plan only God could have come up with...

○   ○   ○

For years, many people — even Christians — dismissed the residents of Detroit's poor neighborhoods as nothing more than welfare cheats and drug abusers getting what they deserved. Inwardly or outwardly, suburbanites condemned city residents as lazy or dangerous. But Jamail and Nicole did not move in to judge their neighbors. They moved in to share God's *mercy* with them. By living, shopping and socializing within the city limits, they slowly won the trust and respect of skeptical residents. Instead of preaching at them from out in the suburbs, they modeled God's mercy in neighborhood markets, barber shops and backyard BBQs. Instead of judging their neighbor's behavior or cultural backgrounds, they extended God's unconditional love: *"Mercy triumphs over judgment."*[3]

Today, City Mission has a staff of over 25 people, with hundreds of volunteers. The Mission provides year-round help that includes a fulltime K-5 school, leadership training and a family development program. Their popular tutoring and mentoring programs have helped countless public school kids catch up and exceed expectations. With 35 full-time students and over 100 more being tutored, their vision is to break the generational cycle of poverty and hopelessness that has a grip on so many families in the area.

Every day, the staff and volunteers are fighting hard to turn things around. But the odds are stacked against them.

Statistics show that 75 percent of children in the Brightmoor community live in poverty. And 75 percent of them will drop out before finishing high school. It's also estimated that half of the 700 families in the Brightmoor area are at least second-generation welfare recipients. For many, living on welfare has become so entrenched they can't remember a single family member who's ever had a job. Poverty is all they know and they have no idea how to break the cycle of dependence.

Their vision is to break the generational cycle of poverty and hopelessness.

The dedicated staff at City Mission bucks this trend with a pair of powerful weapons — sharing God's radical grace and teaching essential life skills to dysfunctional families.

Two of those staff members are Jeff and Dana. After surviving a serious battle with breast cancer, Dana prayed that God would use her for something meaningful: "I am willing Lord. Use me wherever you want." But doors kept closing, and after a while she became frustrated, "Come on Lord, I want to be used *now*."

It turns out that God was asking Dana to learn patience because he had an even bigger plan in mind. When a corporate buyout ended Jeff's booming sales career in computer systems, something strange happened. The couple began to hear God's call to move to the Brightmoor Community and join the staff of City Mission. It was a radical move for the suburbanites, and their friends let them know it was illogical and dangerous. Despite the pressure to reconsider, they sold their beautiful home in an upper-middle-class suburb and moved into the tough Detroit neighborhood.

Some residents can't remember a single family member who's ever had a job.

Like Jamail and Nicole, Jeff and Dana figured they could do a better job of reversing the effects of economic disparity and racial polarization by actually living as members of the community they served.

Today, Dana is Director of Education at City Mission, and Jeff is the Development Director in charge of raising funds. Five years after moving to the inner city, they're both making an incredible impact. But their greatest joy still comes from watching the "everyday miracles" as God changes lives from despair to hope. They've seen families restored, students graduate, junkies get clean and street people get jobs.

Friends and family expected the couple to get discouraged and quit their "noble but hopeless" mission. Even fellow believers predicted they'd come running back to the suburbs. But just the opposite has occurred. Jeff and Dana have been an inspiration to their skeptical friends and to anyone who hears their remarkable story. More importantly, they are instrumental in helping young children break the cycle of poverty and dependence that characterizes life in Detroit.

One of those kids is Antonio...

○   ○   ○

Like too many kids in the inner city, Antonio grew up in a single parent home. Money was always tight. Things were always tough. But despite many obstacles, his mother had big dreams for her son — that he would be the first one in their family to receive a college degree. From kindergarten on, Tabitha hung onto this dream for her son, even though her energy was drained by just making ends meet. Today, this beaming mother has every reason to be proud of her son's academic achievements. And she is thankful for the tutoring he received at no charge. Tabitha says, "City Mission played a big part in his success because they helped him stay focused and led him in the right direction."

Antonio now attends Michigan State University, the recipient of a Michigan Merit Scholarship. From his viewpoint, he credits his mother's tenacity and City Mission's tutoring for his success at college. "Going up to City Mission on Thursdays didn't take away from my time, it actually brought in an important piece," he says. "You're not only going up there to sit and do your homework, you're getting mentored."

That mentoring is grace in action.

For eight consecutive years, a General Motors engineer named Jon was Antonio's friend, teacher and mentor on Thursday nights at the Mission. Jon's consistent friendship was an important factor during Antonio's formative years. By giving up his own time, he patiently modeled Christian manhood — and proved how a caring adult can shape a child's future in positive ways.

When one child breaks out of poverty, it becomes an entire community's success story.

And that friendship is grace in action, too.

Antonio is still deciding which professional direction he will take, but he is certain that part of his post-graduate time will be spent at City Mission helping others. He knows that when one child breaks out of the poverty cycle, it becomes more than just *one* success story — it becomes a community's success story of brighter futures and changed dreams.

○   ○   ○

In the summer of 2010, the Akron Art Museum opened a show called "Detroit Disassembled." This major exhibit features several dozen huge photos of abandoned factories, burned-out homes, and derelict buildings. The show is creating a stir in America and in Europe, where Detroit is seen as ground zero in the world's economic crisis. News groups and filmmakers from dozens of nations have sent teams to chronicle the architectural wreckage of our once thriving city. This bizarre fascination with urban decay even has a trendy new name — "ruin porn."

As people around the world stare at Detroit like gawkers at a car crash, the small army of volunteers at City Mission continues to quietly work behind the scenes. They know that to change a life, a neighborhood, or even a major city requires both individual sacrifice and community effort. More than that, it requires the love and mercy of Jesus Christ — not in some abstract, theological sense, but in the day-to-day lives of ordinary people doing extraordinary things.

These acts of mercy are what Mother Teresa called "small things." Things like teaching a kid to read. Getting a single mom's electricity back on. Helping someone avoid foreclosure. Filling a backpack with school supplies.

Small things. But when they're done in the powerful name of Jesus, they become enormously important.

○   ○   ○

"In this life we cannot do great things. We can only do small things with great love."

— Mother Teresa[4]

III: GRACE IS...

CHAPTER 16:
Grace Is Forgiveness

Joseph Vissarionovich Dzhugashvili ruled with an iron fist. It's no accident the name he adopted for himself — the name you know him by — means "man of steel" in Russian. Before his death in 1953, his secret police routinely snuffed out dissidents by assassination, poisoning and car bombs. But Joseph Stalin's most feared method of eliminating enemies was to arrest them without a warrant and throw them on a train to Siberia. From 1936 to 1950 over 12 million died in his forced labor camps.

And that is where our story takes place...

○ ○ ○

Dr. Boris Kornfield was a member of the Communist Party. If he hadn't been, he would have undoubtedly faced a firing squad for his crime.

Instead, he was sentenced to life in prison.

In those paranoid days before *glasnost* and *perestroika*, all it took to end up in a Russian prison camp was to be accused of having doubts about the infallibility of the Soviet state. For some unknown reason — perhaps a casual remark or a joke overheard during conversation — Kornfield's allegiance to Stalin was questioned. Without warning or explanation, this innocent medical doctor was shipped off to a remote concentration camp for political subversives.

As Russian Jews, Kornfield's family had been persecuted by so-called "Christians" for generations. Life under the anti-Semitic czars was oppressive and countless Jews were executed over the centuries. When the Russian Orthodox Church incited *pogroms* — mob violence — against Jews in the late 1800s, their clergy happily predicted "one-third will convert, one-third will leave the country, and one-third will die." So when the Bolshevik revolution of 1917 promised to replace Christianity with utopian atheism, many Russian Jews hoped for better treatment and became communists out of self preservation.

Ironically, it was behind the icy grey walls of a Soviet prison that Kornfield first began to doubt his communist upbringing. Witnessing the cruelty and corruption of a government labor camp soured his dream of a socialist paradise. Even more ironically, he became friends with a Christian prisoner, an educated man who spoke of Jesus being the long-awaited Jewish Messiah. He taught the young doctor the Lord's Prayer, and he often recited it as he worked. Over time, Kornfield began to change inside and became a Christ-follower himself, despite the abuse his race had endured at the hands of Christian clergy and rulers.

The cruelty and corruption of prison soured his dream of a socialist paradise.

From the first day he arrived, Kornfield was shocked by the inhumanity of the prison guards toward their fellow Russians. As camp doctor, he treated tortured prisoners, starving inmates and exhausted workers with frozen limbs. The senseless beatings angered him, but it was watching guards steal food from the emaciated prisoners that pushed him to the breaking point.

Every day, innocent men died of brutality and neglect. And every day the gentle doctor struggled with thoughts of vengeance.

One night, a member of the hated guards was brought to Dr. Kornfield for emergency surgery. He was bleeding profusely from an injury received in a knife fight. A major artery was slashed.

As he worked on the very man who had killed so many others, Kornfield thought of a dozen ways he could end the guard's life right there on the operating table. Better yet — and safer for him — all he had to do was to loosely tie the suture so it would let go undetected in a few hours, causing the guard to die from internal bleeding.

Suddenly, the words the Christian prisoner had taught him came flooding into his troubled mind, *"Forgive us our trespasses as we forgive those who trespass against us."* Suddenly, the words became his prayer to God, and the hatred he felt for the brute beast on the bloody sheet was replaced by the love of Jesus. He worked quickly to save the guard's life, and in doing so, saved himself from the grip of hatred and vengeance.

A transformed man, Kornfield's values conflicted with the camp's crooked system of bribery and theft. The guards and the orderlies relied on the doctor to sign illegal forms permitting punishments like solitary confinement. As a new believer, Kornfield refused to go along with the schemes. By resisting corruption, he knew he had signed his own death warrant. He knew that every night "uncooperative" men died in their beds at the hands of guards.

> **By resisting corruption, he had signed his own death warrant.**

Soon after becoming a Christian, he was told to treat a prisoner brought to him with intestinal cancer. In great pain, the man looked miserable and hopelessly alone. As he prepped the gravely ill prisoner for surgery, Kornfield shared his love for Jesus with the bearded stranger. Laying out his instruments, he told the story of his conversion from hatred to forgiveness. The puzzled man on the table heard every word then drifted off to sleep under the anesthesia.

The next day, the patient awoke from his successful surgery and heard a commotion in the operating room next door. Through the shouting and chaos he deduced that someone had attacked

Dr. Kornfield during the night and crushed his skull with eight blows from a hammer.

The doctor was dead. But his testimony of forgiveness was so powerful that his patient eventually became a Christian, too. The man with cancer survived the Siberian prison camp and went on to write the monumental exposé *The Gulag Archipelago*. The author's name was Alexander Solzhenitsyn, winner of the Nobel Prize for literature.[1]

○   ○   ○

To fully experience grace in our lives, we must first understand forgiveness and how it can free us from our self-made prisons. Somebody once said the act of forgiving sets *two* people free — you and the person you were angry at. Christian author Lewis Smedes puts it this way, "To forgive is to set a prisoner free and discover that the prisoner was you." Dr. Kornfield was locked up in the worst physical prison an evil system could devise. But his *spiritual* prison of vengeance and hatred was even worse. When he discovered that Jesus forgave him, he was able to forgive others, and the doors of his soul's prison flew open.

After living through the horrors of South Africa's apartheid, Archbishop Desmond Tutu said, "Having asked for forgiveness and having made amends, let us shut the door on the past — not in order to forget it but in order not to allow it to imprison us."

When God sent his Son to reconcile us back to him, he forgave us for all we had ever done and ever would do against him. When? In advance! Before we knew he existed. Before we were born.

Before we even asked him to, he forgave us *"while we were still sinners."* [2]

If anyone had a right to hold a grudge, it was God.

Think about it. If anyone had a right to hold a grudge, it was God. If anyone had a valid reason to withhold forgiveness, it was God. For 75 generations — from the birth of Adam to the birth of Jesus — mankind blatantly ignored him or openly disobeyed him. Yet he still chose to freely forgive us.

o   o   o

When God forgives *us* it keeps us out of literal hell. When we forgive *others*, it keeps us out of emotional hell. It sets us free from the crippling emotions of anger, bitterness and resentment that ruin lives all around us everyday. Irish actor, Malachy McCourt used to say, "Resentment is like taking poison and waiting for the other person to die."

Ideally, forgiveness should be a two-way street. But sometimes you'll extend an olive branch and it won't be returned or appreciated. Do it anyway for your own mental health. I once heard a marriage counselor tell a group of men and women that forgiveness is a two-step process. In a perfect world, it should be about *release* first and *reconciliation* second. But in real life, reconciliation may or may not occur. Step two is not always up to us.

Whoa. What's "releasing" even mean?

Releasing is forgiving someone by saying, "God, I no longer hold this debt over so-and-so's head. They owe me nothing, I cancel their debt forever." It means stop holding it against them. Stop plotting to ruin their life. Stop fantasizing about hitting them with a cream pie or dropping water balloons on them from a tall building or hiding a stinky sardine in their desk. For our own good, God wants us to quickly release anyone who has wronged us from their supposed debt.

> **We want people to grovel a bit before we forgive them.**

Unfortunately, doing this is about as easy as getting an "A" in calculus.

Why is it so hard? Because when someone hurts us, we feel they owe us something. And in a sense, they *did* steal something from us — our childhood, our innocence, our trust, whatever. Maybe they stole our well-being or self-esteem. But whatever the situation, we feel something valuable is missing. Which is why we want people to grovel a bit — to admit their wrongdoing — before we forgive them.

But imposing a prerequisite to forgiveness is a bad idea. They may *never* acknowledge their wrongdoing. They may *never* apologize. In fact, they may *never* even be aware they offended us.

Or they might be dead.

Forgive them anyway — whether they're oblivious or obstinate or deceased.

When you do, according to Desmond Tutu, there's a real bonus: "You can come out the other side a better person. Better than the one being consumed by anger and hatred. Remaining in that state locks you in a state of victimhood, making you almost dependent on the perpetrator. If you can find it in yourself to forgive, then you are no longer chained to the perpetrator. You can move on, and you can even help the perpetrator to become a better person too."

Forgive people. Even if they're oblivious or obstinate or deceased.

This kind of enlightened thinking won Tutu the Nobel Peace Prize. But it definitely falls under the easier-said-than-done department. Especially when we're dealing with repeat offenders. But Jesus doesn't let us off the hook. In fact, he says we are to forgive others at least 77 times. Ouch.

When Peter asked Jesus, *"How often should I forgive my brother or sister? Seven times?"* he thought he was being pretty generous. After all, the rabbis who interpreted the Torah taught the maximum number for forgiveness was three times. Sort of like "three strikes and you're out."

What was Jesus' response? *"Not seven times, Peter, but seventy-seven times."* [3]

Or to quote Buzz Lightyear, "To infinity and beyond."

This unusual number 77 is found only one other time in the Bible, back in Genesis. After Cain (the son of Adam) murdered his brother Abel, Adam's offspring begin to populate the earth. And they were a wild, nasty bunch. One of Cain's descendants named Lamech proudly boasted about taking ruthless personal revenge against anyone who would dare cross him: *"If Cain is avenged seven times, then Lamech seventy-seven times."* [4]

After the fall of Adam and Eve, mankind had become so evil and debauched that God would shortly destroy the world by flood. In that wicked landscape, Lamech's proud declaration of revenge symbolized a cycle of unforgiveness and hatred. But in Matthew 18, Jesus breaks this vicious cycle forever. Instead of getting revenge 77 times, we are to forgive 77 times.

Jesus made it clear that grace and forgiveness will always trump judgment and vengeance. But in case Peter missed his point, he immediately told another story to illustrate our (infinite) need for forgiveness and our need to (infinitely) forgive.

Allow me to paraphrase The Parable of the Unmerciful Servant: *"There once was a CEO whose employee owed him $25 million. The generous CEO let the worker off the hook and cancelled the debt. But that same worker then refused to forgive another worker for a lousy 50 bucks he owed him. In fact, he sent bill collectors over to harass him for it and garnish his paycheck."*

> **Grace and forgiveness will always trump judgment and vengeance.**

By using such wildly disparate amounts of money, Jesus was exaggerating to make a point about you and me. We're perfectly willing to *receive* a huge gift (God's forgiveness for a lifetime of sins) but we're not willing to *give* even a small gift to someone else (by forgiving their measly sin against us).

How does the story end? *"When the CEO heard how stingy and heartless his employee was to a fellow worker, he cancelled his offer to pay back the $25 million and the employee ended up losing everything and declaring bankruptcy."*

Forgiveness is not a suggestion, it's a command. And it carries a threat.

In actual scripture, the unmerciful servant's punishment was even more severe: *"In anger his master turned him over to the jailers to be tortured, until he should pay back all he owed."*

Jail? Torture? Gulp. Jesus warned his listeners: *"This is how my heavenly father will treat each of you unless you forgive your brother from the heart."* [5]

What can we learn from this story?

1. The sin debt we owe God is staggering and incomprehensible, and we could never pay it back.

2. God's forgiveness is equally staggering and incomprehensible, and we could never earn it.

3. Refusing to forgive is not an option.

Somebody once said that God gave us the Ten Commandments, not the Ten Suggestions. Same is true here. The advice to forgive others is not just a suggestion or a good idea, it's a *command*. And it carries a threat within it that most folks overlook. That threat is most clear in Matthew's version of the Lord's Prayer: *"If you do not forgive men their sins, your Father will not forgive your sins."* [6]

Read that verse again, and if it doesn't make you feel squirmy inside, read it again until it sinks in. Then pick up your cell phone and forgive someone.

American journalist Christopher Morley wisely noted, "If we discovered we had only five minutes left to say all that we wanted to say, every telephone booth would be occupied by people calling other people to stammer that they loved them."

○ ○ ○

I screw up so often that I'm tempted to think that maybe God is going to stop forgiving me someday. But that whole "77 times" thing is proof that God's supply of forgiveness is like the bottomless pasta bowl at Olive Garden. It just never runs out.

Personally, I'm thrilled to the bone that God's forgiveness is infinite. Even if we think we're a pretty good person, we've got *lots* to be forgiven for. By God's standards of holiness, even the squeaky clean among us need his forgiveness 77 times a day, if not per hour.

I'm guessing you're not a bank robber or a homicidal maniac, but unless your name is Jesus, I know for a fact you're not perfect. Which means God is persistently and freely forgiving you for things like, well, let me take a wild guess — *worry, grumbling, apathy, selfishness, stinginess, crankiness, impure thoughts, prayerlessness, jealousy, bragging, temper tantrums, irritability, road rage, failure to floss and hogging the remote.* Just a shot in the dark.

My own list of sins goes on and on, way past yours, but it could never be too big to be covered by what Jesus did on the cross. In fact you could say *forgiveness is the whole reason Jesus came to earth in the first place.*

Here's what I mean: We not only need to forgive other people, we need to ask God to forgive us. Why? Although our sins do tons of horrible damage to each other, they ultimately hurt God himself.

How could my little shortcomings hurt the omnipotent Creator of the universe? Does God even notice, let alone care?

Yes! In Genesis 6, we see that God *"was grieved in his heart"* over the wrongs that men inflicted upon each other. He was grieved enough to enter human history as a baby and pay the ultimate price 33 years later on the cross.

It's beyond our understanding, but God is so holy, so sinless,

> **Our sins do tons of damage to each other. But they ultimately hurt God himself.**

that he grieves at the mere thought of evil. Which means we could not stand in his presence for one nanosecond unless he first forgave us for our sins. However, because of God's perfect justice, he can't just wave a magic wand and make sin disappear. Justice demands that every wrong must be accounted for. God doesn't dismiss our sin; he *assumes* our sin, and suffers for it on the cross *"to demonstrate his justice."* [7]

Legitimate forgiveness requires legitimate restitution. That's why Jesus died in my place. His suffering and death validated the legal transaction. The cup Jesus drank at the Last Supper represented the blood he would shed the next day to purchase my forgiveness: *"For this is my blood of the new testament, which is shed for many for the remission of sins."* [8]

In the ultimate act of love, God not only grieved over our sins, he paid the entire penalty for them. All *we* need to do is to accept his free offer. It's there for the taking. But he won't force the issue. We're free to reject Jesus. But if we do, we are declaring that we do not want to be reconciled with God — here on this earth or in eternity to come.

God doesn't drag anyone kicking and screaming across the line of faith.

God doesn't drag anyone kicking and screaming across the line of faith. He wants you to step over, he's pleading for you to step over, but it's got to be voluntary. God offers his grace to everyone. But if you don't accept his gift, it sits there like an unopened birthday present. As theologian Dietrich Bonhoeffer said, "Jesus himself did not try to convert the two thieves on the cross; he waited until one of them turned to him."

And what happened when the crucified criminal turned to Jesus? Jesus immediately replied, *"Today you will be with me in paradise."* [9]

This last-minute conversion blows a lot of traditional performance-based religions right out of the water. That's because the human mind cannot grasp the amazing, unimaginable love of God expressed through Jesus Christ. If you're new to the Bible, make John 3:16 the first verse you memorize, *"For God so loved the world that He gave his only begotten Son, that whoever believes in Him should not perish, but have everlasting life."* [10]

Notice it doesn't say "for God so tolerated the world," or "despised the world," or worst of all, "ignored the world." He *loved* the world.

It's been said the opposite of love isn't hate, it's apathy. And that describes the theology of those who believe God created the universe and then abandoned it. They see God as the great "clockmaker" who created the clock, wound it up, and cut it loose. To them, God is ambivalent, uncaring and uninvolved. In a word, apathetic.

Scripture says they're wrong. He is a personal, attentive God who knows the number of hairs on your head and offers you forgiveness like a loving parent. [11]

It's our free choice to accept or refuse or ignore God's loving forgiveness, but at the end of this short life, we *will* ultimately be held accountable for all the sins we've ever committed. And here's the kicker — you can only choose forgiveness on this side of the grave. Two seconds after you die is two seconds too late.

> **We can only choose forgiveness while we're alive. Two seconds after we die is too late.**

Maybe right now you're struggling to forgive someone for deeply hurting you. But before you can do that, you need to feel the freedom of God's forgiveness for *yourself.* Here's how: If we acknowledge our wrongdoing and ask for mercy, God has promised to forgive us — no questions asked: *"If we confess our sins, He is faithful and just to forgive us our sins, and to cleanse us from all unrighteousness."* [12]

○   ○   ○

When the Pharisees quizzed Jesus about why he hung out with sinners, he responded by telling several stories. They're all found in Luke chapter 15, and they all paint the same picture — something was lost and now is found. A lost sheep, a lost coin, a lost son. All pictures of how deeply God cares for people who are separated from him. Remember, they're not separated because they're evil; they're separated because they haven't (yet) accepted his offer of forgiveness. And as we've seen, people don't repent and turn from sin because we *judge* them, but because we *forgive* them — and tell them about God's grace.

The "lost" stories prove that despite our disobedience, the Father desires reconciliation and restoration more than anything. They are beautiful illustrations of his patient, persistent, almost relentless pursuit of those who are far from him. They demonstrate what author G.K. Chesterton called the "furious love of God."

While each "lost" story contains a similar message, the parable of the Prodigal Son is the most illuminating. Why? Because most of us have played the role of each of the three main characters at some point in our own lives.

First, it's easy to identify with the **PRODIGAL SON**. Restless and bored, he leaves the comfort of home in search of something more satisfying and fulfilling. He has all the gifts a loving father can provide, but he takes them for granted and blows through his inheritance in no time. Haven't we all done that at some point? Set off in search of something more fun or exotic or exciting than what we have? It's this itch that some people scratch by cheating on their spouse, or changing jobs or buying a bigger boat. Discontent with our status quo, we too set off for a "distant country," hoping we'll find more sizzle in life. By separating ourselves from God, we squander the gifts and blessings he has provided, and eventually end up empty and unfulfilled. Fortunately, when we finally come to our senses and head back home, the Father is waiting with open arms.

Second, there's the **OLDER BROTHER**. It's not so easy to

admit we have something in common with this character. After all, no one likes a party pooper. But if we dig deep enough into our own hearts, we realize we're a bit like the ticked-off sibling. Instead of being happy that his brother is back, he pouts and whines and refuses to go to the welcome home party his dad throws. Can you relate? When we see someone heading off to a "distant country," we warn them of the dangers. And if they insist on going anyway, we pray they snap out of it and come back to safety. But truthfully, part of us also hopes they get what they deserve, that they face the music, pay the piper, whatever. Of course we want them to repent and return home to God, but we want them to eat some crow in the process. We want to see them suffer some suitably humiliating consequences for skipping out and leaving us to mind the farm. We want to see justice, baby, not a barbeque in their honor.

Finally, there is the **LOVING FATHER.** Despite heartbreaking disappointment over his youngest son's disobedience, he still has hope. Every day, he longingly gazes down the road, grieving for his lost child and praying for his safe return. Months — maybe years — later when the son returns, the Father abandons any sense of dignity or pride and runs as fast as he can down the long dusty road to meet him (in Middle Eastern culture, it was unheard of for any adult male, let alone a wealthy landowner, to run). Then, instead of scolding him, he hugs the boy, kisses him and enthusiastically welcomes him back into the family. Dressing him in the finest clothes, Dad throws a neighborhood block party to celebrate his son's return.

In our daily lives, do we have this kind of gracious reaction when somebody who's wronged us wants to patch things up? Do we accept them back unconditionally, or do we rub a little salt in their wounds first? When somebody comes to us and admits they've been wrong — a rebellious son, a wayward spouse, a reckless friend — we want to see reparation before reconciliation. Yet before the Prodigal Son can even open his mouth to apologize, the Father embraces him, letting him know how much he is loved despite his failure. Before he can volunteer to work as a slave in his family's fields, his Father shoves the royal ring of authority onto his prodigal finger! This proactive display of grace is a picture of God's love for us and an example of how we should forgive others.

The Pharisees of Jesus' day (and today) were a lot like the Older Brother. They worked hard and played by the rules and thought they deserved the Father's blessing. But their pride in accomplishment made them look down on others. They acted godly, but they didn't truly love God, because loving God *means* loving others, especially those who have wandered off. Ironically, they were the ones far away from God but didn't know it. Full of pride and hubris, they were as lost as the Prodigal Son in the distant country and as bitter as the Older Brother upon his return.

○   ○   ○

Releasing is up to us. But when it comes to *reconciliation*, it takes both parties.

As we've seen, forgiveness is ideally a two-step process of *release* and *reconciliation*. Releasing is up to us, independent of anyone else. But reconciliation takes both parties. There is great freedom in releasing, and even greater joy in reconciliation. So if the other party is willing — and this is beyond your control — go for it! Anyone who's been reconciled with a formerly estranged family member or friend knows the thrill that comes from a restored relationship.

I learned this the hard way.

My own son, Chad, had a prodigal moment the summer before his senior year of high school. He moved out to live with a friend because the home life we provided was "too restrictive." The distant country, only a few miles away, looked much more promising. Yet the adage "you don't know what you've got till it's gone" proved correct. Away from the love of his family, he saw a harsh picture of life in a home without grace. He saw favoritism, criticism, judgmentalism (is that even a word?) and other negative "isms" in the span of only four days.

Unfortunately, I was not like the Prodigal Father. I did not stand out in my driveway straining to see if Chad was coming home. Instead, I spent my time crafting a punishment that would ensure he would forever regret taking his parents for granted. Instead of extending him grace in advance, I played the part of the Older Brother. I wanted retribution. I wanted consequences. There was no way I was letting him just skate back into our home again unconditionally. I began to draw up a written agreement — an actual printed contract for him to sign — that would clearly spell out the conditions necessary for his return.

It was a very godly, mature response. *Not.*

Thankfully, I remembered the story of the Prodigal Son. Truthfully, I was mad at God for drawing my attention to it. I told him, "There's no way I'm welcoming Chad back here without a signed agreement." But God was patient, and gently reminded me where I would be without his unconditional love.

"Oh yeah," I recalled, "I once played the part of the Prodigal Son, too." Only in my case, the role lasted for decades, not days.

I tossed out my contract.

God showed me that the grace portrayed in the parable was the only way something good could come out of my son's disobedient adventure. As Chad's father, I was God's main influencer in the young man's life. If he didn't see a clear picture of grace in me, how could he experience its power in his own life? If I could not forgive him for his minor transgressions, how could God forgive me for my major blunders?

During several quiet, reflective mornings, God melted my hard, obstinate heart and reshaped my will. When Chad returned, I was ready to play the part of the Prodigal Father.

The result? Embraces and tears of joy led to hours of discussion about the invaluable lessons he had learned. His spiritual growth during the week away was amazing. He sought God for answers. He came home with the resolve to do things God's way, and began to experience new levels of joy and peace. He became more respectful at school, more diligent in his work, and more confident in who he was — a child of God deeply loved by his fathers, both heavenly and earthly.

And I could have blown it all with my Older Brother attitude!

○   ○   ○

During the height of our rebelliousness, God forgave us and welcomed us back.

Paul tells us in Romans that God forgave us *"when we were far too weak and rebellious to do anything to get ourselves ready."* [13]

That means during the height of our rebelliousness, God forgave us and welcomed us back — without condemnation, reparation or signed contracts. Like the Prodigal Son, there is nothing we can do to reconcile ourselves to the Father except come to our senses and turn back home. It's this turning back — this repenting — that God is looking for in us. Every day, he longingly looks down the road, knowing that if we return, our lives will be blessed in ways we can't imagine.

The American rabbi, Harold Kushner, describes forgiveness as a powerful tool for change: "The ability to forgive and the ability to love are the weapons God has given us to live fully, bravely, and meaningfully in this less-than-perfect world."

To live bravely.

What an incredible premise. One that flies in the face of a culture that often portrays forgiveness and mercy as signs of weakness.

Throughout scripture, forgiveness is presented not as timidity or lack of resolve, but as a sign of courage and strength. Joseph, ruler of Egypt, forgave his 11 brothers who sold him into slavery. Moses, deliverer of Israel, forgave his brother and sister for opposing him in the wilderness. David, king of Israel, forgave his rival's family for rebelling against him. Paul, the mighty apostle, forgave his supporters who deserted him. Stephen, the first Christian martyr, forgave the mob that was stoning him. And Jesus, Creator of the universe, looked down from the cross and forgave the crowd who was crucifying him: *"Father, forgive them, for they do not know what they are doing."* [14]

With this same Jesus living in our hearts can we do anything less?

○   ○   ○

"Forgiveness liberates the soul. It removes fear. That is why it is such a powerful weapon."

— Nelson Mandela[15]

III: GRACE IS...

CHAPTER 17:
Drive-By Dad

A head-on crash between two vehicles traveling 60 mph is roughly equivalent to hitting a brick wall at 120 mph. Chances of survival are slim to none.

The long stretch of highway was dark and unpatrolled. Traffic was moving fast, no cops in sight. As Rex drove home from work, he watched the oncoming headlights and calculated the highest speed he could possibly hit before tugging the steering wheel to the left, crossing the center line and ending 38 years of pain. With a click he released his seatbelt and shoved the accelerator pedal down hard into the carpeting. The rush of speed pushed him back into his seat. Signs blurred by. The speedometer pegged in triple digits and controlling the Buick became difficult. Then, mysteriously, perhaps miraculously, vivid pictures of his children appeared in his mind, and he realized the awful tragedy his death would cause for his family.

He slowed down, pulled over and chalked up another failure.

○   ○   ○

Rex grew up in a household with two brothers and one sister. He was not close to any of them. He was an island to himself, and he pursued life's achievements for one purpose only — to please his father.

Unfortunately, Rex's workaholic dad was hardly ever around. And when he *was* home he had no time, no love, and no affirmation for his son. Driven to please an un-pleasable dad, Rex excelled at many things — academics, sports, you name it. He won victories on the gridiron, trophies in the gym and top grades in the classroom. But during his entire schooling, his father never attended a single football game, golf match or parent-teacher conference.

Worse yet, he never once said he was proud of his son.

Instead, the absentee father was prone to fits of rage, and more than once, Rex was beaten black and blue for his transgressions. Often the beatings were so brutal he had to wear long-sleeve shirts and blue jeans in the blistering heat of summer to hide the bruises. The physical abuse made Rex bitter toward his father, but it also made him more determined to find a way to please him.

Rex's absentee father had nothing but criticism for his high-achieving son.

Years rolled on and Rex racked up more awards and honors, but his father remained a distant and cold disciplinarian who had nothing but criticism for his high-achieving son.

Rex remembers visiting his grandparents every summer at their beautiful seaside home on the New Jersey shore. It was a restful escape for the young teenager, the one place he could count on for peace and tranquility. It was such a contrast to his anxious home environment that he could hardly wait to return each year. The windswept seashore provided a welcome relief until one sunny afternoon when Rex made a thoughtless comment to a female cousin. When his father heard about the inappropriate remark at a family party, he gave the teen an ultimatum: *Retreat to your room with no food and no interaction with guests, or face the wrath of a severe belt whipping.*

Clenching his teeth, Rex chose the beating.

But he was unprepared for the consequence.

When he limped back to the party, filled with guilt and

shame, he realized this magical summer retreat had suddenly lost its charm. The one peaceful, joyous place in his entire life had been taken away.

And along with it, his childhood.

In spite of (or maybe because of) his dysfunctional home life, Rex went on to achieve numerous accolades. He was smart, competitive and driven to succeed. College came easy and professors predicted success for the bright student. After graduation, his father asked him to join the family business, and despite the years of verbal and physical abuse, Rex accepted the position. It was a chance — maybe his last chance ever — to show his father he had what it took to make it in life. Besides, as an adult, he convinced himself that he had long since forgiven his father for his rotten upbringing.

Working 50 to 60 hours a week, Rex drove the oil and chemical company to new heights and was promoted multiple times. As president, he doubled the profits of the 85-year-old firm in less than five years. In his words, "We were knocking it out of the ballpark." But continuous struggles with his father over the direction of the business took its toll on Rex and his family life, "I had everything that describes success. Luxury cars, country club memberships, world travel, big home, all the toys. But many nights, I sat in the dark with my head in my hands, crying."

Rex started hitting the local bars after each day's grim battle.

Eventually the company fell on hard financial times, and the stress heightened tensions between father and son. Struggling to prove his worth to the man who mattered most, Rex started hitting the local bars after each day's grim battle. Compounded by his drinking problem, worries about the business plunged Rex into a deep depression.

The malaise grew, and dark, crazy thoughts haunted him

until the night he almost ended his life in a car crash. When visions of his kids snapped him out of his suicidal funk, he arrived home with a new resolve to seek counseling and get help for his depression. Taking ten weeks off from work helped revive him, and for the first time ever, Rex started looking to God for answers. His family began attending a church regularly and hope returned to his life. After praying and listening for God's guidance, Rex concluded he needed to exit the family business permanently. His father was outraged, angry that his son would leave him stranded in a time of financial distress. Threats and insults followed. But Rex knew he needed to move away and find a fresh opportunity.

As he worked on establishing a new career away from his father, the bitter memories of their rocky relationship faded, and Rex convinced himself he had forgiven his dad for the years of hurt. But his wife suspected otherwise and challenged his sincerity. Rex tried to persuade her that he was an emotional superman who had "moved on" by sheer willpower, but she wasn't buying it.

Finally, in a heated discussion, Rex blurted out that he positively *knew* he had forgiven his father because it was "the right thing to do." Isn't that what Christians do? Forgive and forget?

Isn't that what Christians do? Forgive and forget?

But it was apparent to his wife that Rex had not forgiven. He had only forgotten, by stuffing the bad memories deeper into his soul.

Bottom line? His wife was right. In fact, Rex could *not* forgive his dad. Night after night, questions flooded his mind: *Exactly what had his dad taken from him? His happiness? His self esteem? His chance for a normal life?* Without knowing this part of the puzzle, it was impossible for Rex to cancel the debt. It was like receiving an invoice without any "amount due" indicated.

Rex lived in this relational limbo until years later when he attended a men's retreat called "Story Weekend." One by one, the guys in his group voluntarily shared their life journey. Rex was not sure if he would join in, but when it came his turn to speak, he uncorked years of anger and pain. Words rushed out in a torrent of anguish. For the first time in his life, he became openly, publically angry about his father. For the first time, he allowed the bitterness and rage he had suppressed since childhood to come out verbally in a tearful confession that lasted nearly an hour.

As emotions churned and old memories surfaced, Rex realized his father had stolen his childhood that summer day on the Jersey shore. But there was an even bigger, more important debt his father owed him — the love and approval he never received. This all-important blessing that every father absolutely needs to give his children had been intentionally withheld.

Listening to himself speak, Rex realized how this total lack of affirmation had triggered the vicious cycle of a child striving to earn his father's approval over and over for 38 years, only to be disappointed. And with this new understanding of what he had suffered, Rex began to grasp how he could finally — for real this time — forgive his father.

The key to a life of freedom dangled right in front of him, but first he had a choice to make: *Would he seek vengeance or forgiveness? Would he behave like his earthly father or his heavenly Father?*

Sometimes, difficult and destructive people can influence us so much that we become just like them. The oppressed becomes the oppressor. The emotional quicksand of an absentee father or an abusive mother can suck us down and ruin us if we don't keep our eyes on God. Fortunately, we have a far better example to follow. Like Rex, Jesus didn't get the affirmation or approval he deserved, either. After three years of healing the sick, feeding the poor and raising the dead, people wanted to kill him! However, Jesus did not allow other people's insults, ingratitude or unbelief to make him bitter or turn him into someone else. His focus was

Jesus didn't allow insults, ingratitude or unbelief to make him bitter.

on pleasing his heavenly Father, not on pleasing people.

Rex explained to the men how his father had failed as a parent, a business partner and a friend. Fortunately, we have a God who knows exactly how that feels. The people Jesus trusted most let him down, too. But he didn't allow those horrible experiences (rejection, betrayal, desertion) to defeat him, take him off mission or push him to revenge. He continued undeterred.

As Rex told his life story, he felt the bottled-up emotions of anger, bitterness and disappointment boil up and spill over. These negative emotions were real and valid, but he did not want to stew in their acidic juices forever. Instead, he began to let them go by initiating forgiveness and intentionally acting in the opposite spirit toward his father — with kindness, honor and forgiveness.

Rex perceived that he had allowed himself to become a "victim." Without knowing it, he had given his dad the power to define him as worthy or unworthy, depending entirely on whether or not he spoke words of approval. And perhaps we *all* do this to some extent. We become victims whenever we give another person the power to define our worth. We become victims whenever we make approval, or possessions, or addictions, or activities responsible for our feelings of happiness, self worth and lovability.

We become victims by giving another person the power to define our worth.

Like Rex, we have a choice. We can try to find our happiness, value, peace, security, lovability and self worth through people, things, activities, and substances. Or we can feel happy, valued, peaceful, secure, lovable and worthy through connection with the God who created us and loves us unconditionally.

○   ○   ○

Rex learned that part of being a healthy person is the ability to make decisions for yourself without feeling the need for your parent's (or anyone else's) approval. Sometimes doing the right thing will bring disapproval, but you need to do it anyway. In Mark 1, Jesus went to Peter's home to take a break from the crowds.[1] However, when word leaked out he was there, a huge gang of sick and needy people were soon banging on the door for help. Jesus went out and ministered to them, but there wasn't enough time to treat them all. The next day, there was an even bigger crowd of people. But instead of healing them, Jesus went to Jerusalem!

Excuse me? That means lots and lots of people were disappointed and let down and maybe even angry at Jesus for leaving town.

If the all-knowing all-powerful Son of God can't please all the people all the time, what makes us think *we* can?

Rex knows now that what happened to him was not his fault. He was a child. But as an adult, what happens next *is* up to him. When a parent (or spouse or authority figure) withholds their approval, we can feel frustrated, despondent, guilty, useless, unlovable, shameful and bitter. When that happens, we can overcompensate by becoming a high achiever like Rex or we can shut down and become a social dropout. Either way, we're going to be miserable until we learn to forgive the perpetrator. The only way we can keep this poison from ruining our lives is to fight back with good: *"Do not be overcome with evil, but overcome evil with good."* [2]

And the "goodest" thing you can ever do is to forgive someone.

Thankfully, Rex has been able to receive and embrace the love of his heavenly Father. Unfortunately, many men can't. They are virtually incapable of receiving grace and love as an adult because they were never shown it as a child. Dads, listen up: If our kids don't receive love and affirmation from their *earthly* father, it will be very difficult to receive it from their *heavenly* one. Act accordingly!

Over time, Rex came to understand that despite his father's failings, he is a beloved son. God has shown him that he "has what it takes" to be an exceptional man, husband and father. By extending forgiveness toward his father, he's found forgiveness for his own shortcomings, too. And while it is difficult to undo years of pain, the power of Jesus can heal and restore broken lives.

Rex would soon see that power in an unusual reunion with his estranged father...

o   o   o

I was at the Story Weekend retreat where Rex first shared his life story with a small, trusted group of guys. The process of healing *began* that weekend, but the real breakthrough came later when the same group met at a place we called the "Man Cave." In this private, supportive setting, Rex uncovered more painful, emotional junk — crammed in, trash-compacted and warehoused in his heart. To make peace with his past, he resolved to meet with his father in person and try to get a handle on their volatile history.

> **If Jesus couldn't please all the people all the time, what makes us think *we* can?**

Rex booked a flight to the family's winter home in Naples, Florida. There, he heard his dad's story for the first time. His father had grown up in a military academy, and the conditioning process he went through in boot camp was sheer hell. Under the control of a particularly savage instructor, the new students were beaten severely as a test of their manhood. To survive the abusive training, Rex's father learned to fight back and soon developed a reputation as a tough SOB who could punch his way out of any situation. With a red-hot temper and a fast right hook, the young Texan became the unofficial enforcer to keep the incoming students in line. In his world, violence solved everything and he had no compassion for weaklings or whiners. He was taught by the faculty that this was how you "became a man." You learned to live with pain and punishment and you kept your mouth shut.

Many recruits broke under the pressure, but his father survived and became a tougher man in the process. After graduating, he went on to play middle linebacker for a Big Ten college team and helped them win the Rose Bowl in his senior year. Later, he took that same smash-mouth philosophy and applied it to raising his kids, especially the boys.

As Rex listened in amazement to his father's story, he finally understood the torment of his dad's early life. And with this release, the reconciliation process began.

Rex has done his part in the two-step forgiveness process. He has *released*. But *reconciliation* depends on his father. To experience true reconciliation with his son, this classic alpha male will have to ask for forgiveness. And for dear old closed-off dad, that will not be easy.

As a Christian, Rex's desire was to forgive his dad and be reconciled. But what if his father never accepts responsibility for the damage he caused? God is not commanding us to have close friendships with those who hurt us, but he does ask us to love them, honor them, and forgive them anyway.

Why? Because when we forgive an undeserving parent (or spouse or sibling or boss), it protects us from being crippled by negative emotions. When we forgive someone, we please God and we stay emotionally healthy. Doing good to our enemies may not make a difference in them, but it will definitely make a difference in *us*. As Dutch botanist Paul Boese said, "Forgiveness does not change the past but it does enlarge the future."

o   o   o

Apologizing to Rex will not be easy for his elderly father. It may never happen. But Rex is no longer bound by the chains of his past. He is learning to trust. He is learning to love. He is willing to risk being vulnerable in relationships. He no longer believes the lies about himself. He makes sure Satan does not have a louder voice in his head than God's Spirit does. He is parenting with tenderness and approachability. He is an attentive husband and "on-site" father who intentionally dishes out approval and affirmation to his kids.

○　　○　　○

Forgiving demonstrates God's grace to a world that's bent on getting even.

We sometimes think forgiveness is letting someone "off the hook." But as Rex will confirm, the greatest benefits are for the *forgiver*, not the forgiven. Refusing to forgive leads to unresolved anger and bitterness, simmering emotions that will resurface at pressure points throughout our life. When we hold a grudge, we develop a chip on our shoulder, the nagging feeling that the world is against us. And that's a guaranteed recipe for self-centeredness and repeated disappointment.

As writer Robert Brault says, "Life is too short to hold a grudge, also too long." If that's too cerebral, comedian Buddy Hackett hits closer to home, "I never hold a grudge. You know why? While you're busy carrying a grudge, they're out dancing."

Worst of all, unforgiveness gets in the way of our relationship with God. When we "cancel the debt and tear up the contract," it allows Jesus to do his wonderful work in us and through us. Just as Rex is now a role model to his sphere of friends, forgiving others is the best way we can model God's grace to an entire world that's bent on getting even.

As we saw in chapter 5, Dietrich Bonheoffer was a German pastor who founded the anti-Nazi resistance movement among clergy during Hitler's rise to power. In 1943 he was arrested, and at age 39 he was hanged, just eleven days before his prison was liberated by U.S. forces. His final letters from prison often spoke about forgiveness: "Live together in the forgiveness of your sins, for without it no human fellowship, last of all a marriage, can

234

survive. Don't insist on your rights, don't blame each other, don't judge or condemn each other, don't find fault with each other, but accept each other as you are, and forgive each other every day from the bottom of your hearts." [3]

○   ○   ○

Just 30 years after the death of Jesus, Spartacus led a doomed revolt of slaves against the Roman Empire. When the Legions of Rome easily defeated his untrained fighters, all 6,000 rebellious slaves were crucified along the Appian Way. Every hundred yards for 350 miles, a captured prisoner hung from a cross. So Jesus wasn't the only man who had nails pounded through his wrists and feet. But Jesus *was* the only man who ever willingly, voluntarily went to the cross — and the only one who could bear the sins of the entire world.

If there ever was an incalculably large debt to be paid, it's the sin debt that humanity owes to God for our disobedience and unbelief. But God "cancelled our debt" 2,000 years ago, when he nailed all of our sins — past, present and future — to the cross along with his Son.

The total number of people who have ever lived on earth is estimated to be 106 billion. Yet Jesus found it in his merciful heart to forgive you and me and Rex's father and all the other bazillion human beings ever conceived on this planet — just as we should forgive those who trespass against us.

That's grace in its highest form.

○   ○   ○

"You will know that forgiveness has begun when you recall those who hurt you and feel the power to wish them well."

— Lewis Smedes[4]

III: GRACE IS...

CHAPTER 18:
Grace is Compassion in the New Economy

Forget seatbelts. Heck, forget seats. This is a mission of mercy and a test of manhood rolled into one.

From where I'm riding, the moving cityscape of rickety apartments and crowded markets is a bouncing blur. I try to focus on individual faces but hundreds of beggars and vendors and hawkers are shouting up at me simultaneously. Smells of garbage, incense, cattle and curry swirl up to baffle my nose. Signs scrawled in Hindustani and Sanskrit cover every wall with bargains and warnings indecipherable to me. I'm hanging on for dear life, but the workers sitting next to me are laughing and joking like kids on a rollercoaster. Among natives, the rule of travel in India is simple: Climb up to the highest and most dangerous point of any moving object — trains, buses, hay carts — and ride there in total nonchalance.

Far below me, three-wheel taxis and motorbikes with entire families onboard careen recklessly in and out of our path. Unfazed by the danger, bicycles and bullocks seem bent on being crushed under our wheels. Brakes screech and motorized rickshaws weave and honk in clouds of choking blue exhaust until traffic thins, then disappears like lifting fog.

Relieved to be out of the city, I recall that 90,000 people a year die on India's roads and wonder if we've just added to that tally.

Headed for the coast, our ragtag convoy rumbles down a

rutted road lined with clumps of scrawny palm trees. Each of our five flatbed trucks is loaded to capacity with 70-pound bags of rice and a crew of workers balanced precariously on top of the cargo. Several hundred pots and pans clatter noisily as we pitch back and forth on the sun-baked clay. I squint hard in the noonday brightness. I flinch as road dust stings my cheeks. I speculate if my kidneys will ever be the same.

Somewhere up ahead, the beautiful Indian Ocean looms, and our drivers scan the horizon for the seaside village that is our destination.

We had travelled for 15 bone-jarring hours and our tsunami relief team was anxious to arrive before dark. Communications were out and we'd been warned to beware of marauding bands of survivors looking for food. After another half hour of hard driving, I could smell the saltwater and hear seabirds wheeling overhead.

After 15 bone-jarring hours, our tsunami relief team was anxious to arrive before dark.

As the convoy came to a halt, I jumped down from the lead truck to find out why we had stopped before reaching the village. Ahead of me, I could see the ocean waves crashing onto shore, but figured we must be lost since there were no signs of a fishing village. I looked up and down for huts or buildings, but couldn't see any signs of habitation. All I saw were several men sitting on their long wooden boats, patching holes and replacing damaged boards. As I walked toward the surf, the road suddenly ended in a jagged cliff. I peered over the drop-off to the beach about twelve feet below me. Confused, I told my driver that the tsunami must have washed the road away. But why would the road extend out to the beach in the first place? Wouldn't it lead into the village?

When our translator caught up with us, we motioned toward an elderly man, the apparent leader of the boatmen. His brown face was etched and wrinkled from years in the hot Indian sun. As I got closer, I could see that tears had recently streaked his dusty cheeks. Eager to distribute our emergency food, we asked him for directions to the fishing village and why the main road ended so abruptly at this place.

He winced at our question, and water welled up in his sad, red eyes. Speaking softly, he explained that the village we were seeking was built on a small peninsula that jutted out into the ocean for another kilometer or so. When the tsunami hit, a wall of water crashed over the entire land mass, destroying everything and then sucking it back out into the ocean, taking the village and hundreds of lives with it. On its retreat, the water left its destructive high-water mark where the road was sheared off. The look on his face betrayed what he was about to say next. Gazing past us toward the ocean, he whispered that the only survivors were a few fishermen who happened to be out in their boats that day and a handful of women who had gone inland to the market.

Everybody and everything else was gone.

○   ○   ○

Do you remember the Asian Tsunami of 2004? It was one of the worst natural disasters in human history. Over 230,000 people lost their lives in 14 countries. Shocked nations from every corner of the globe rushed in tons of food, medicine and relief. In all, $7 billion in humanitarian aid was donated and reconstruction efforts continue to this day. Images of the destruction dominated world media round the clock and it ranks as one of the biggest news stories of the twentieth century.

Every single day, 30,000 children die from poverty.

I'll never forget it because I was there, involved in Indian relief work with a team from my church. I personally witnessed the indescribable destruction from this disaster, and it's etched in my memory forever.

Yet there's a far bigger disaster story occurring right now and it goes by virtually unnoticed. Every single day, 30,000 children die from poverty. That's the equivalent of one Asian Tsunami striking every eight days. That's one poor child dying every 2.8 seconds or 21 per minute or 1,260 per hour or 30,240 per day or 211,680 per week or 846,720 per month or 10.8 million per year.

Death on this scale should be front page news. Trouble is, these kids die invisibly. They starve to death quietly in developing countries far from the cameras and the news teams and the industrialized nations who could change it virtually overnight if they chose to.

How is that possible? According to UNICEF, the additional amount of money it would take to meet basic human needs in all developing countries is $13 billion for basic health and nutrition, $9 billion for water and sanitation, and $6 billion for basic education.

Sounds like big numbers. Impossible numbers. Until you compare them to what some of us spend on our pooches. According to *Business Week*, Americans spend $41 billion a year on their pets. That's more than the gross domestic products of most countries! Pfizer sells an obesity control drug for dogs while Eli Lilly markets a drug for canine separation anxiety. Pet plastic surgeons now offer eye lifts and nose jobs while pet dentists offer canine braces and crowns. Beyond the demand for gourmet pet foods, Americans shell out big bucks on cancer treatments, MRIs and even psychotherapy for their pets. Doggie slippers, cat bikinis and health insurance are hot sellers. Meanwhile, a shift of a few billion from organic chew toys to human medicine could eradicate tuberculosis worldwide and save two million lives a year — that's equal to Nebraska's entire population.[1]

Half the world lives on less than $2.50 a day.

○   ○   ○

America suffered a recessionary dip in 2008-2009 that left 10 percent of the nation unemployed. Tough times caused most of us to make cutbacks in our budgets. But even at our lowest point, we have never experienced the kind of grinding poverty that dominates most countries. Almost half the world — over three billion people — lives on less than $2.50 a day. At least 80 percent of humanity lives on less than $10 a day, a meager annual income of $3,560. In America, we flip on a light switch or open our refrigerator or set our thermostat without giving it much thought. But 1.6 billion other people — a quarter of all humanity — live without electricity. American kids spend $12 billion a year on video games. But 1 billion other children live with starvation, rampant disease and unpredictable violence.

One out of two kids face starvation, rampant disease and unpredictable violence.

That's one out of two kids on the planet.

Why such disparity between the world's rich and poor? Why is the gross domestic product of the 48 poorest nations less than the wealth of the world's three richest people? Why is this divide getting wider and deeper?

Because we're still operating on what I call the "Old Economy."

In the last decade, the world has become a much smaller place. In his groundbreaking book, *The World Is Flat: A Brief History of the Twenty-First Century*, Thomas L. Friedman analyzes globalization. As the title suggests, Friedman views the new high-tech world as a level playing field for commerce because communication technologies have reduced historical, cultural and geographic boundaries between countries. He argues that the rise of personal computers, the fall of communism, the explosion of outsourcing and the Internet's instant access to information give all competitors an equal opportunity.

In a sense, Friedman's correct. Globalization *has* brought people together like never before. Phone operators in India can answer questions about my new Blu-ray player that was assembled in China that I purchased in America and took home in my Japanese car running on fuel from Venezuela paid for with my credit card issued by a bank in Belgium. International trade *is* allowing certain segments of poorer countries to experience the fastest growth in their economic histories. The standard of living for those at the top is being raised dramatically. The technology boom that started in the late 1990s led economists and market analysts to conclude that a "New Economy" was at work — one that would trickle wealth down to the poor.

But it hasn't worked out that way.

Despite the label "New Economy," the same old principles that applied thousands of years ago are still at work today: Create something of value and the forces of supply and demand will set the price accordingly. The main difference, however, is that market size has increased exponentially as new consumer bases open up. Yet at its core, this "conditional" economy has been operating since the creation of man. The conditional economy goes something like this: If I give something to you, I expect something in return. Therefore, I have no value in the economic or social system unless I have something to offer. The value I possess is determined by how much what I have to offer is in demand by others. And that works whether your product is slate (Fred Flintstone) or computer software (Bill Gates).

There is, however, a *genuine* New Economy — an absolutely revolutionary economy — ushered in by Jesus 2,000 years ago. The principles he laid out are in stark contrast to the conditional economy that still drives commerce today. His "unconditional economy" goes like this: Each and every one of us has unsurpassable worth regardless of what we have to offer to the marketplace. Our value is not determined by man, but by God. It doesn't depend on our bankbooks, our paychecks or our situation in life.

In Mark Twain's novel, *The Prince and the Pauper*, the rich boy and the beggar are switched out only to discover that despite their vastly different circumstances, they are equally clever, intelligent, resourceful and courageous. That was a shocking storyline to set in medieval England. But God takes it one step further — an heir to the throne and a destitute commoner both have equal and inestimable value to their Creator.

The three main pillars in God's New Economy are:

1. Give to others and expect nothing back in return.

2. Forgive those who have wronged us just like God has forgiven us.

3. Love unconditionally and demonstrate it through compassionate action.

These key principles are not found in your standard MBA textbooks, but when practiced, they produce a return on investment that puts Wall Street to shame.

○   ○   ○

Those of us in business were taught that if we got a good education and worked hard, we would develop a certain value in the economy. The better the schools, the harder the work, the greater our value would be. The greater our value, the greater our earning power. And if those earnings were high enough, we could accumulate the fruits of our labor — big houses, luxury cars, hot motorcycles, cool boats, electronic toys, the whole SkyMall catalog.

The promise of the American Dream leads only to a thirst for more.

Conspicuous consumption is deemed to be the right of those privileged few who succeed. After all, they earned it, right? But I dare you to ask anyone who's reached the top, "Have you found true happiness in life?" The majority will tell you the promise of the American Dream leads only to a thirst for more. And that pursuit ultimately leads to an emptiness that cannot be fulfilled by anything here on earth. But don't take my word for it. Andrew Carnegie said, "Millionaires seldom smile." John Jacob Astor said, "I am the most miserable man on earth." And John D. Rockefeller said, "I have made many millions, but they have brought me no happiness."

In the world today there are 10 million millionaires. Of these, 85,000 are what's called "extreme millionaires" with financial assets of over $30 million each. But the mega-rich of our day couldn't hold a candle to the immeasurable wealth of King Solomon. According to 1 Kings, Solomon received an income of 46 tons of gold per year (gold prices fluctuate but are over $1,300 per ounce at the time of this writing!). Yet he described being the world's richest man as pretty much a wasted life. He sampled every possible pleasure, both moral and immoral, and came up empty: *"I denied myself nothing my eyes desired; I refused my heart no pleasure. My heart took delight in all my work, and this was the reward for all my labor. Yet when I surveyed all that my hands had done and what I had toiled to achieve, everything was meaningless, a chasing after the wind; nothing was gained under the sun."* [2]

If that passage doesn't rock your view of chasing the American Dream, read it in this Message translation: *"Everything I wanted I took — I never said no to myself. I gave in to every impulse, held back nothing. I sucked the marrow of pleasure out of every task — my reward to myself for a hard day's work! Then I took a good look at everything I'd done, looked at all the sweat and hard work. But when I looked, I saw nothing but smoke. Smoke and spitting into the wind. There was nothing to any of it. Nothing."* [3]

Doesn't that describe our daily grind?

So many of us just go through the motions of life, hoping to find purpose and fulfillment and happiness that always seem just one step away. We work hard and many of us play hard, but nothing seems to bring any lasting satisfaction. We feel empty inside but can't put our finger on what it is we're longing for.

I submit that what we're missing are the dual joys of *giving* and *forgiving*.

We can never get enough of anything to fill the hole in our soul.

Why are people in America so unhappy and stressed out? Because we can never get enough possessions to fill the hole in our soul, and we can never get enough retribution to satisfy our thirst for getting even. As long as we focus on ourselves — hoarding up wealth or hoarding up anger — we will be miserable. As long as our hearts are fixed on gaining treasure or gaining revenge we are turned completely inward.

But switch the perspective from "It's all about me" to "It's all about *others*" and everything would change overnight. If we could truly grasp just how forgiven and blessed we are, we would forgive and bless others.

A self-centered person says, "I deserve this lavish lifestyle. I worked hard for it." An other-centered person says, "Every good thing I have came from God. Now what do you want me to do with it, Lord?"

Radio talk show host Rush Limbaugh uses a humorous tagline to describe himself: "With talent on loan from God." Whether he means it sincerely or it's a tongue-in-cheek promotion, it's a true statement. We need to recognize that every gift we have, including the ability to succeed in our careers, is on loan from God. Everything we accumulate is actually God's possession, to be used for his purpose: *"Both riches and honor come from you, and you rule over all."*[4]

Frankly, we get so full of ourselves that we forget the true source of our "riches and honor" (and everything else) is God. The money and possessions we have are not simply a sign of how hard we work or how smart we are, but how generous God has been to us: "If you start thinking to yourselves, "I did all this. And all by myself. I'm rich. It's all mine!" — well, think again. *"Remember that God, your God, gave you the strength to produce all this wealth."*[5]

What if we really believed that to our core? Imagine how that spirit of gratitude and humility would impact the financial inequality between people groups around the earth. For example, think about the current food situation. Some countries, like the United States, have crops in abundance. Others seem to suffer in perpetual famine. The biggest problem for much of world's population is finding enough food each day to stay alive. But for many of us, the problem is finding new *diets* so we can squeeze into our designer jeans. We have so much excess food so easily available that Americans spend around $30 billion a year on weight loss products and services.

Is this how God designed the world? With some barns meant to be overflowing and some meant to be empty? No. Not if you believe that all people have equal dignity and worth to Jesus. Paul wrote a letter to the (temporarily) well-off believers in Corinth to assist the (temporarily) needy in Jerusalem: *"At the present time your plenty will supply what they need, so that in turn their plenty will supply what you need. Then there will be equality."* [6]

Americans spend around $30 billion a year on weight loss.

People complain, "If there is a God, why does he let people starve? Why doesn't he do something about world hunger?" The answer is: *He did. He made us.* And he placed us in the richest nation in the history of the world. I can imagine God's response, "There's plenty to go around. More than enough. But some of you are storing up your treasures on earth and not in heaven. You aren't sharing."

Jesus warned against this kind of selfishness: *"Don't hoard treasure down here where it gets eaten by moths and corroded by rust or — worse! — stolen by burglars. Stockpile treasure in heaven, where it's safe from moth and rust and burglars. It's obvious, isn't it? The place where your treasure is, is the place you will most want to be, and end up being."* [7]

So how do we get our treasure up into heaven? Is there a ladder tall enough? Or an angelic Brink's truck to pick up our deposits? No, God means that by sharing our wealth with others in *this* life, we are earning an eternal reward in the *next*.

We will all eventually part with everything we own and every dollar we have.

Remember, no matter how stingy we are, every one of us must eventually part with every single thing we own and every single dollar we have. The only question is *when* — at our death (when it's too late to be transferred to our heavenly account) or now while we're alive (thereby transferring it upstairs).

Like the old joke goes, you never see a U-Haul trailer behind a hearse.

In his book, *The Treasure Principle*, Randy Alcorn describes the fate of our earthly riches this way: "You can't take it with you — but you can send it on ahead."

By giving to others in need, we make investments that will be paying dividends to us for millions and billions of years to come. But if we selfishly cling with our Gollum arms to what we accumulate in our "three score and ten" down here, we will lose it all: *"Whoever wants to save his life will lose it, but whoever loses his life for me will save it. What good is it for a man to gain the whole world, and yet lose his very self?"*[8]

In my professional life as a senior portfolio manager, I buy and sell stocks for my clients. When I see danger or a downward trend in a particular company, I move their assets out of it into a better investment. Likewise, we need to see the difference between the high-risk market on earth and our guaranteed-safe market in heaven. Leaving your assets in an account that's soon going to be worthless is just plain crazy. Depositing them where they will earn *"thirty, sixty, or even a hundred"* times what was invested (with dividends being paid forever) is just plain smart.[9]

Jesus commands his followers to give. And the rewards he promises are high. How's that working out?

Surprisingly awful.

The average church attender only gives $100 a year to his church. And about 20 percent of believers don't give anything at all. Nada. Zip. Zero. Despite the clear need, despite the clear teaching, despite the clear rewards, only about one in twenty Christians tithes 10 percent of their income to God's work.

Something doesn't add up here.

Somebody said that if every Christian chipped in just $20 a month we could eradicate poverty in America — without relying on government programs. So what's stopping us? In an article named *Why Christians (Don't) Give,* sociologist Dr. Christian Smith said: "Many people have little perspective on how wealthy they are, and view themselves as just getting by." He says our reluctance to give can be traced to a lack of teaching, a lack of trust, and plain old-fashioned greed. "In our culture, money is sacred; for some people it can replace God." He concludes, "If American Christians gave generously, it would produce more than $100 billion a year to do whatever the givers wanted to do with it. American Christians have been blessed with unbelievable amounts of wealth compared to Christians throughout church history and the rest of the world today." [10]

If Christians chipped in $20 a month we could eradicate poverty in America.

I recently read a report saying Americans spend over $23 billion a year storing their excess junk in those new self-storage facilities.

$23 billion. For what? To hang onto our extra stuff for a little longer? Imagine if we solved our storage problem by giving that stuff away to the needy and donating the $23 billion in rent to solve world hunger.

How big is a billion? A billion seconds ago it was 1959, a billion minutes ago Jesus walked the earth. Those billions would go a long way toward feeding the 800 million people who go hungry every day.

By adopting the New Economy principles of Jesus, we would keep less and give more. We would reject materialism. We would reject wretched excess of every kind. We would know the difference between needing and wanting.

There's a new term in pop culture, the antonym for consumerism. It's called "enoughism" and it's the theory that when consumers finally possess everything they could possibly need, buying more stuff will actually make their life worse instead of better. Even among nonbelievers there's a growing rejection of greedy, unrestrained consumption and the workaholic race for wealth. The late comic George Carlin lampooned our unquenchable urge for more stuff in a classic routine: "A house is a pile of stuff with a roof on it. Your house is just a place to keep your stuff while you go out and get... more stuff!"

○   ○   ○

Just before telling the Parable of the Rich Fool, Jesus made a controversial statement to those who accumulate things only for themselves: *"Watch out! Be on your guard against all kinds of greed; a man's life does not consist in the abundance of his possessions."* It was an inflammatory idea in those days, and it still is: *"Life is not defined by what you have, even when you have a lot."* [11]

As the crowd reeled back on their heels, he told them a story: *"The farm of a certain rich man produced a terrific crop. He talked to himself: 'What can I do? My barn isn't big enough for this harvest.' Then he said, 'Here's what I'll do: I'll tear down my barns and build bigger ones ... I'll say to myself, You've got it made and can now retire. Take it easy and have the time of your life!'"* [12]

Sound familiar? Some of us who've been successful are busily tearing down our barns and building bigger and bigger ones. It may not be a literal barn; it could be a savings account or a retirement

We can't hold on to possessions. They hold on to us. And ruin us.

fund or a second home or whatever bigger, faster, flashier, more expensive symbol of achievement suits us. The common thread is that we build these "barns" for ourselves, all so we can hold on to more and more possessions for longer and longer.

And that's the problem with possessions. We can't hold on to them. They hold on to us. And ruin us. The end of the parable is a knock-out punch reminder of how short-sighted we are: *"Just then God showed up and said, 'Fool! Tonight you die. And your barn full of goods — who gets it?'"* Looking around at the well-dressed, well-fed, well-connected Pharisees in his crowd, Jesus cautioned them, *"That's what happens when you fill your barn with Self and not with God."*[13]

○   ○   ○

Giving is half the beauty of the New Economy. The other half is *forgiving*. And we need both to live the full, free life God imagined for us.

So how do we deal with our debtors? Not debtors who have borrowed money from us, but those who have grabbed something even more valuable. Maybe your innocence was taken through sexual violation. Maybe like Jimi in chapter 13, your self esteem was stolen. Maybe like Rex in chapter 17, your childhood joy was robbed. Under the "Old Economy" principles, you would put that hurt and pain into your barn and hold on to it forever, guarding it, adding to it, and releasing it only if the person responsible begged for forgiveness. If they eventually "earned" your forgiveness, then maybe, just maybe, you could reconcile.

> **Giving is half the beauty of the New Economy. The other half is forgiving.**

Under the New Economy principles, your actions would be quite different. The new way to live says "Forgive, just as God has forgiven us." This unnatural response is what Jesus demands of us who choose to follow him. In fact, you jeopardize your own forgiveness and incur his anger *"unless you forgive your brother from your heart."* [14]

Picture Jesus hanging on the cross. Was there ever a more undeserved punishment? Jesus loved everyone he came in contact with, yet his reward was death in the most brutal form imaginable. But even as he hung there, wrists spiked to the roughhewn crossbeam, he pardoned those who condemned him: *"Father, forgive them, for they do not know what they are doing."* [15]

Even in this moment of excruciating agony, Jesus was interceding on our behalf to the Father. Imagine that — asking forgiveness for the very people who lied about him to the Sanhedrin and slandered him before Pilate. For those who plotted his death and sold him out. For those who whipped him and pummeled him and hoisted him up on a stake. If he could do that, how much more should we be able to forgive those who have wronged us? Wrongs that are petty compared to the galactic injustice borne by Jesus.

Human nature says people should have to bow down and earn our forgiveness by working for it. But *grace* says give your forgiveness to others as a "free gift they don't deserve and could never earn."

Living in the New Economy requires thinking differently about everything. The Old Economy is based on unredeemed human nature. The *Wall Street* mantra of Gordon Gekko — greed and selfishness — has not changed since mankind fell in the Garden. But the New Economy, with

> **Do we approach poverty, sickness and injustice like Jesus did?**

its unique potential to change our thinking, has its roots in Jesus Christ. Inviting him into our heart and letting him take over our lives allows us to change from the inside out and become new people. People who can give generously and forgive easily.

For those of us who call ourselves believers, those who know God's love at a personal level, I have some hard questions: *Are we living out that love in the world around us? Do we approach poverty and sickness and injustice in the same manner Jesus did?*

I'm pointing the finger back at myself with this last question: *Are we more concerned with our comfort or our character?*

To paraphrase author Brennan Manning, Jesus did not endure poverty, nakedness and pain so that we could become rich, well-clothed and spared from suffering.

It's not just our "happiness" that's at stake. Happiness is a fickle, fleeting emotion that comes and goes with our circumstances. It is our *joy* that's at stake — the abiding joy of a life lived for others in the New Economy.

○   ○   ○

"We make a living by what we get, but we make a life by what we give."

— Winston Churchill[16]

CHAPTER 19:
Jesus Plus Nothing

Every architecture student asks the same question: "How do I come up with a truly original design?" And most look for inspiration from the same fictional architect.

Since its debut in 1943, Ayn Rand's novel *The Fountainhead* has sold over six million copies. This perennial bestseller is the story of a talented young architect's battle against mediocrity and his sometimes violent dedication to excellence.

The hero of this inspiring tale is Howard Roark, a rough-cut prodigy struggling to achieve purity of form, architecture not watered down or compromised by clients or committees. With a backbone as strong as a steel girder, he represents the triumph of individualism over collectivism. From the beginning, Roark stubbornly refuses to conform and is kicked out of school for his fresh imaginative style. When he refuses to copy the classical designs of past eras, the dean expels him, taunting, "You want to stand against the whole world?"

This intransigent rookie chooses to toil in obscurity rather than compromise his personal artistic vision. He champions modern architecture, defying an establishment that worships traditional styles. Rather than work for bosses who oppose his creativity, Roark opens his own office, but his designs are too revolutionary and he attracts few commissions. When he is finally chosen to design the most important new skyscraper in Manhattan, he turns down the commission rather than permit adulteration of his design.

Against these odds, Roark eventually rises from unknown architect to prominent designer. (It's thought that Rand modeled Roark's character after Frank Lloyd Wright. Wright's family motto was "The truth against the world.")

Howard Roark goes on to design many landmark buildings, and near the end of the book, a former classmate begs him to design a huge public housing project called Cortland Homes. After completing a highly innovative plan for low-cost construction, Roark allows his rival to covertly submit the blueprints as if they were his own. His only demand is that the plans are not to be altered in any way. Unfortunately, while Roark is away on an ocean cruise, competing architects are hired in to alter his design. When Roark returns, he is livid that Cortland was not built according to his original vision.

That night, he dynamites the defaced masterpiece and allows himself to be arrested.

At his trial, Roark chooses to eschew lawyers and defends himself in a powerful courtroom speech defining the difference between the "creators" and the "parasites" of society. In the 1946 Hollywood version of *The Fountainhead*, matinee idol Gary Cooper tells the jury what a true artist is: "He serves nothing and no one; he loves only himself."

Roark's rebellious rhetoric convinces the jury (and millions of readers and viewers) that the only true virtue is selfishness and that we should live for ourselves on our own terms. He argues that the caveman who discovered fire was "probably burned at the stake he had taught his brothers to light."

In the end, he persuades the jury and is declared innocent.

At first glance, it appears that Ayn Rand wrote *The Fountainhead* as a tribute to the creative freethinker. After all, Howard Roark is a rugged individualist whose radically new designs are rejected by society. Like many inventors and original thinkers (Galileo, Copernicus, Tesla, etc.) he fights against those afraid of change, the unthinking masses blindly following the status quo. That noble ideal is to be greatly applauded. But there's another, more troubling theme that runs throughout the 752-page book — the philosophy of Objectivism.

Rand first introduced this concept in her novels and later through the work of the Ayn Rand Institute. In the appendix to her 1957 epic, *Atlas Shrugged*, she wrote, "My philosophy is the concept of man as a heroic being, with his own happiness as the moral purpose of his life, with productive achievement as his noblest activity, and reason as his only absolute."[1]

An outspoken atheist, Rand believed an individual's primary moral obligation is to achieve his own well-being — a total rejection of religion's universal imperative that we live for the sake of others. Rand's Objectivist ethics are summed up in the oath her *Atlas Shrugged* character John Galt adhered to: "I swear — by my life and my love of it — that I will never live for the sake of another man, nor ask another man to live for mine."[2]

> **Ayn Rand believed man's primary moral obligation is to achieve his own well-being.**

Embracing this philosophy of "rational self-interest" results in a kind of dog-eat-dog world where one's class status and monetary success are leveraged exclusively for one's personal enjoyment. Expressions like "He who dies with the most toys wins" hint at this creed's inherent narcissism and consumerism. (I love the alternative bumper sticker that reads "He who dies with the most toys still dies.")

The philosophy Rand brought to life in her wildly popular novels is the polar opposite of the New Economy we looked at in the previous chapter. The New Economy that Jesus ushered in is based on *selflessness*; the Old Economy is based on *selfishness*.

You could tidily sum up the competing systems as "grace versus greed."

Don't get me wrong — I do agree with some of Rand's philosophy. For instance, I believe the Declaration of Independence gives us the right to exercise our liberty and to pursue our happiness — including our financial fortune — without government interference. No more taking orders from an unelected king or a socialist politburo. And I believe each of us *is* free to live for himself. But a higher moral code dictates that we use that freedom to help those less fortunate than ourselves.

Objectivism teaches that my own life and happiness are my highest values, and that I do not exist to serve the interests of anyone else. It describes our self-absorbed "me generation" perfectly and it's a core value of secular humanism. Compare this fashionable love of self to the Apostle Paul's love of others: *"Love cares more for others than for self ... doesn't want what it doesn't have ... doesn't have a swelled head ... doesn't force itself on others ... isn't always 'me first.'"* [3]

> **Objectivism describes today's self-absorbed "me generation" perfectly.**

The Old Economy (selfishness) says, "I deserve everything my money and power can buy." The New Economy (selflessness) says, "I choose to set aside my own interests to serve others."

If I want to live like Jesus, I need to see that the interests of God and the needs of society have greater moral significance than my own. As a Christ-follower, I must see myself fundamentally as a servant, existing to serve the weak, the poor, and the marginalized: *"Jesus Christ laid down his life for us. And we ought to lay down our lives for our brothers. If anyone has material possessions and sees his brother in need but has no pity on him, how can the love of God be in him?"* [4]

Ever drive by one of those scruffy guys on the street corner with a cardboard will-work-for-food sign? Or step over a homeless man on the way into an expensive restaurant? I have. It's real easy for me to embrace Bible verses that promise me blessings, but kind of tough to remember ones like: *"If you see some brother or sister in need and have the means to do something about it but turn a cold shoulder and do nothing, what happens to God's love? It disappears. And you made it disappear."* [5]

Well-meaning Christians (me included) can be seduced by the temptations of the Old Economy. My friend, Greg Gibbs, puts it this way, "The American spiritual cancer is that we presume the beauty of Christ is me getting everything I want." But God is not a cosmic vending machine. His kingdom is not an outlet mall. And heaven is not a big Costco in the sky. In fact, our leader himself, the Messiah, owned virtually no earthly possessions. And instead of retiring with a fat IRA, he permitted himself to be arrested and tortured as Roman soldiers gambled for the clothes off his back.

Blame it on TV evangelists or lingering Yuppie zeitgeist from the Boomer generation, but lots of Christians think following Jesus is not about giving up our lust for *things* but getting on a fast track to acquire them even quicker. And many of us who are spiritually mature enough to reject the slick health-and-wealth preachers still have a corner of our brain that thinks God owes us a comfortable lifestyle without speed bumps. But in reality we are promised just the opposite: *"In this world you will have trouble. But take heart! I have overcome the world."* [6]

> God is not a cosmic vending machine. His kingdom is not an outlet mall or a big Costco in the sky.

Lots of decent people have been confused by preachers hinting (or outright proclaiming) that Christianity is a shortcut to financial security. This so-called "prosperity gospel" plays out pretty well in America where the standard of living for most citizens is sky high. But it's an insult to tell believers in Somalia or Cambodia that faith in God will bring financial riches or material possessions.

Here's the proof that most "health and wealth" preaching is misguided: Five out of six people alive on the earth today will live their entire life in poverty — whether or not they are Christians. Whether or not they send money to a TV ministry.

If some big-haired preacher promises you heaven on earth, run his claims by this truth detector: If a spiritual principle is true *anywhere*, it has to be true *everywhere*, in every culture. Scripture says God doesn't play favorites or show partiality between races or nations or geographic regions.[7]

What's true in oil-rich Houston has to be true in dirt-poor Haiti.

Or it's totally bogus.

Five out of six people alive today will live their entire life in poverty.

I don't know about you, but I get real uneasy when I see ministers who have more in common with Ayn Rand than with Jesus Christ. Instead of multiple homes and a private jet, Jesus had zero homes and a public donkey: *"The foxes have holes and the birds of the air have nests, but the Son of Man has no place to lay his head."*[8]

Another word for this New Economy (and one Objectivists choke on) is *altruism* — unselfish concern for the welfare of others. Not only is this kind of giving voluntary, it's often anonymous, done for the pure joy of serving others. Admittedly not a core value in consumerist societies, it's still a traditional virtue in many cultures, and a central (but often overlooked) teaching of most religious traditions. Pure altruism is a form of pure grace — giving freely without expecting to get something back in return.

Fictional architect Howard Roark lived by his own rules and for his own selfish interests. He lived for his work and defined "success" as being able to do exactly what he wanted to. Another architect I know — a real flesh-and-blood architect — has quite a different definition of success. And it's all about serving others...

○   ○   ○

Mike and Robyn were living the dream. Dual incomes, big house in the suburbs and nice cars in the driveway. A graduate of Lawrence Technological University's prestigious School of Architecture, Mike was an up-and-coming designer with a bright future at a top firm.

As an architect, he planned to leave his mark on the world by designing impressive structures that would last for generations. But God had another plan to leave a legacy that would last for eternity.

Even as young, upwardly mobile newlyweds, Mike and Robyn sensed they had a future calling to follow Jesus in a way that would require great sacrifice. Initially, they believed this call meant they would serve overseas on the mission field. And why not? Missions were a high priority in their church. And Mike's own brother and sister-in-law were missionaries in Ecuador. As they sensed the growing urgency of God's call, they grew more and more excited. They often discussed what it would be like to pack up their belongings and move away to a foreign country.

Instead of a private jet, Jesus had a public donkey.

But God had other plans.

For starters, no mission organization would accept them. Robyn's background in graphic arts seemed like a gift they could use, but the sending agencies were unsure about what to do with Mike and his architectural degree. Disappointed by this "closed door," Mike dived back into his lucrative career. In their free time, he and Robyn poured themselves into various youth and family ministries at their local church.

While they performed this "temporary" service, they kept asking God what he ultimately had in store for them. Growing up in Christian families, they had both prayerfully agreed to serve God in whatever way he wanted, wherever he wanted. At this point, that meant serving him through their local church in a variety of volunteer roles. However, they felt particular satisfaction from helping families in crisis. As they counseled and mentored couple after couple, their desire to see healing in marriages slowly replaced their desire to live overseas.

What had started as a way to fill the time while waiting for God to start their missionary careers had become their life's true calling.

This irresistible, almost magnetic, attraction to helping families was what author Bill Hybels calls a "firestorm of frustration." According to Hybel's book, *Holy Discontent*, each believer has a particular area of this broken world that drives them bonkers. When they see it or hear about it, it frustrates them to the point that they are driven to help solve the problem. It's as if God personally opens your eyes to a certain need then kicks you off the couch with a size 50 boot directly into the game. If we ignore this nagging feeling of holy discontent, it frustrates us. If we *surrender* to it, it can fuel us to follow God's leading, even when it looks risky or doesn't make sense.

For some Christians, the holy discontent is world hunger. For others it's social justice or poverty. For Mike and Robyn, it was broken families.

As teenagers, Mike and Robyn had grown up in churches with a strong focus on overseas mission work. Now, their hearts were being drawn to more local needs, to reach hurting families living all around them. At the same time, the "seeker church" movement was revving up in Metro Detroit, with the goal of reaching adults who'd given up on traditional religion. These new churches were intentionally designed to attract a skeptical generation who described church as "irrelevant, boring and hypocritical" in surveys. One of these unconventional start-ups was Kensington Church, founded in 1990 by Steve Andrews, Dave Wilson and Mark Nelson.

Kensington's grace-based format was a perfect environment for Mike and Robyn to minister in. The unique platform for "loving their neighbors" — especially their un-churched neighbors — was exhilarating. As Mike would later say, the energy and excitement of the new movement gave them an empowering new game plan — to be "a follower of Jesus plus nothing."

Seeing Jesus as their all-sufficient provider allowed them to stop worrying about their future and focus on what God wanted them to do one day at a time. Along the way, other believers poured into the young couple. In particular, their friends Chuck and Laurie helped them to grasp the most fundamental teaching of Jesus: *"Love the Lord with all your heart, soul, mind and strength, and love your neighbor as you love yourself."* [9]

This ancient confession of faith — recited by Jews every morning and night since Moses — became their marching orders. Formerly ho-hum days became exciting adventures in walking with the Holy Spirit and learning new skills along the way. Unknown to them, the Spirit was preparing them for the road ahead. Author Ron Ash writes, "We are where we need to be and learning what we need to learn. The things we experience today will lead us to where he wants us to be tomorrow."

God only shows us the future on a need-to-know basis.

We'd all love to see God's plans for our entire life all nicely printed out in chronological order and handed to us by a big hand coming down from the clouds.

But that's not how he works.

God only shows us the future on a need-to-know basis. We have to trust him for the rest. The important thing is that we keep moving and let God re-direct us as we go. As we complete each step, God continues to reveal more and more of his plan. Sometimes his plan will surprise us. The disciples were on a journey they thought was going in a certain direction. Their plan was to see Jesus crowned as an earthly, political king who would rescue the oppressed Jews and defeat the occupying Romans. But their journey was detoured to Calvary's cross. What they thought was a *deviation* was God's *true destination* all along.

So we need to be flexible.

While the young couple was busy counseling others, they were experiencing rapid spiritual growth in their own life. With each local family they touched and helped, God was equipping them with specific life skills they would later need to follow his plan. *"For we are God's workmanship, created in Christ Jesus to do good works, which God prepared in advance for us to do."* [10]

Things were going along great. Mike was being promoted at work and Robyn was enjoying their two young children at home. They liked their house and loved their neighbors. And best of all, they were serving God in their spiritual "sweet spot," doing exactly what they loved with families who needed their help.

The couple would be tested on Christ's teaching of radical humility and total dependence.

But they would soon be tested on Christ's teaching of radical humility and total dependence.

As is often the case (just ask Jonah), God was preparing them for something they had not anticipated. Mike was pursuing his successful career in architectural design, and Robyn was progressing with her graphics. In the evenings and weekends they mentored and counseled families. They enjoyed the balance of professional careers and volunteer ministry. But as time went on, ministry to families took more and more of their time.

Juggling work and ministry got tougher and more stressful until finally they felt that to be fully obedient, something had to give. After praying, they decided to cut back drastically on their professional work hours. The resulting extra time for ministry helped for a while, but it still wasn't enough. Finally, after the birth of their third child, they made a "point of no return" decision — they would step out in faith, quit their day jobs, and pursue what it meant to love God and others full time.

With no guarantees except the promises of scripture, they

decided to rely totally on faith and use the gifts God had given them, however raw and undeveloped they were.

It was difficult for many of their friends and family members to understand how the couple could walk away from their safe careers and step into the great unknown. Truthfully, Mike and Robyn didn't quite understand it either. They had no real plan of their own, just a desire to follow God with their whole heart.

Experts on how to start a ministry advised them to create a prospectus, to print up a slick brochure with bullet points and graphics and an eye-catching logo. They were told they needed a press kit, a media packet to portray a compelling vision of their ministry and to drum up financial support. But Mike and Robyn resisted pressure to market themselves. They knew God was only interested in them getting to know him better — by simply abiding in his goodness, like children on the lap of a beloved parent. Mike says, "The deeper we know him, the more we can enjoy him and trust him, and the more we can benefit those he loves."

Sounds good, doesn't it? Quit your job, trust in God and don't worry about a thing. Except even heroes of the faith have to pay their gas, electric, water and phone bills. They have to put food on the table for hungry kids. They need gas in their cars and oh, yeah, the mortgage doesn't magically disappear either.

Even heroes of the faith have bills to pay. And mortgages don't magically disappear.

With no income, Mike and Robyn knew they had to simplify their lives. But switching to generic brands wasn't enough. Dialing down the thermostat wasn't enough. Eliminating vacations wasn't enough. Even brown bag lunches and hand-me-down clothes didn't solve the money problem. In another giant leap of faith, they put their beautiful home on the market, hoping it would sell fast. They were ready to cut back, ready to do without in order to serve

God. But things didn't quite go as planned. Weeks, then months, went by and the house did not sell. When the house didn't move, they tapped into their life savings until their bank accounts were empty. Eventually they did what every financial professional in the world (including me) tells you *not* to do — they dipped into their 401k retirement account. They survived on this nest egg until it too was gone.

Their faith was severely tested. What had been only theoretical was now very real and very difficult. But during those lean days, they came to understand that obeying God can mean giving up everything.

They went from following "Jesus plus good jobs and financial security" to following "Jesus plus nothing."

It was a new way to live — spend only what you have and never know what's coming next. On many occasions, they literally spent their "last dollar," and with empty wallets they would celebrate what God was going to do next. If they were to survive, he had to show up.

If they were to survive, God had to show up. Big time.

After all, it was his plan, not theirs.

After a year-and-a-half on the market, their house finally sold, and soon after that God blessed them with their fourth child. They moved into a small fixer-upper not far from their previous home, excited to see who God would bring into their lives. They named their ministry "Abide" — a word that accurately described 18-months of living with no visible means of support. Many times, people prompted by God would spontaneously show up with bags of groceries or a monetary gift for the fledgling ministry. Over and over, when the cupboards were bare or the baby needed formula or the bills were due, people showed up at exactly the right time to "coincidentally" meet a specific need — a need they were not even aware of.

○   ○   ○

By trusting only in God's grace, Mike and Robyn were experiencing the kind of supernatural provision that sustained one of my faith heroes, a man who lived in England during the time of Charles Dickens. During the 1830's, a horrific cholera epidemic swept the British Isles. Thousands died and children who lost their parents wandered the streets begging for food. Seeing the suffering in his town of Bristol, a young pastor named George Muller decided he must do something about it. With almost no food or money for his own kids, Muller opened up his family's house to 30 orphans! Sustained entirely by God's daily miracles, his *ad hoc* "Breakfast Club" grew to a huge orphanage that eventually rescued over 10,000 children.

In the beginning, church members and city officials predicted disaster for Muller's unfunded idea to help orphans. Undeterred, he prayed for every single item the children needed (food, clothing, textbooks, even the rent) and recorded the requests and the answers in a prayer diary. He seldom had more than a few days operating expenses on hand but he never complained.

One morning he was faced with having no food for the orphans. 300 hungry children were seated at the dining tables, staring at empty plates. When a child asked where breakfast was, Muller replied "God will supply." Then, without a crumb in sight, he asked the children to bow their heads and give thanks for their meal. Suddenly there was a knock at the door. When he opened it, the smell of fresh bread swept in. A baker holding trays of bread blurted out, "Mr. Muller, I couldn't sleep last night. I kept thinking I was supposed to get up and bake for you. So I got up at two o' clock and baked three batches. I hope you can use it."

By his death at age 92, George Muller had prayed in millions of dollars for the orphans without ever asking anyone directly for money. He took no salary during the last 68 years of his ministry, but trusted God to move on people to send him whatever the ministry needed.

He never took out a loan. He never went into debt. And his

Muller never took out a loan. And his 10,000 orphans never went hungry.

orphans never went hungry.

Like Muller, Mike and Robyn have faced numerous challenges along the way, but the couple's bold move has led to amazing blessings for them and others. Their four children have watched and learned as their parents "pray in" each necessity of life. They have come to understand the true value of a dollar — what it can buy and what it can't. They have seen how sacrificing a lavish lifestyle in order to help others leads to a priceless treasure few people understand. They know the value of listening and obeying the voice of God. And they fully understand the simple New Economy idea of making themselves and their resources freely available to others.

Today, the ministry of Abide still depends solely on the grace of God and the help of supporters. As Mike says, "We have what we need when we need it. I believe this is how God wants many of his people to live, trusting him daily."

Without government funding or a financial safety net, Mike and Robyn have touched hundreds of lives — like Joe and Kappy in chapter 9 — through marriage mentoring and family counseling. By donating countless hours of free, compassionate care, they have helped restore broken lives. One man they helped was just days or hours away from totally self-destructing...

o   o   o

Steve was a hard-working minister in an old-fashioned church that was very legalistic and controlling. As he intensely pursued his career in ministry, his marriage suffered. When his wife filed for divorce, Steve's world came crashing down. His self worth and identity in life were tied to being a husband and minister. When that fell apart, he completely lost hope. Struggling to maintain his home, he was burdened with crushing debt and haunted by loneliness and guilt. As he withdrew from human contact, his despair deepened to depression.

As darkness closed in, he tried to kill himself. Miraculously, his suicide attempt was thwarted by an urgent phone call from an acquaintance. The caller later revealed he had just arrived home from work that day when God told him to phone Steve immediately — for no apparent reason!

Steve spent the next two months in the hospital. There, Mike and Robyn helped him get back on his feet as he received professional help for his depression.

Over the course of several months, other families began to embrace Steve, surrounding him with support and acceptance. They gave him food and odd jobs to help pay his bills. But most importantly, they gave him their unconditional love. Following the pattern established by Abide Ministries, they generously gave their time and non-judgmental respect. In the months that followed, they helped restore Steve's faith in God and brought him renewed hope for a functional future.

Several years later, Steve now has a refreshed and enlightened view of Christianity. He's turned away from his old works-based religion and has a grace-based relationship with God. Because of his own hardships, he is a humble man who understands the pain that broken people feel, and he reaches out to them with invaluable understanding. This man who once felt worthless and used up has a future of unlimited potential in Christ.

Steve's dramatic recovery is evidence of God's grace. And the proof that it's the "real deal" is his devotion to a group of hurting people that polite society prefers to forget. Today, Steve is an officer in the Salvation Army, serving as Correctional Ministries Director for Eastern Michigan, heading up the prison and jail ministry. He has focused his compassion on incarcerated men, understanding their deep need for community and love. His "holy discontent" has translated into his ongoing efforts to change legislation and improve programs in Michigan's rehabilitation process for prisoners and parolees.

For Mike and Robyn, a man like Steve is the reason they stepped out of life in the fast lane and into the spiritual journey of a lifetime. To witness a human being restored to a life of passion and purpose is a constant reminder of grace in action. Over the years, the loving volunteers they've enlisted in their mission have seen how even the simplest acts of kindness can renew faith and hope in people. And how those people can go on to affect others in an ever-widening ripple effect.

Restoring a person to a life of passion and purpose is grace in action.

To be sure, Mike and Robyn can tell many stories that don't have such a happy ending. Whenever we enter into people's lives — going in below the surface — we are bound to find the consequences of bad decisions. People make awful choices in life because of selfishness or ignorance or lack of role models. For under-resourced families, generations of poverty, addiction and hopelessness have devastating effects. But wealthier families have problems too, suffering from addictive behaviors, co-dependency issues and misplaced priorities.

Either way, these dysfunctional mindsets are hard to break.

According to Mike, this downward spiral of negative thoughts and poor decisions can only be broken through *sacrifice*. First, the sacrifice of a perfect God who died for imperfect people. And second, the sacrifice of people willing to leave their comfort zone, take a risk, and trust God to help them change some very messy lives. Mike says, "Love requires sacrifice. Otherwise it's not really love." Beyond their counseling and direct assistance, Mike and Robyn invite people to experience God's grace firsthand by accepting his free gift of salvation.

And that can take some time.

One aspect of extending grace that's often overlooked is giving the healing process enough time to take hold. People who have struggled for years cannot always change overnight. They experience setbacks, remissions, mistakes and slip-ups that try our patience. But grace means giving people the freedom to fail and the encouragement to try again.

Deceptive influences are shouting defeat and discouragement at them day and night. Peers are often tempting them to fall back into destructive behaviors. Unless the positive voices (and loving actions) of people willing to go the distance are louder than these negative voices, there's little chance of recovery.

Which is why God calls us to be in the lives of others on a daily basis, to live in authentic community with them and point them toward truth with extreme patience.

> **Grace means giving people freedom to fail and encouragement to try again.**

As Mike recently told me, "We are the hands and feet of Jesus. If he lives in our heart, we take him with us wherever we go. Often his very presence in a crisis moment or in a spiritual breakthrough is simply the result of our willingness to be physically present in the lives of others. In other words, avoid the 'holy huddle' — you've got to hang out with the people who need Jesus."

He added, "To be able to extend grace, we must have first received it ourselves and recognize it as a free gift. That means we are no better than anyone else. So being humble is step one. Step two is admitting we're not smart enough to solve somebody else's problem. It's only by asking for God's wisdom that we can know how best to love and help those around us. Don't just barge in without asking God what to do. And don't try to do it in your own strength."

As Mike and Robyn demonstrate, grace can be extended to others in many forms. With the selfless mindset of the New Economy, it can mean sharing our prosperity with the needy. It can mean sharing our knowledge with those who need a mentor.

It can mean sharing our time with someone who is lonely. In its simplest definition, grace is about giving something good to someone *who can't earn it and doesn't deserve it.*

Which, by the way, is every single one of us.

Remember the movie *Pay It Forward*? Grace is like that. It is an endless circle. When we extend grace, we receive it back in ever increasing portions. That's the secret weapon of the New Economy — the more you give away, the more you get in return.

Buddha said, "Thousands of candles can be lit from a single candle, and the life of the candle will not be shortened. Happiness never decreases by being shared." Neither does grace.

○　　○　　○

We find ourselves living in an incredible time in history. Breakthroughs in technology, transportation and communications have created a level of prosperity previously unimaginable. Today, we could literally feed the world, stamp out childhood diseases and provide hope to the hopeless — if we had the willpower to do it. But many of us don't, because we ignore or deny the central truth of life: *That we are to love God and to love others more than ourselves.*

Like the Pink Floyd song, we've become comfortably numb.

Like the Pink Floyd song, we've become "comfortably numb." Some days I am oblivious to the suffering around me but laser focused on getting the next new application for my iPad. Other days I'm blind to my neighbors who are far from God but an expert on the latest episode of *30 Rock*. Can you relate?

During a sermon one Sunday, my pastor set out six empty chairs on the platform. Each chair represented one billion of the over six billion people living in the world today. The first chair represented the one billion who live on less than $1 a day. Another pair of chairs represented the two billion who live on less than $2 a day. The audience grew quiet as he explained that half the world lives without basic sanitation, running water or plumbing. Lined up in a pool of light, five of the six chairs stood for five of the six billion humans who subsist on less than $10 a day — about $3,600 a year. As he sat down in the last chair, he said it represented us, the fortunate few who control the vast majority of the world's resources.

If we're lucky enough to be sitting in that last chair, the only question that matters is "Why me?"

The answer is painfully obvious: *To bless the people in the other five chairs.* He concluded by saying that if Americans gave up ice cream for a year, the $20 billion dollars we saved could provide clean water, sanitation and basic health care for the rest of the world (and probably prevent some coronary problems for us).

Why has God singled us out to be born into wealth and safety?

Advances in science, medicine and farming could make life so much better for the world's poor, but the majority of people still chase the false dream of the Old Economy. Today, each of us sitting in the "last chair" has the ability like never before to make a difference, now and for eternity. It only requires us to receive God's grace, and then give it away — to be the hands and feet of Jesus Christ to a fallen and broken world that will go to bed hungry tonight.

Thousands of books have been written by brilliant philosophers like Ayn Rand, trying to chart a moral course for humanity. But the choice for me boils down to a three-word question: *Grace or greed?*

Do we choose to live for others or for ourselves?

Mike and Robyn made a life-changing decision to switch

from getting to giving. From comfortably numb to fully alive. From the Old Economy to the New Economy. And by doing so they discovered that Jesus plus nothing equals everything.

○　○　○

"I used to ask God to help me. Then I asked if I might help Him. I ended up by asking Him to do His work through me."

— Hudson Taylor[11]

CHAPTER 20:
Grace Is Incomprehensible Love

In ancient times, a nation about to be attacked would dump poison into all nearby sources of drinking water. Without a safe water supply, the invading army would be much less effective. This preemptive battle tactic was called "poisoning the well."

Today the term is used when we poison a conversation or a relationship with preemptive information that works to our advantage.

For example, imagine a worker sets up a meeting to ask for a pay raise. His boss opens by saying, "I'm thinking about reducing our staff size by 30 per cent next week. Now, what was it you wanted to discuss?" He has poisoned the well. He has instilled fear in his employee.

We see it all the time, especially in politics. Suppose two candidates are asked to debate on law and order. The first debater opens by saying, "Let me remind you that my opponent is an ex-convict." He has poisoned the well. He has undermined the man's credibility.

A poison preferred by spouses is the "faulty dilemma." Let's say a man tells his wife, "I want to buy a motorcycle. If you don't let me get a Harley it means you don't love me." His either-or proposition has poisoned the well. His wife may have legitimate concerns about his safety or their limited budget, but now if she raises an objection she tags herself as unloving.

The poison list goes on and on, and it can ruin the chance for open and honest dialogue on just about any subject: *If you're against higher taxes, you're against poor people. If you're not pro-choice, you don't support women's rights. If you don't drive a hybrid, you don't care about the environment. Blah, blah, blah...*

The strategy of poisoning the well is deployed every day.

One powerful king who understood battle strategy was King Solomon. His standing army had 1,400 chariots and 12,000 horsemen ready to defend his kingdom. But he was also a great intellect, possibly the wisest man in history. Some of his sayings are found in the Book of Proverbs, including advice written to his own son. First, he encourages the boy to pursue God and to avoid the pitfalls of youth. Then, in one final instruction he writes, *"Above all else, guard your heart for it is the wellspring of life."* [1]

To our modern ears his advice sounds strange. But what he's actually saying is: "Above everything else, don't let anyone poison your well (heart). Keep your own well (heart) safe and don't poison anyone else's, either. Recognize the sources of poison and avoid them."

At our family property in northern Michigan, a natural spring of sweet water bubbles up out of the ground near the Ausable River. Since the property was purchased in 1915, this sand-spring fountain has produced some of the best-tasting water in the state. Since I was a boy I've enjoyed sipping the cold refreshment straight from the "wellspring." So when I read this passage in Proverbs, I understood what Solomon was talking about. If chemicals or pollution ever seeped into the underground source of our spring, the water flowing out would become contaminated and undrinkable.

If contaminated junk seeps into our heart, whatever flows out of us will be impure.

In the same way, if we let contaminated junk seep into our heart, whatever flows out of us will be impure, too. As we encounter people in our daily lives, we'll soak them with toxic spew — anger, insults, bitterness, cursing, slander, gossip, weird lines from Will Ferrell movies, whatever.

Back in the early days of computer programming there was a saying, "Garbage in, garbage out." It meant you couldn't blame the computer for bad output if you input the wrong data! The same is true of our heart. Put in garbage (anger, insults, bitterness, cursing, slander, gossip — sound familiar?) and you'll get garbage out. Jesus put it this way: *"The good man brings good things out of the good stored up in his heart. And the evil man brings evil things out of the evil stored up in his heart. For out of the overflow of his heart his mouth speaks."* [2]

Maybe you're like me. Maybe you figure you can have it both ways. Most of the time I say *"good things."* I bless people; I encourage them and compliment them. I watch my tongue and I guard my heart. But sometimes I come across some jerk who really needs to be put in his place. You know the type. So I let him have it.

> **When I lose my temper and cut loose, it's like I have a split personality.**

I give him a verbal lambasting that turns the air blue. When I encounter a rude driver or an unfair referee, words pop out of me that I can't print here. I'm a Christian but when I lose my temper and cut loose, I'm not representing Christ very well.

It's like I have a split personality.

What does the Bible say about this dichotomy? James says it's unacceptable: *"With the tongue we praise our Lord and Father, and with it we curse men who have been made in God's likeness. Out of the same mouth come blessing and cursing. My brother, this should not be."* [3]

Nobody's surprised during an R-rated movie when an actor drops the f-bomb. Nobody's surprised in a bar when a drunk peppers his speech with four-letter words. But what if your pastor cussed from the pulpit? You'd be shocked. Because a renewed heart should produce renewed speech. A pure heart should produce pure speech. But guarding our hearts isn't just for "professional" Christians, it's for all believers.

James goes on to ask, *"Can both fresh water and salt water flow from the same spring?"* The answer (sadly) is "Yes, it can, but it shouldn't." The fact that I occasionally use salty speech means there's still some poison in my heart. It means I've got some cleaning to do. It means I'm not letting God's Spirit totally control my thoughts and actions and speech.

Something or someone has poisoned my well.

○　　○　　○

What would happen if we carefully guarded what flows into our heart? What if we kept our eyes and ears away from what we know to be impure, and instead filled our heart with things from "above" as Paul writes? *"Set your minds on things above, not on earthy things ... put to death whatever belongs to your earthly nature: sexual immorality, impurity, lust, evil desires and greed ... you must rid yourselves of anger, rage, malice, slander and filthy language."* [4]

Good plan, hard to pull off. Especially today in the digital Information Age.

Before I leave home for the office, I scan the newspaper and TV news. In five minutes my mind is filled with fresh stories of crime, disasters and scandals. I have breakfast with a side order of murders, rapes and foreclosures. Driving to work my radio blares more bad news of oil spills, financial meltdowns and international tensions. Between Twitter, Facebook and podcasts I can't escape the flood. And now when I'm pumping my gas or waiting at the bank, newly installed video screens give me even more discouraging news.

No wonder prescriptions for antidepressant drugs have tripled in the last decade, reaching over $40 billion in annual sales. Americans now spend more money on antidepressant therapy than the gross national product of two-thirds of the world's countries.

But what if we changed our focus from the bad news of this fallen world to the good news of God? What if our time was spent focusing on *"whatever is true, whatever is noble, whatever is right, whatever is pure, whatever is lovely, whatever is admirable?"* Paul says we should *"think about such things."* [5]

Americans spend more money on antidepressants than the GNP of most countries.

It sounds simplistic, and of course we can't live in a bubble. Nor should we. God wants us fully informed, fully involved and fully active as his agents of change in the earth. But we can engage the world around us and still drastically cut down our intake of disturbing news, celebrity gossip and inappropriate entertainment.

If we do that, Paul says *"the God of peace will be with you."* [6]

And I'll take Paul over Prozac any day.

o   o   o

Erwin McManus, in his book *Soul Cravings*, writes that our heart was designed for one purpose — as a reservoir for God's love. Just as a glass was designed to hold water, our heart was designed to hold love. If our heart is filled to overflowing with love, that love will spill out over those around us. But if our heart is filled with pride and selfishness, our friends will get splashed with some pretty nasty stuff. If our hearts are filled with bitterness or unforgiveness, they'd better back off because the toxins are building up. Instead of sharing love, peace and joy, we'll be pumping out verbal pollution.

I know, it's only a metaphor. But it works. Whatever we take in through our five physical senses is what ultimately gets stored in that metaphorical heart-shaped container meant for love. If we cram our souls full of negative news and impure thoughts, that's what will ooze out onto innocent bystanders.

I'm an outdoorsman, and I enjoy camping in the wilderness. Sometimes after a hard day of trekking, I'll come across a creek or a mountain stream. Miles from any civilization, the cool, rushing water looks safe. The temptation to fill my canteen from it is overpowering. But as experienced campers know, the crystal clear water that looks so clean to the naked eye is home to millions of invisible micro-organisms that can make you very sick. Even though the water looks pure, I know it might contain yucky protozoa and gross bacteria like Salmonella and E. Coli.

No matter how parched I am, I remind myself that untreated water can host scary little hitchhikers like pinworms and tapeworms. But it's not just fecal contamination that worries me. Once I was hiking up into the hills above a riverside campsite where people love to swim. About a hundred yards upstream from the party, the rotting carcass of a huge deer lay in the water. The river was flowing right through the exposed ribcage of a dead animal on the way down to that clean-looking swimming hole!

My point? *Sometimes poison in the water (and in our hearts) can be awfully hard to detect.*

And that's the tricky part. What we're putting into our inner man might appear harmless to the naked eye, yet still be dangerous to our spiritual well being. Like physical poisons, some spiritual toxins — from things we watch and read and listen to — don't seem to hurt us at first, but build up over time to dangerous levels.

Unfortunately, peer pressure makes them almost impossible to resist.

Media has the power to influence us without our knowledge or consent.

I'm not here to bash movies, magazines or cable TV. I'm not down on pop culture, social networking or video games. Media is neither inherently good or evil. But like my pastor friend Chris Zarbaugh warns, "Media has the power to influence us without our knowledge or consent." So choose wisely. Just because publishers or producers or programmers tell us something is acceptable or safe or mainstream doesn't mean we should partake.

When I'm camping, I don't trust the water unless I run it through a special filtered container. Fortunately, the Bible gives us a filter, too. Before you put something into your heart that may or may not be pure, run it through God's spiritual filter. Ask yourself if it meets Paul's definition of love found in 1 Corinthians 13: *"Love is patient, love is kind. It does not envy, it does not boast, it is not proud. It is not rude, it is not self-seeking, it is not easily angered, it keeps no record of wrongs. Love does not delight in evil but rejoices with the truth. It always protects, always trusts, always hopes, always perseveres."*[7]

That kind of love is pure and transformational. Drink it up!

○   ○   ○

Paul wrote scores of letters to the early churches, including a cautionary note to the disobedient, quarrelling believers in Corinth. In this letter, Paul admonishes the baby believers with firm discipline. He knows that only God's transformational love can empower them to live together as a unified community. To instruct them, he describes what love *is*

> **Love is the ruling principle of God's kingdom and the ultimate code of conduct.**

and what it *isn't* in the now famous "love chapter" quoted above. After listing the defining characteristics of real love, he compares it to other spiritual gifts God put in the church. Then he ranks them by saying *"the greatest of these is love."*[8]

Why is love the greatest?

Because long after the other spiritual gifts have become unnecessary, love will still be the ruling principle of God's kingdom and the ultimate code of conduct for eternity. It describes who God is and how he operates.

If you've attended 100 weddings, you've probably heard Paul's iconic "love chapter" read at 99 of them. Next time a bridesmaid or preacher quotes it, listen carefully. On one level, Paul is painting a picture of ideal love between two humans. But he is also describing what God's love for *us* looks like, and how it must be the motivation for everything we do. Paul says, *"If I have the gift of prophecy ... and if I have a faith that can move mountains, but have not love, I am nothing. If I give all I possess to the poor and surrender my body to the flames, but have not love, I gain nothing."* [9]

In other words, we can have great spiritual gifts, incredible knowledge and unwavering faith, but they're all useless without love. We can do great works or make amazing sacrifices, but none of it is meaningful unless we have love. We can distribute food and build clinics and adopt orphans, but if we do the right things for the wrong motives, Paul says they amount to exactly "nothing."

If we want to show the world that we are followers of Jesus Christ, we have to do *his works* with *his love*. When God lives in our hearts, our speech and our action will demonstrate his love and grace to others. The kind of love Paul describes in chapter 13 is exhibited by both what we DO (trust, patience, forgiveness, compassion and mercy) and by what we DON'T do (envy, pride, jealousy and ego trips). And as all wedding planners know, verse 8 of the love chapter says, *"Love never fails."*

At a recent wedding ceremony, my mind started racing: *Okay, I get it, God. But if your love is in me, and "love never fails," then why do I fail so often?*

I shouldn't have to work and sweat and struggle to show love. It should be easy, like breathing. It should be a natural by-product of Jesus living in me, an inevitable outpouring of what fills my heart to overflowing. Which raises other questions: *Am I showing true love to my family, friends and neighbors? Or am I just faking it? Do I love others out of obligation? And why is it so stinking hard to love unlovable people?*

The grace I extend to others — the culmination of all the characteristics of God's love — should simply be a reflection of God within me. Like standing in front of a full-length mirror.

Theoretically.

But Houston, we have a problem: The junk we have stored in our heart (our love container) blocks God from filling it. It may be poison we voluntarily ingested, or poison dumped in by someone else. However it got there and whatever it is — anger, guilt, pride, ingratitude, judgment, revenge or inability to forgive — this blockage prevents us from having a healthy love life.

We shouldn't have to work and sweat to show love. It should be easy, like breathing.

If we detect toxins in our heart — our wellspring — Paul gives us a simple prescription: Flush them out. *"Get rid of all bitterness, rage and anger, brawling and slander, along with every form of malice."* [10]

That's a tall order, but Doctor Paul is right. It may be difficult, even painful, but they need to be removed. It may require professional Christian counseling, or it may be something you can do in your one-on-one time with God. But either way, be like Nike and *Just Do It*. As the heart opens up, it creates what I call "space for grace" and God's love will fill the vacuum.

With God's love in our heart, we can begin to love others.

To be sure, our best efforts to love others will fall far short of God's. And our human love is admittedly flawed and tainted. But because God works *through us*, we get to be a pipeline of his pure love to a world that is absolutely starving for it.

When you lay in bed at night wondering how you can make the world a better place, remember that *love* is the most primary human need. Mother Theresa said, "The most terrible poverty is loneliness and the feeling of being unloved."

If a cardiologist said my pulmonary arteries were dangerously clogged, I'd probably make an appointment for surgery right on the spot. Why? Because we know how critical our physical heart is to our well-being. So when contamination clogs our *spiritual* heart, why do we let it sit there, occupying valuable space meant for God? Why don't we just as hastily book time with the spiritual surgeon, Jesus, and go under his knife? The operation's free to us, and there's no co-pay.

Jesus paid it in full on the cross.

○   ○   ○

In chapter 5, we learned the Greeks had four distinct words for "love," all with different meanings. Three of them describe an emotional attachment we might feel for a person or an object. But when the divine love of God is described, the word used is *agape*. It means unconditional, self-sacrificing love — the fundamental characteristic of grace. Author Greg Boyd puts it this way: "By sacrificing himself for us, God ascribes unsurpassable worth to people who in and of themselves have little apparent worth. In doing this, God reveals his nature, which is eternal, unsurpassable love." [11]

If that last statement makes your head hurt, join the club. It's deep. To help us grasp the ungraspable, God gave us the ultimate object lesson: *"This is how we know what love (agape) is: Jesus Christ laid down his life for us. And we ought to lay own our lives for our brothers."* [12]

If you've ever had a crush on someone, you know that love — even puppy love — is powerful. As a human emotion, it can make us do unexplainable things, awful things, crazy things. It can even make us sing along to really embarrassing music. (When I Googled "cheesy love songs," I got 281,000,000 results to choose from.) But when we experience *agape* love, it's a whole different story! It makes us do wonderful things, gracious things, unselfish things. God loved us before we loved him — with no strings attached — and gave us his ability to love others in return.

Not to get all theological on you, but in the interest of balance, consider this: Love is a key attribute of God. But equally important are his attributes of holiness, justice, and righteousness. That means God's love is a holy, just and righteous love. Which means his hatred of sin is just as strong as his love of mercy. Which is why he cannot permit sin or evil in his presence. Which is why we could not approach God on our own merit. As unrighteous beings, we'd be toast if it wasn't for grace — the unearned, undeserved gift from a Savior who shed his blood to *"purify us from all unrighteousness."* [13]

Grace encapsulates everything that is amazing about God: his mercy, kindness, forgiveness, encouragement, healing, redemption, compassion — I could go on for pages. There's just no way

> **God's hatred of sin is just as strong as his love of mercy.**

our finite brains can begin to understand God's infinite greatness and goodness, let alone describe them. Words can only fumble toward the unknowable. So when we try to communicate all that God is and all that he's done for us, we will always come up short.

But one thing's for sure. Among God's limitless attributes, love is the central focus of Jesus in his earthly ministry. Like I said, all of God's attributes are equally important. But it's his *love* that propels and energizes the New Testament narrative. Not a fickle, mushy, faint-hearted love, but a wild, unstoppable, swirling love that would chase any one of his children across the universe to restore them back to fellowship.

As a weekend handyman, there are three things I can't do without — Super Glue, Gorilla Glue and Elmer's Glue. They hold my projects together. But God's love is what holds it *all* together. And by "all" I mean *everything in the universe*. Grace is the crowning jewel of this incomprehensible love — the love that prompts a father to make a monumental sacrifice so his children can be freed from their sin nature to experience the intimacy with him that he planned for them eons before creation.

When Adam sinned, he ran and cowered in the bushes. But Jesus came to reverse the effects of the Fall. To restore everything that was broken by sin. So there's no need to hide from God anymore. No need to try and win his approval, either. Since we are loved by God, let's recklessly love him back. And share that restorative love with everyone we meet.

○   ○   ○

"Man is born broken. The grace of God is glue."

— Eugene O'Neill[14]

CHAPTER 21:
Life on the Streets

It's the world's oldest profession.

And one of the riskiest.

Experts say 80 percent of prostitutes have been sexually assaulted; some raped as often as ten times a year. Although it's portrayed by Hollywood as a glamorous occupation (remember Julia Robert's *Pretty Woman*?), the reality is often a grim story of drugs, beatings and exploitation.

Like any retail business, selling your body has a hierarchy of earnings and status. At the very bottom of the prostitution barrel are the classic street walkers. They account for only 10 percent of all prostitution in America and thrive in decaying neighborhoods where they can openly solicit drivers from curbside. It's no coincidence the sidewalks they work are littered with used condoms and syringes — at street level, sex and drugs go hand in hand. Sharing needles and customers, these bottom-rung ladies of the night expose themselves to ravaging diseases that often go unreported and untreated.

At the opposite extreme, high-priced call girls operate out of five-star hotels and can make thousands a day from well-heeled clientele. Many of these paid companions are highly educated; some are earning six-figure incomes. They are medically certified, stylishly groomed and well compensated. But street prostitutes have a far lower price range. They typically charge $20 to $75 depending on the act. And if they're a crackhead, anything goes.

The price for sex with a drug addict is as low as the going rate for a single rock of crack cocaine.

A girl working for a fancy escort service might enjoy a luxurious night on the town with her carefully-screened client. But for a street hooker working Cass Avenue in Detroit, the usual transaction is 10 minutes in a car with a total stranger. A deluxe package is 20 minutes in a dark alley, cheap motel or abandoned building.

It's no surprise that street walkers are usually in some sort of personal decline — running away from home, strung out on drugs or becoming less physically attractive. Most are uneducated, poor and have a myriad of health problems. Many use heroin or crack or both and turn to prostitution to support their habit. They usually start in their teens but age quickly in the hostile environment, trolling the streets for a half dozen clients a night. They may promise themselves it's only temporary, but what starts as a way to make quick cash becomes an endless cycle of turning tricks, getting arrested, paying fines and returning to the streets.

Street walkers are despised by almost everyone, including other prostitutes.

Pimps make that cycle even tougher to break by using addiction and violence to control their employees. Police say pimps take up to 70 percent of a girl's earnings and intimidate them with threats and physical abuse. But like battered wives, prostitutes don't report assaults by their pimps because they fear retaliation. Likewise, when a "john" or "trick" attacks them, they're afraid to report it because the police will charge them with solicitation.

Overworked and underpaid, street walkers are despised by just about everyone, including other prostitutes. Like modern-day lepers, they are rejected by society and neglected by religion. But they *do* have an unlikely advocate — a white-haired grandma with nerves of steel and a heart of gold...

○   ○   ○

Disco diva Donna Summer sold 130 million records worldwide, including her smash hit about prostitutes, "She Works Hard for the Money." But tonight, I'm seeing prostitution through the eyes of *another* Donna. This Donna doesn't drive around in a limousine; she drives around in a beat-up van handing out sandwiches to hookers.

Cruising with Donna in her signature white van, I couldn't help but marvel at her team of volunteer women. Three times a week, they tool up and down the toughest streets in Detroit looking for prostitutes. Stocked up with fresh food and gift bags of toiletries, they pull over to women on the sidewalk and ask if they can pray for them. Dressed in high heels, micro minis and revealing tops, the girls approach the van. Some dash over, some approach warily. Some are strangers, some are old friends, but virtually every woman welcomes Donna's prayer.

I felt honored to be with them that night, the only male in the van, and one of the few men to ever accompany Donna on her midnight missions of mercy. In her own words, "Bringing guys downtown to pray for female prostitutes is probably not the best way to reach them!" It had taken years to build trust in the neighborhoods, and Donna was protective of her acceptance among the working girls.

Donna has earned her acceptance among the working girls.

On the night I rode along, we encountered Sophia, Seannie, Rochelle, Shawna, and Emma Jean. When Emma Jean came up to the van window, one of the volunteers asked if she could pray with her. As I watched from inside, Emma Jean began sobbing, tears flowing down her heavily rouged cheeks. She explained that between clients she had been earnestly praying that the white van would come that night. She wanted to change her life. Desperately. Donna handed her a ministry card and said to contact her in the morning.

Donna promised she would get her into a great rehab program where she could break free from her addiction. As the volunteers prayed for Emma Jean, they told her how valuable she was to God and how much Jesus loved her. By the time they were through, everyone was crying. I was overwhelmed by the love this van full of suburban women had for an unloved girl who most people would pity or ignore. I sensed that maybe this night would mark a new beginning in Emma Jean's tragic life.

As we pulled away from the curb, Donna turned to me with a wise and knowing smile. Gently, she tempered my elation with the harsh reality of the situation. Her team often experiences emotional encounters with hurting women who sincerely want to change. But for a variety of reasons, the girls are unlikely to follow through. When presented with a chance to make a complete turnaround, they stick with their familiar life (as awful as it is) rather than step into an unknown future. It's as if they prefer the hell they know to the uncertainty of heaven. When the tears are dry and the emotion fades, many of Donna's girls fall back into their routine, despite the emotional pain and suffering they endure.

I can understand why.

When you endure humiliation and degradation on a daily basis, your self esteem bottoms out. When you engage in criminal activity and live in constant fear of being arrested or injured, your heart hardens. It's perfectly natural for prostitutes to believe Satan's lie — that they are worthless scum, with no value to anyone, and no hope for change. As Donna says, "They need to be taught a new way of thinking, to stop listening to the lies of the evil one and to accept God's forgiveness." But for many of them (and many of us), forgiveness is not easy to receive. On that hot, muggy night, I silently prayed that Emma Jean would be

When you endure humiliation and degradation daily, your self esteem bottoms out.

the exception, that she would take the important step toward life change and call Donna the next day.

Donna could see that I was deflated. The thought of this precious woman who God sees as infinitely valuable slipping back into the shadows of her dangerous occupation broke my heart. Patting my shoulder, she reminded me that even though things looked bleak, God's grace would be sufficient for Emma Jean.

And Donna knows what she's talking about...

○   ○   ○

When she was only seven years old, her mother did the unthinkable. To make ends meet, she sold her daughter to male acquaintances. Her twisted customers were sick men who could not fathom the deep scars their pedophilia would leave on a small child. But God is good, and he met Donna in the midst of her nightmare. When she was eight years old, she had an encounter with the living Christ who whispered into her ear, "No matter what they do to you on the outside, they can never change who you are on the inside."

Thirty years later, Donna was living a life apart from the God who had comforted her in childhood. Working for the financial services firm, J.P. Morgan, she attended church only now and then. If God was real, he seemed distant and unconcerned about her. When a friend asked her to check out a new church, she went reluctantly. She was unprepared for the sermon she heard. It was based on the famous Parable of the Talents, the story Jesus used to illustrate that we all have a unique gift from God and that he expects us to use it.[1]

If God was real, he seemed distant and unconcerned.

As Donna listened, she wondered if *she* had a gift from God. She had heard the message many times as a child, but never connected it to her own life. Certainly, other people had gifts — singing, speaking, writing, painting, parallel parking, whatever. But as she racked her brain, she couldn't think of a single outstanding talent or skill she possessed.

Apparently, she was born without a gift. Or so she thought.

As she reflected on the message that evening, she ran a mental inventory. The only possibility she came up with was her love for people. Could that be her gift? And if it was, so what? What could God possibly do with that? She was confused, but she was sure about one thing: God was trying to get her attention. He wanted her to slow down and simply listen — he would soon be whispering in her ear again.

From that night on, she *did* listen and eventually heard about a small group of volunteers that went out into the streets to help prostitutes break their cycle of addiction. Almost lost among the high-profile charities and fund-raising telethons, this little-known cause stood out to her. In the heartbreaking world she grew up in, Donna had many friends who'd succumbed to a life on the streets. Maybe joining this group was a way she could give back.

Donna started accompanying the team once a week. She enjoyed the work, and over the years, she became a recognizable friend to the local ladies of the night. Her God-given "talent" for loving people was a major asset as she counseled on the sidewalks. But there was one problem. Since starting to attend her friend's new church, she had recommitted her life to Christ. She was convinced that the Jesus who rescued her could rescue anyone. So whenever she encountered a street walker, she would end her time of listening to their troubles with a prayer.

Unfortunately, the group was a secular organization and prayer was forbidden. Donna was reprimanded nearly every night. The volunteers complained that if the organization's main financial supporter found out about her, their funding would be in jeopardy. Eventually, she was asked to either stop praying or quit the group. By then, Donna knew her true calling and she decided to follow her heart. She left the organization, determined to start her own part-time street ministry with a group of women from her church.

In September of 2001, Donna gathered several of her bravest friends together for what would be their first trip into the Detroit neighborhoods she had become so familiar with. Despite being nervous, her rookie team met with ten

Donna was asked to either stop praying or quit the group.

prostitutes that inaugural night. When they asked if they could pray with the girls, all ten grabbed their hands and gave them a resounding "Yes!"

She's been "working the streets for God" ever since. In her own words, "That one simple act of loving God and loving others was the turning point in my spiritual walk and the ministry has grown in ways that are truly humbling."

Donna now does three outreach drives per week in three different neighborhoods. Her well-recognized white minivan has become her trademark on the streets. When the women see her van, they spread the word. Even though they jokingly refer to her as "the church lady," they know Donna is a loving friend who is not there to judge but to help.

Kind of like Jesus, some would say. After all, he was known for reaching out to lepers, tax collectors, criminals and ... prostitutes.

Like Jesus, Donna knew the Father's love was unconditional, undeserved and unlimited. So quoting Jesus in Matthew 18, she named her ministry "70x7" as a reminder to her team that it might take 490 (or more) times before these precious women could accept God's grace.

As God blessed Donna's efforts, the ministry soon outgrew her ability to run it by herself. With her business background, she enjoyed managing the operation, but sometimes found herself alone on her nightly pursuits. Despite the many friends who would ride along whenever possible, she knew she needed someone to share the ministry burden with. So she began to pray for the "someone" she knew God would bring. At the same time, she also began to pray for coats. Winter was fast approaching and the women she encountered on her late night drives did not have adequate protection to survive the plunging temperatures.

Miles apart and worlds away, a woman named Lauren was attending midweek service at a local suburban church. That evening the pastor talked about the food baskets they would be passing out on Thanksgiving Day. Lauren signed up to volunteer and helped deliver baskets to needy families. As she went from house to house, she noticed how many of the children and adults did not have good winter coats. Prompted by God, she quickly organized a successful coat drive. Donated coats piled up in her church's lobby, but she was unsure how to distribute them. Then a friend suggested she call Donna. A meeting was arranged between them to transfer the coats. When the two women met for the first time, Donna looked into Lauren's eyes and said, "I have been praying for winter coats for months."

Lauren saw the compassion in Donna's eyes, and swears she felt God nudge her heart: *This is who I want you to invest your life with. You belong here.*

Donna would later admit she felt a similar holy urging: *Lauren belongs here. She just needs time to figure that out.*

After 22 years, Donna's day job ended. Abruptly.

Two months later, Lauren was all in, accompanying Donna and her dedicated gal pals on their midnight escapades through the rough Brightmoor area of Detroit.

With new blood and fresh troops, the ministry was thriving. Life was good, work was good, and Donna was enjoying a time of stability and financial security.

Then one morning her day job ended. Abruptly. After working 22 years at J.P. Morgan, Donna's job was eliminated in an all-too-familiar corporate reshuffling. But rather than feeling angry, she felt calm, knowing it was God's way of prodding her into full-time ministry. Today she is supported by many big-hearted people who have seen the importance of 70x7. She has developed wonderful relationships with the local drug treatment centers and cultivated deep friendships with hundreds of women trapped in the cycle of prostitution. But there have been heartbreaking challenges along the way. Some of her girls have been kidnapped. Some have been murdered. Others have died of HIV AIDS.

Donna has been threatened by angry pimps, hostile drug dealers and gang members.

Over the years, Donna has been threatened by angry pimps, hostile drug dealers and gang members armed with automatic weapons. She has had pistols and knives waved in her face and obscenities shouted at her van. She has witnessed drug overdoses, domestic violence and needless tragedy.

She has *also* witnessed countless stories of restored and rebuilt lives. One such story is Yvonne...

○   ○   ○

Tall, leggy, and looking for business, Yvonne stood shivering on her street corner on a cold December night. Despite the chill, she was dressed in tight shorts and a tube top. From inside her van, Donna could see she was trembling from the frigid cold. Never one to mince words, she rolled down the window and yelled, "Put some clothes on, girl!"

They became instant friends.

In and out of foster homes as a child, Yvonne was molested by a foster father at the age of twelve. She ran away from that home to live on the streets, and never saw the inside of a foster home again. At 18, she got involved with a street gang to support her fledgling drug habit by selling the product herself. When a dope deal went bad, a gang fight broke out and Yvonne was stabbed multiple times. According to her, she was slashed "nearly in half" and left for dead. Bleeding profusely, she was miraculously saved when a friend carried her limp body to the emergency room of a nearby hospital. Weeks later, when the doctors finally released her, she vowed to quit the pharmaceutical business.

Instead, she switched to prostitution.

Donna met Yvonne during her first year of hooking. By then she was "hungry and homeless." Her tricks barely financed her heroin and crack addiction. She liked Donna, but was too proud to accept her help. She figured she needed to do life on her own terms. In her mind, no one could be trusted. Not cops, not pimps, not even white ladies coming around with free tampons and bags of soap. Soon after, however, she found herself arrested for prostitution and sitting in a jail cell, staring at the concrete walls. Totally broke and unable to score, her desperate hunger for drugs made her skin crawl and her stomach churn. Shaking and sweating, she wanted to die. The minute she got out, she called Donna.

Tired of turning tricks and shooting dope, she wanted a new beginning. She called Donna.

She wanted a new beginning.

Donna got Yvonne enrolled in a rehab program, and she seemed to do well with the first phase. When she was released into the halfway program, she was able to get a job and pay for an apartment. But like so many broken people, Yvonne was only "playing the game," and her addiction to drugs raged back full force. Eventually she lost her job and her apartment, and Donna discovered her back out on the street.

To save her life, Donna took a radical step — she actually prayed that the cops would arrest her young friend again. Donna knew that if they did, Yvonne could ask to be part of the new rehab program called "Fresh Start." If any addict asked for this option, the police had to comply by enrolling them in this innovative treatment that seemed to be having great results. A few days later, Donna's prayer was answered — Yvonne was busted and she requested the "fresh start."

Toward the end of the 90-day program, Donna received a call from Yvonne. Excitedly she said, "Donna, I finally get it. I now have tools for life." Donna was ecstatic and invited Yvonne to a new inner-city church. Before long, it was Yvonne who was doing the inviting. She attended every week, brought visitors and even performed the public devotionals. At first, she would describe her success by saying "I did this and I did that." But her testimony soon became "God did this and God did that for me."

Despite her newfound reliance on God, Yvonne realized she could no longer live in Detroit. Too many temptations. Too many reminders of her past. So Donna helped her move to her brother's place across the state in Grand Haven, Michigan. Things went great. She got a job, an apartment and a bicycle to ride to work. Sadly, it turned out her brother was not a positive influence, and Yvonne called Donna to let her know. Seems her brother's girlfriend had strongly suggested, "Get down from your high horse and join me and my friends in hooking and doing drugs."

Without missing a beat, Yvonne responded, "Girl, I don't do that no more. I am celibate. You need to put that stuff away and find Jesus."

Donna could not believe her ears. She lifted the phone toward heaven and said with a beaming smile, "Thank you, Jesus!"

That Christmas, Donna received a holiday card from Yvonne. Inside she had written the simple words, "Thanks for praying and caring for me." One life touching another. Winning against all odds. Imagine how many Yvonnes there might be if we had more Donnas.

○   ○   ○

Recently, Donna began attending a new church. On her first visit, a petite redhead in her early sixties came up to her. "I know you," she said. "You're the woman with the white van." Then without pausing, she rolled up her sleeves to show Donna the years of needle tracks and scars up and down her arms. "Look what God did for me. I have been clean for over five years now. If God can save me, he can save anybody."

She showed Donna the needle tracks up and down her arms.

Tearfully, Cindy told Donna her story, how she reached a point where she knew she had to change or die. She was in such bad shape from drugs and malnutrition that paramedics took her to a local hospital. There she met what she called "an angel," someone who introduced her to Jesus. Cindy surrendered immediately, accepting Christ's forgiveness and the promise of a new life. According to the former addict, she changed her identity from "Satan's Slave" to "Slave for Jesus" right on the spot. After sharing her miraculous conversion, Cindy told Donna, "I'd like to help you reach those who think it is hopeless."

And just like that, Donna had a new recruit for her midnight army. Cindy has been instrumental in reaching drug addicts who think change is impossible. All she does is roll up her sleeves and explain how Jesus saved her life. Talk about street cred!

○   ○   ○

Love is an action verb, and it usually requires us to step out of our comfort zone to truly experience it. Sure, we can say "I love you" to someone, but talk is cheap. The only way those three little words have any real, lasting impact is when they're backed up by authentic action.

Donna backs up her words with right-now in-your-face action. Sometimes the action is dangerous, sometimes it's scary.

Sometimes the action is uncomfortable, sometimes it's awkward. But it's almost always *effective* because God is right there in the middle of it. And by letting him call the shots, she gets a glimpse of just how unconditional God's love is for people.

> **Out on the streets, love is an action verb.**

Next time you're nervous about inviting a neighbor to church, think about Donna's team of volunteer housewives proclaiming Jesus on the gang-infested streets of Detroit at midnight.

Next time you're afraid to chat with a friend about Jesus, think about Donna's team risking everything to talk to pimps and prostitutes right where they live. Then take courage from their example. God may not call you to the same location, but he is calling you to the same *message* — that there is plenty of grace for everybody.

It's hard to imagine an environment where sin is more visible, more rampant than in a drug den or a hotbed of prostitution. But when a believer like Donna rolls in with a message of grace and forgiveness (instead of judgment and condemnation) sin can't win: *"Sin doesn't have a chance in competition with the aggressive forgiveness we call grace. When it's sin versus grace, grace wins hands down."* [2]

Prostitutes exist because men are after pleasure and power. But *redemption* is what God is after — the redemption of one life at a time, even when common sense says it's hopeless. And he's using a white van full of juice boxes and unconditional love to make it happen.

o   o   o

"I know God will not give me anything I can't handle. I just wish that he didn't trust me so much."

— Mother Teresa [3]

III: GRACE IS...

CHAPTER 22:
Grace Is Power to Transform

There are two sure signs of summer in Michigan.

One is finding a patch of milkweed in full bloom. The other is finding the tiny critter that depends on the plant for survival. After an hour of searching fields and roadsides, we spotted the telltale pink flowers at the edge of a hay meadow. We rushed up and carefully scanned the milkweed's oval-shaped leaves until we found our treasure.

It was exactly how I remembered it as a kid.

About an inch long, the colorful creature had yellow, black, and white stripes. Clinging to the topmost leaf of a four-foot plant, a solitary monarch caterpillar was happily munching his all-day meal.

To say the monarch depends on milkweed is an understatement. The female butterfly lays its eggs on the plant, and when they hatch, the growing larvae eat the leaves (the milky toxins don't hurt the baby caterpillars but make them poisonous to predators). Later, the monarch caterpillar attaches itself to the hairy underside of the leaves to pupate. It even eats the flower's nectar as an adult butterfly.

But I'm getting ahead of myself.

My daughter Kira found the first caterpillar. A moment later, I found another. We were excited. Prized by collectors, the famed king of butterflies has grown less plentiful in the Midwest as civilization encroaches on its winter hibernating grounds in

Mexico. It had been years since we last spotted the migrating royalty out in the wild. Now we had two "future monarchs," each in their own glass Mason jar with holes punched in the top.

For the next few days, our caterpillars ate constantly, nibbling away at the fresh leaves we dropped in each morning. Then an amazing thing happened. On day 5, they both climbed to the top of their jars, spun a small button of silk, and hung upside down from it like a letter "J." Precisely 12 hours later, each caterpillar split open its skin to reveal a squirming green pupa. In a few more hours, the pupa's skin hardened and smoothed over to become a chrysalis. In this early state, the protective covering was jade green, with flecks of amber and a gold stripe near the top.

By day 12, each chrysalis had become transparent and we could make out the colors and details of developing wings inside. On day 17 we woke up to find two beautiful monarch butterflies hanging from their empty shells. As their new wings slowly unfurled, the orange and yellow patterns were as brilliant as the morning sun. Kira and I sat and stared at the insects for hours, amazed at the transformation that had taken just over two weeks. We unscrewed the lids of the jars and gently turned them over onto the patio table. The butterflies wobbled at first, but quickly gained enough strength to stand steady in the gentle breeze, drying their wings in the sunlight.

And then, without saying goodbye, our houseguests flew away.

○   ○   ○

The butterfly is often used as an analogy for Christianity. As we surrender ourselves to God, we are transformed into new people. Our old selves become our new selves, like a caterpillar morphing into a butterfly. But perhaps it's more of a *restoration* than a transformation. Under his care, God restores us back closer to the original condition he had intended for us. The psalmist spoke of this intimacy, *"The Lord is my shepherd ... he leads me beside quiet waters, he restores my soul."*[1]

God knows our souls have been bruised and damaged by life. And when we let him lead us to places of quiet and solitude — places where he can speak to us — he will *restore* us. Imagine the joy of a car collector discovering a 1962 Ferrari sitting in somebody's barn. It's dented and rusty and squirrels are living in the trunk, but he doesn't care. The tires are flat, the seats are torn and the glass is broken, but he doesn't mind. He is thrilled. He is ecstatic. Why? Because he knows he's found a diamond in the rough. His joy is to clean away the grime, repair the damage and gently restore the priceless treasure to its original pristine condition.

The butterfly is often used as an analogy for Christianity.

This is God's goal for our lives, too — that we'll invite him to clean us up, repair our damage and completely transform us from the inside out. With a spiritual makeover that puts the monarch butterfly to shame.

o   o   o

Why is this happening to me?

Hiding under the covers, pretending to be asleep, the nine-year-old child trembled in the darkness. But it wasn't the cold night air that made her shiver. It was the sound of footsteps coming down the hallway.

Most kids her age were afraid of the dark. But for Amy, darkness was her friend and the monster that frightened her wasn't imaginary. By turning out the lights and being totally silent she hoped to trick this real life boogeyman into thinking that she wasn't there.

He came into her room a lot, doing things to her she knew were wrong. Angry, confused and most of all ashamed, she never said a word to anyone, not even her best friends or favorite teachers. She desperately wanted people to think everything was fine with her family, so she learned to invent stories and put up a good front. She did not want to be a burden, especially to her mother who was battling breast cancer.

During the days preceding his nighttime visits, he would belittle her and call her awful names when no one was looking. Sometimes he would kick her or punch her in the face when he got angry. On those days she could usually absorb the blows without crying and bravely pretend nothing happened. Even when he called her a "dirty little whore" she kept her feelings bottled up inside.

Truthfully, she didn't even know what the words meant. All she knew was that when he touched her she felt sick and dirty in a way she couldn't wash off.

Tonight, lying in her bed, Amy listened for footsteps and thought about God. *Where is he? Why is he letting this happen?* Her mother was a good Christian woman and took the kids to church when she wasn't too weak or sick from chemotherapy. There, Amy heard Bible stories about a loving God, and she wanted to believe in him. But she suspected he was far too busy with bigger needs and more important people to have any time for her.

She suspected God was too busy to have time for her.

She prayed anyway, just in case, until the sound of a hand turning her doorknob interrupted her whispered words.

○   ○   ○

Amy's real father left when she was a baby. She had little memory of him, but imagined he looked a lot like Mr. Brady on TV. He had been a successful retailer, but when things went bad and he lost his shoe store, he couldn't cope with the stress. Although he loved his wife and kids, the shame of failing as a provider was too much. He filed for divorce and moved to Nevada, leaving a single mother with four children to raise. Her mom never spoke an unkind word about him, and after his disappearance, Amy continued to receive gifts from him for birthdays and Christmas.

The toys were a welcome relief for a cash-strapped single parent, but couldn't fill the void of a missing dad. This kind of abandonment causes a "father wound," and it often scars a child with a lifetime of deep emotional pain and low self esteem. When a birth father is absent or abusive, his children — even his adult children — tend to see themselves as unworthy and unlovable.

Because she was so young when her dad left, Amy didn't fully know what she was missing. But her older siblings did. They were angry and disappointed about losing their father. It didn't seem fair and it couldn't possibly be right that their mom had to work two jobs just to put food on the table. Divorce was rare in those days, and her six-year-old brother in particular wanted a dad like the other kids on the block.

That vacuum would soon be filled.

When Amy was in kindergarten, her mother started dating a man she thought would ease her burdens and be a good father figure to her children. Although he was rough on the outside, the mother believed he had a "good heart and was just misunderstood." Amy's grandparents and two oldest siblings were less enthusiastic.

Unfortunately, their concerns about his character were overruled by the mom's desire to get a new father for the family.

They would have been better off without one.

After the wedding, the family moved into his house. Within weeks, Amy's older brother and sister went off to college, leaving her and her eleven-year-old brother to defend themselves against an increasingly hostile man. As spankings escalated to beatings, Amy watched her brother do his best to make a stand for the family and fight back. She called him her hero. But eventually the brave boy was intimidated by the harsh stepdad who kept loaded guns and big hunting knives around the house as threatening symbols of his total control. The man's previous wife had committed suicide, and his dark ramblings and violent temper made the house a living hell for the two children.

Behind his wife's back, the surrogate dad bullied and provoked his stepson constantly. Amy sensed that the emotional harassment and physical attacks were staged as an example of what would happen to her if she didn't fully submit. Sadly, Amy's mom was legally deaf and missed the stream of insults and profanities aimed at her kids. When she was out of earshot, her new husband even bragged about "being able to kill someone and get away with it" in front of the frightened children.

Amy couldn't realize it then, but abusers like her stepdad often use a variety of coercive tactics designed to scare spouses or children into submission. He was a classic case — giving threatening looks, smashing things in front of the kids and putting weapons on display. His clear message to Amy and her brother was: *If you don't obey there will be violent consequences.*

The climate of fear was tangible. Like most abusers, the stepdad did all he could to make his victim — in this case, Amy's brother — feel bad about himself and defective in some way. After all, if you believe you're worthless and that no one else will want you, you're less likely to leave or tell anyone. His name-calling, shaming and put-downs were designed to erode the young boy's self-esteem and make him feel powerless.

Then, just short of Amy's tenth birthday, her stepfather turned his awful attention to her. The secret horror lasted on and off until her mother died and Amy left home to live with her oldest brother. The escape felt like sanctuary, but by then the twin traumas of sexual abuse and parental loss had scarred her deeply.

So deeply, that to this day, she "remembers every detail" of her childhood, but rarely speaks about it.

It's no surprise she doesn't want to dredge up the horrific details. She was simply trying to survive. When asked to describe her childhood in one word, Amy says "dark." Too dark to reveal to anyone. Even when she was going through it, she never mentioned it to anyone — and *especially* not to her mother. A remarkably strong woman, her mom bounced back from the pain of losing her first baby during childbirth by having four more children. And after being divorced by her husband of 19 years, she supported the family by

> **No wonder she wanted to protect her mom from the truth.**

sheer hard work. Forced to become the breadwinner, she juggled parenting and working between cancer operations and radiation therapy. Her example taught Amy how to survive and be self reliant.

No wonder the girl wanted to protect her mom from the truth.

That was noble. But there was another reason for Amy's silence. She hid her stepfather's actions to conceal how damaged and branded she felt. This sense of shame is so strong that survivors of sexual abuse often feel that people can tell they have been molested just by looking at them. This combination of guilt and embarrassment makes most victims very secretive. In Amy's case, make that secretive and *angry*. During the attacks, Amy was completely powerless. This feeling of helplessness could have persisted into her later years if it wasn't for one thing — her anger.

Anger is a common (and sometimes healthy) reaction for a survivor, and Amy's rage helped her get control of her life back. But as she grew older, her thoughts of outrage turned to thoughts of vengeance. She wanted her abuser dead.

Not reformed, not rehabilitated, *dead*.

Although Amy was able to outwardly function in society, her mind was a swirling mix of emotions. On any given day she had to deal with uninvited feelings of anger, confusion, bitterness and betrayal.

Worse yet, she didn't think God cared about her. It seemed obvious his love and concern were reserved for other people. Special people. Of course she was wrong, but considering her two "earthly" fathers — one absent, one abusive — it was tough to imagine a virtuous "heavenly" father who loved her.

A year after her mother died, a tearful Amy finally broke down and asked her brother if she could see a psychologist. As she confided in this stranger, years of pent-up shame, guilt and rage came out in torrents of sobs for the first time. Next, she shared the awful truth with her oldest brother and sister. Last of all, she shared it with her youngest brother — the brave boy who had lived through the darkest days with her. All three siblings embraced her fully. Fortunately, their love was just the beginning of a steady stream of support from people who would help rebuild the teen's confidence and self-worth.

Slowly and sometimes painfully, the healing process was set in motion. Her high school English and theatre teacher took special notice of Amy after her mother died. She respected her for what she had gone through, and asked the bright student to use her experience and maturity to mentor others going through similar struggles. For the first time she could remember, Amy felt that maybe, just maybe, she could get beyond her tormented childhood.

In addition to using her siblings and a favorite teacher, God was assembling another "restoration team" behind the scenes. For instance, during high school she worked at a local motel on the cleaning crew. Her boss there was a trustworthy, caring person who genuinely took an interest in her life. When Amy's old car broke down (a frequent occurrence), he would loan her his vehicle or have his mechanic fix hers on a special payment plan. He even made sure she stayed on top of her homework so she would graduate. In these simple but meaningful gestures, he was "ascribing unsurpassable worth to her life" and was one of many people God would use to restore her shattered soul.

While it was impossible to make sense of the horrible evil she was subjected to, Amy was finally able to forgive her mother for not protecting her. She even forgave God for apparently being too busy to care. This progress brought some inner healing and was a major step forward. But it definitely did not cause her to pursue religion or seek a relationship with God the Father.

More healing came as family and friends offered her the love and security she had desperately needed and deserved as a child. But most of her improvements were coming from within, from the iron will she inherited from her mother. Strong and self reliant, Amy worked hard to build a life for herself — a life she recalls "didn't need God, friends, or a husband to protect me."

> **Amy became an expert at compartmentalizing her life.**

In time, Amy became an expert at compartmentalizing her life, She coped by stuffing the bad old days into a deep corner of her psyche, and then, in her words, "cementing over it." Instead of actually dealing with the issues, she was simply packing up the junk from her childhood and burying it. As long as she kept it locked away, she figured there would never be a need to open up the box of anger, deception, fear, confusion and dysfunction.

The dirty little whore was stuffed away forever. Or so she thought.

○   ○   ○

As the darkness of Amy's childhood receded, her inner beauty began to shine through. Her close friends noticed the change as she blossomed into womanhood. Others noticed, too. One of her admirers was a gifted musician named Danny who was finding success in the Detroit music scene. Amy was waitressing at a local jazz club, and at first she wasn't interested in Danny's overtures. She figured musicians were all about wild parties, substance abuse and loose morals. But he was persistent and they eventually became friends. As they talked between Danny's music sets, she sensed that "this intense guy was really interesting." On their first date, she remembers, "We talked about music, art, philosophy and religion."

And somehow she knew he was the one for her.

A sought-after drummer, Danny was busy playing concerts and all-night recording sessions, but he diligently pursued Amy between jobs. Because of his late hours and out-of-town work, they couldn't always date like normal couples. But despite his wacky schedule they soon became engaged and were happily married within six months.

Before she met Danny, Amy had become good friends with a local businessman named Alan. When Alan started dating a young lady named Angela, he called Amy with the good news. His new flame was a former Broadway actress blessed with an incredible singing voice. He suggested that Amy introduce Angela to Danny. The talented pair hit it off immediately and started writing, recording and performing together. About a year later, Alan and Angela invited Danny to play at a Friday night concert series called "The Listening Room," hosted by the local church they had joined.

It was an invitation that would change his and Amy's life.

Although Amy and Danny were not attending any church at the time, Danny agreed to play the unusual "gig." Shortly after this concert introduction, Danny was asked back to Kensington Church — this time to play drums at their Easter weekend. It was a whopping eight services spread over two days. During the rehearsals and between performances, Danny hung out with a gang of musicians, singers, actors and stagehands. In many ways they were just like him — talented, dedicated and a little crazy. Backstage and during breaks, they shared their spiritual journeys (the highs and the lows) candidly with Danny. Although none of them claimed to be anywhere near perfect, he could see they were each trying their best to follow

They were just like him — talented, dedicated and a little crazy.

God. This impressed the young musician. And when he heard the pastor's Easter message titled "Coming Home," he broke into tears.

> **Danny announced his life was changed forever.**

When Danny got home after the services, he announced that his life would be changed forever because of what he had just experienced. He told Amy that God was whispering to him that it was time for him to live his life differently, like the people he met backstage. He felt he was being handed an invitation to return to the God he knew as a child but had walked away from as an adult.

Amy was skeptical. She listened politely but expected her husband's unexpected enthusiasm to quickly fade.

And why not? Danny was a well-meaning, good-hearted man and he openly showed his love for Amy. But he was no angel. His lifestyle as a working musician made things difficult, especially after they added two active little boys to the equation. And despite his newfound excitement about God, Danny didn't lose his faults overnight. There were enough setbacks to make any spouse doubtful. From her front-row seat, a wary Amy watched to see if this "Christianity thing" was the real deal or not. But soon it was undeniable — Danny's life was being transformed right before her eyes.

As weeks went by, she watched her husband surrender his heart to God and obey his call. And as the evidence of Danny's life-change mounted, Amy decided to make Kensington her church as well. Sunday after Sunday, she was moved to tears as she felt God's love expressed through this community of believers. As his Spirit stirred in her heart, she realized that perhaps she really *did* have a heavenly Father who loved her deeply and had a plan for her life.

All was going smoothly until one day in the summer of 2004, when the couple received a fateful email. Without warning, this brief, unsolicited letter would forever convince Amy that God himself was personally pursuing her in a strategic and profoundly meaningful way.

○   ○   ○

By that spring, God had become the center of their lives, and the excited couple decided to get baptized at a public beach along with hundreds of other believers. On a warm afternoon in June, Amy and Danny went under the water, symbolizing their new life in Jesus Christ. Emerging wet and dripping in the summer sun, the couple knew the ancient ritual was a powerful moment in their spiritual journey together. "We both had the feeling we were in for a life of adventure with God," says Amy.

Neither guessed how quickly the ride would begin.

"Like we were jumping into a waterslide that we would ride the rest of our lives — not knowing the twists and turns, getting wet, getting scared, but safe in God's hands."

Neither guessed how quickly the ride would begin.

The following day, they were cleaning out their garage when they came across a dusty pile of unused "baby stuff" — strollers, cribs, car seats and high chairs. Like all parents, they paused nostalgically to reflect on how quickly their kids were growing up. Standing among the reminders of their boy's infant years, they confirmed to each other that they were over and done with having children. It was a hard discussion because they loved their kids so much and were reluctant to close the door forever on the possibility of having more. Because of her tough childhood, Amy talked about wanting to be a foster parent. But Danny felt the eventual separation from a foster child would be too difficult for him. He said he favored adoption instead.

The impromptu conversation ended with them agreeing to pray about expanding their family. But it was something they both felt was far down the road —"maybe when the boys are older" — if ever.

Two days later, Danny opened up an email at work. It was from a family involved in supporting an orphanage in Omoa, Honduras. The subject line of the email read: "Will someone adopt this little girl?" Danny nearly fell out of his chair. He quickly forwarded the email to Amy at home. Nervously they wondered if God was extending another of his clear invitations to them. To find out, they took a small step of faith and contacted their friend who had originally sent the email. A longtime supporter of foreign missions, Jan explained that a work trip

The couple felt like God was moving in some "mysterious way."

to Honduras was being organized and she wondered if Amy and Danny wanted to go. The couple felt like God was moving in some "mysterious way" and they quickly signed up for the trip. But again, they both agreed adoption was not in their immediate future — if it was to occur at all.

They just wanted to check out what God was up to in Honduras.

On the trip, Danny worked with a team of volunteers building a structure for a new ministry called *La Casa de Esperanza* — the House of Hope. The ministry was designed to provide a safe place where older girls from the local orphanage could live after they turned 18. By training the girls in a vocation, the House of Hope could help transition young women into a productive life outside the orphanage. If the teens left without job skills there was a chance they would have to resort to begging, prostitution or drug dealing to keep from starving. Worse yet, Honduras has the highest murder rate in the Western Hemisphere and women are often the targets. The thought of precious young girls being victimized after leaving the orphanage energized Danny to work even harder in the tropical heat.

While Danny was busy cutting lumber and stacking cinder blocks, Amy was busy inside the orphanage conducting Vacation

Bible School with other volunteers. On the second day of their trip, the exhausted couple talked excitedly about how God was nudging their hearts. With a boldness that could only have come from God, Amy shared with Danny that there were several girls at the orphanage she felt drawn to and would consider adopting. And even though Danny had not spent the day with Amy, he knew *exactly* which girls she was talking about — and identified them all by name! This mutual attraction to the same orphans at the same time felt like dramatic confirmation that God's plan for them might be a whole lot bigger than a ten-day mission trip.

The idea of adopting multiple kids at one time was crazy. The idea of adopting teenagers instead of toddlers was insane. On top of that, none of the girls could speak English. Nothing like this had ever been done, and the international legal hurdles involved in pulling it off would be enormous. But God continued to give Danny and Amy miraculous reassurances that seemed to say, "Yes, I'm with you, keep going."

Nothing like this had ever been done. The international legal hurdles were enormous.

Amy recalls hearing God speak directly to her heart: "About six days into the trip I was standing in the back hallway of the orphanage alone. Thoughts were screaming in my head, *Am I crazy? Am I hearing voices? Why would God ask us to adopt teenage girls? Why would I risk everything? This doesn't make any sense. I'm not prepared. Can't someone else do it?* Then, for the first time in my life I heard God speak to me and it stopped me cold. In my thoughts I heard '*Amy, it is okay. I've prepared you with the perfect compassion for this task. You've been through a similar fire. I kept your heart safe with me and provided for your life. I have given you a family, a home, and love beyond your dreams. I've prepared you uniquely and perfectly for this task.*' And I knew it was going to all work out."

Amy reflects back, "That was the ultimate revelation that

God had always been there in my life. In those darkest days, he was there. He had protected my heart and had not abandoned me — and he never would. It was like a veil was lifted because I had always thought God was busy somewhere else. He really did get me through all that, and then fulfilled my dream of a good husband, a great family and a secure home."

It was there, in the muggy streets of Honduras, that Amy first connected her childhood experiences with her ultimate purpose in life. God didn't *cause* her rotten home situation, but he *used* it for his greater purposes: "*We know that in all things God works for the good of those who love him, who have been called according to his purpose.*"[2]

Seeing it from God's perspective gave Amy strength to persevere in the adoption process.

And it would take every ounce of strength she had.

For the next four years, Amy and Danny fought their way through miles of red tape and mountains of documents. They flew back and forth to Honduras ten times to try and complete their adoption. Negotiating with local government officials and working through a confusing legal system, Amy stayed in Honduras for weeks at a time. The couple spent thousands of dollars, hit dozens of dead ends and battled discouragement for 48 months as lawyers and judges told them it was impossible. During the struggle, Amy and Danny saw many miracles with finances, relationships, legal systems and governments. But the battle was uphill all the way. As years dragged on, the outcome seemed so hopeless that well-meaning friends asked them to reconsider and redirect their energy and resources into other worthy causes.

Could their friends be right? Had they only imagined that God had spoken to them? If it was his idea how come it wasn't working out?

From the first day to the last, doubts crept in. But God's answer was always the same: "Keep going. I didn't tell you to stop." So they kept pushing and praying.

Just because God asks us to do something doesn't mean it's going to be easy or that things will go smoothly. In fact, the opposite is often true. Yet too many times we use challenges as an excuse to give up or question our calling. We're tempted to think: *Maybe I misunderstood God's will. Maybe I didn't hear his voice in the first place.* But hitting a barrier doesn't mean we're wrong or that God wants us to quit.

Somebody said that when God closes a door he opens a window somewhere else. Or maybe he wants us to lose weight and climb through the keyhole!

Just because God asks us to do something doesn't mean it's going to be easy.

Bucking the system, Amy and Danny trusted God and relied on his grace to sustain them. Finally, in 2008, they brought three beautiful adopted children back to Michigan and welcomed them into their family. It was the culmination of an amazingly difficult spiritual journey — one that began the day after they first set foot on Honduran soil when God whispered a plan to the two new believers. Although they didn't understand how he would accomplish his will, they dedicated themselves to obeying it. In the end, God's perfect plan brought hope and a future to three remarkable Honduran girls: *"For I know the plans I have for you', declares the Lord. 'Plans to prosper you and not harm you. Plans to give you a hope and a future.'"* [3]

o   o   o

When we step out in faith to help someone else, we usually end up being helped ourselves. As a child, Amy had a difficult home life. But when she dedicated herself to providing a loving home for *other* children, she found true healing for her painful past. Even as a believer she struggled with the nagging question, "Where was God during my greatest need?" But when she turned her focus outward to helping others, God gave her the answer: *I was right there with you, preserving your life and preparing you to lift others out of their despair.*

The God who knows the future gave Amy a wonderful husband to protect her and a loving family to care for. And he gave her the ability to move beyond a personal history that most would consider insurmountable. When she fully surrendered her life to Jesus, God redeemed her deepest pain and allowed her to share her greatest treasure — her loving home — with five loving children.

God wants to heal the wounds in our life and restore whatever has been destroyed by our parents, spouses, siblings, bosses, whoever. If you're suffering from a father wound or other emotional trauma, think of Jesus as your "wounded healer." In the Messianic prophecies, Isaiah portrayed Jesus as the "suffering servant" who would leave heaven to live on earth as the *"man of sorrows."*

As a man, Jesus experienced suffering so he could know our suffering: *"He was looked down on and passed over, a man who suffered, who knew pain firsthand. One look at him and people turned away. We looked down on him, thought he was scum. But the fact is, it was our pains he carried — our disfigurements, all the things wrong with us."* [4]

As a man, Jesus experienced temptation so he could know our temptations: *"Because he himself suffered when he was tempted, he is able to help those who are being tempted."* [5]

As a man, Jesus was laughed at, humiliated, rejected, tortured and crucified. So he fully understands — from personal experience — any pain you've ever experienced. And best of all, he's promised to help. If you invite him into your anguish, he can heal the memories, regardless of who wronged you: *"By his wounds you have been healed."* [6]

Jesus understands — from personal experience — any pain you've ever experienced.

Regardless of what your earthly father was like, your heavenly

Father is loving, caring, accepting and totally trustworthy. This next statement might seem obvious, but it's important you know and believe this to down to your toes: *You can totally trust what God says about you.*

When God says he will *"never leave you or forsake you,"* believe it! When he assures you he will *"never let you down, never walk off and leave you,"* believe it! [7]

The Bible doesn't say we will always *feel* loved, but it promises we *are* loved —regardless of emotions or circumstances. There are hundreds of voices in the world (and inside your head) that will try to discourage you and make you feel like you're a "dirty little whatever." But God says you are his beloved child, chosen by him before you were even born. The world may whisper (or shout) that you're worthless and insignificant, but God says you are valuable and precious. The world may say you're a failure and a loser, but God says you're *"more than a conqueror."* [8]

What God thinks about you is the only opinion that matters.

When friends or family belittle you, when co-workers or leaders snub you, when the hallway mirror or the bathroom scale depresses you, remember this: What God thinks about you is the only opinion that matters: *"Let God be true and every man a liar."* [9]

Amy suffered from hurtful words and hurtful actions. But God showed her how to take her eyes off of her past and onto his future. Once we realize that God has forgiven us and redeemed us and has an eternal inheritance lined up for us, then we can start moving past the pain toward freedom.

But there's one more step needed to complete the transformation.

And it's the hardest step of all.

When Jesus looked down from the cross, he uttered the most unexpected, most unexplainable words ever spoken: *"Father, forgive them, for they do not know what they are doing."* [10]

God's grace — in this case I mean his enabling power — can even help us forgive the perpetrator. God's grace allows us to see even depraved people through his eyes of compassion and mercy. When we realize that God loves fallen people (which includes all of us) and that his grace is available to popes and predators alike, we can start to forgive our transgressors.

> **From the cross, Jesus uttered the most unexpected, most unexplainable words ever spoken.**

Sound familiar? Smack dab in the middle of the Lord's Prayer, Jesus injects, *"Forgive us our sins, as we forgive everyone who sins against us."*

According to Jesus, forgiving is a mandatory, ongoing process: *"Keep us forgiven with you and forgiving others."* And it's the only thing that can free us from the bitter poisons of hatred and vengeance: *"Forgive us our debts, as we also have forgiven ... and have given up resentment against our debtors."* [11]

○　　○　　○

Amy and Danny's lives have been transformed. God's life-giving grace was the spark in Amy's dead existence that resurrected every good thing that had been snuffed out in her as a child — hope, trust, innocence and joy. And it even allowed her to begin forgiving her deceased stepfather for his horrendous crimes. For Danny, God's grace unleashed musical and leadership gifts in him that have blessed thousands through his inspired songwriting, recordings and performances. Today, he's the full-time Music Director at Kensington — leading worship on the same stage where God touched his heart during his first "Easter gig" back in 2000!

In turn, Amy and Danny, along with their two sons, have initiated a transformation process in their three new daughters.

Though her own journey is ongoing, Amy's story has now come full circle. God is using her childhood suffering as a way to validate and acknowledge the pain others face and to become part of their healing process.

Amy's life proves that God's grace can turn tragedy into triumph. But if you're wondering why tragedies occur in the first place, you're not alone.

A survey asked hundreds of random people what they would ask God if they could ask him just one question. The number one response was: "How can a loving God allow evil and suffering in the world?" A simplistic answer is: *This is not the world as God created it.* It's fallen. It's broken. It's a hot mess. If man hadn't rebelled, there would be no cancer or kidnapping or child abuse. The world would still be a utopia and we would live forever in perfect health and harmony.

God could have created us as robots, programmed to obey him. But he didn't want automatons, he wanted loving children. And love is only real if it's voluntary. *Stepford Wives* wouldn't do. Because he loves us, God created us with a free will. Like Adam, each of us can choose to return his love or reject him. And like Adam, we have a supernatural enemy called Satan who actively encourages us to turn away from God. History attests to the consequences of man's willful disobedience — pain, poverty, disease, crime, war, the whole depressing list.

Sometimes we bring suffering on ourselves through bad choices. Sometimes we just bump into it because it's all around us and we're not immune to it. That's because the entire planet is under a curse brought on by man's rebellion back in Genesis.[12] The effects of this curse are universal, with every living thing in *"bondage to decay."* That's why every living thing wears out, breaks down and eventually dies. Certain species of mayfly live for 30 minutes. Certain species of pine trees live for 5,000 years. But they're both under the same death sentence. Someday God will renew the physical universe to its former state of perfection, but until then *"the whole creation has been groaning as in the pains of childbirth."* [13]

There is no easy answer to the complex question of suffering. And questioning God in times of stress doesn't make you any less of a believer. But know this: When we're struck with a pain so deep that we can't imagine how a loving God could allow it, *grace is there*. When it seems like things cannot possibly get worse and there's no chance they'll ever get better, *grace is there*.

Author Frederick Buechner shares how suffering and grace intersect: "The grace of God means something like this: 'Here is your life. You might never have been, but you are because the party wouldn't have been complete without you. Here is the world. Beautiful and terrible things will happen. Don't be afraid. I am with you. Nothing can ever separate us. It's for you that I created the universe.'" [14]

Beautiful and terrible things.

We've all seen our share. But take comfort. Even though suffering is real and awful and often unexplainable, it is also temporary. It will all end someday. When unbearable heartache crushes our dreams, we can turn to the last book of the Bible for hope: *"God himself will be with them ... He will wipe every tear from their eyes. There will be no more death or mourning or crying or pain, for the old order of things has passed away."* [15]

○   ○   ○

As the adoption process dragged on, Amy and Danny often prayed for their problems to be solved or roadblocks to be eradicated. Some were, some were not. Victories and setbacks alternated. But all during the struggle, God showed them what he showed the Apostle Paul — that when we are at our weakest, he is at his strongest. The miracles that occurred in Honduras proved that what can't be done through human effort can always be done by his unlimited strength.

In one case, Paul begged God three times to remove a hardship he was facing. But God chose not to. Instead, he replied, *"My grace is enough; it's all you need. My strength comes into its own in your weakness."* [16]

If you're reading this at the gym or on your treadmill at home, I can imagine you asking, *So the weaker I get, the stronger I become?*

Being weak and submissive almost sounds un-American. The sure ticket to failure. But it's only when we submit to God's plan and ditch our own strategy that the power of his grace is unleashed. That's the meaning of *"my grace is enough."* If you feel like you're hitting your head against a brick wall and nothing you do seems to be working, remember this: When we submit to God's plan (and his timetable) we experience peace that passes understanding and joy that's not dependent on our current circumstances.

Paul asked for relief. God said, "No." Paul's reaction to God's reply is still the best advice on how to deal with hardships in life: *"Once I heard that, I was glad to let it happen. I quit focusing on the handicap and began appreciating the gift. It was a case of Christ's strength moving in on my weakness. Now I take limitations in stride ... abuse, accidents, opposition, bad breaks. I just let Christ take over!"* [17]

○   ○   ○

I'm not a lepidopterist (official butterfly geek), but scientists say the majestic wings of a monarch are created from its own excrement as a caterpillar. Likewise, God takes the awful smelly stuff in our lives and transforms us into a new creature that can fly instead of crawl: *"If anyone is in Christ, he is a new creation; the old has gone, the new has come!"* [18]

When we invite Jesus to forgive our sins and live in our hearts, we become as different from our old self as a butterfly is from a caterpillar. God takes what is ugly, painful, toxic —

everything that is contaminated — and turns it into something more beautiful than we could ever dream. God is *able to do immeasurably more than all we ask or imagine, according to his power that is at work within us."* [19]

During its caterpillar stage, a young monarch is small and unimpressive. Its only activity is binge-eating milkweed. Then the creepy crawler pupates, and inside its chrysalis the lowly insect is mysteriously transformed into the king of butterflies. The caterpillar cannot transform itself — and neither can we. We can only be changed by grace — the transforming power *we do not deserve and cannot earn.*

> **The caterpillar cannot transform itself. Neither can we.**

A butterfly emerging from its chrysalis is a picture of our new birth here on earth and hints at the glorified bodies we'll receive at the return of Jesus. Talking about this miraculous change, Paul says we're already *"being transformed into his likeness with ever-increasing glory."* Another translation says our lives are *"gradually becoming brighter and more beautiful as God enters our lives and we become like him."* [20]

As a child, Amy couldn't possibly know that her hardships were preparing her for future service. But God did. Years later, the injustice she endured became an incentive to rescue other children from lives of despair. God's grace saved her, sustained her, and ultimately prepared her to survive 48 months of legal combat to get custody of her adopted daughters. Personally, I doubt I would have been strong enough to hang in there that long.

But Amy was.

Sweet on the outside, tough on the inside, she prayed and worked and negotiated and refused to quit until the three young ladies were legally and forevermore her adopted children.

Like Amy, a monarch butterfly may look delicate and fragile as it flits from flower to flower. But it's also tough enough to migrate 3,000 miles from the mountains west of Mexico City to the northern wilds of Nova Scotia. The monarch is light — three adults weigh less than a dime — but it can fly 30 mph for ten weeks to reach its nesting ground. This long-distance champ has a brain smaller than the head of a pin, yet it navigates to the same wintering habitat its ancestors travelled to — often to the exact same tree!

The injustice Amy endured became an incentive to rescue other children.

How? Only God knows for sure. But there's an old saying that applies to people and butterflies: "The adventure you get is the one you're ready for." To paraphrase the Boy Scout motto, the Christian life is all about being prepared: *"If a man cleanses himself ... he will be an instrument for noble purposes, made holy, useful to the Master and prepared to do any good work."* [21]

Amy was ready. God had prepared her. And the adventure of a lifetime brought three girls over 1,700 miles from Honduras to Michigan.

What has God's grace prepared *you* to do?

○   ○   ○

"We talk about heaven being so far away. It is within speaking distance to those who belong there. Heaven is a prepared place for a prepared people."

— Dwight L. Moody [22]

Epilogue — This Ends Tonight

By Karl Nilsson

"Relax, zipperhead. I'm not going to shoot you."

Can a beer-guzzling racist who hates his neighbors and spouts ethnic slurs help us understand the grace of God?

In chapter 2, we turned back to 1862 for the amazing example of grace found in Victor Hugo's bestseller *Les Miserable*. Now let's fast forward 147 years to an R-rated movie starring one of Hollywood's most notorious tough guys. The top-grossing flick is Warner Brothers' *Gran Torino*, and the star is Clint Eastwood.[1]

Eastwood is best known for playing macho guys who take the law into their own hands. His most memorable role was Detective Harry Callahan, the central character in a series of three "Dirty Harry" movies (*Dirty Harry, Magnum Force*, and *Sudden Impact*) starring the slit-eyed sleuth who carried a huge revolver instead of a business card. To a society disillusioned with legal loopholes and liberal judges, his shoot-now-ask-questions-later approach to police work was a welcome relief. For millions of law-abiding citizens, watching Harry whack fictional crooks eased the frustration of watching high-priced lawyers get actual bad guys off the hook.

Typically a man of few words, Detective Callahan would occasionally wax philosophical. In the 1971 classic, *Dirty Harry*, he discusses the meaning of life with a bad guy, *"I know what you're thinking: 'Did he fire six shots or only five?' With all the excitement I've lost count myself. But being as this is a .44 Magnum, the most powerful handgun in the world, and would blow your head clean off, you've got to ask yourself one question: 'Do I feel lucky?' Well ... do ya, punk?"*

Turns out the punk did not feel lucky, and he grudgingly

surrendered. He shouldn't have. Harry's humongous gun was empty and his famous bluff is forever etched in movie history.

In real life, most cops work their entire career without firing a single shot outside the practice range. But in an Eastwood movie, lawmen can unleash a string of wisecracks or a hail of bullets with equal ease. In a film career spanning 55 years and 66 movies, Eastwood's cold-blooded vengeance was dished out against hundreds of outlaws, drug dealers, crooked cops and would-be assassins. Taking the express lane of law enforcement, he appointed himself judge, jury and executioner, making sure criminals got what they deserved and audiences got what they wanted.

What can a Hollywood legend possibly teach us about grace?

So what can an 80-year-old Hollywood legend possibly teach us about grace? The answer may surprise you.

Gran Torino opens on a funeral service in progress at a Catholic church located in the working-class neighborhood of Highland Park, Michigan. At the front of the church, retired Ford auto worker Walter Kowalski (Clint Eastwood) stands ramrod straight near the closed casket containing his late wife. From the pulpit, a boyish, overly eager priest asks the mourners, *"Is death the end, or the beginning?"*

Walt snarls in disgust.

He is unimpressed with religion in general and especially with the cherub-faced priest he calls *"an overeducated 27-year-old virgin who likes to hold the hands of old ladies who are superstitious and promises them eternity."* When Father Janovich makes a surprise house call to invite Walt to confession, the scrappy senior tosses him out the door.

A decorated Korean War veteran, Walt is disgruntled that his formerly all-white neighborhood is now populated with dark-skinned strangers. The Polish and Irish families of his youth are gone, replaced by Blacks, Latinos and Asian immigrants.

EPILOGUE

The local stores are derelict or boarded up, and the once proud homes are shabby. Crime has gone up and decent families are harassed by rival gangs who cruise the streets in hopped-up cars, brandishing Uzi machine guns.

Walt spends most days polishing his prized 1972 Ford Gran Torino and drinking Pabst Blue Ribbon on the front porch with his dog. Between sipping beer and spitting tobacco, Walt is an equal opportunity bigot. He despises his non-white neighbors for being lazy, the parish priest for being clueless, and his own sons for driving Japanese cars and retreating to the suburbs. But most of his venom is focused on the family next door, a group of Hmong immigrants he openly calls "gooks" and "slopes." The Hmong people lived in the mountains of Laos and Thailand, and helped American troops during the Viet Nam war. When the U.S. pulled out, they were forced to flee and many relocated to the Midwest.

The unlucky targets of Kowalski's over-the-fence tirades are a matronly grandma, a single mother, and two teenage kids — the quick-witted Sue and her shy brother, Thao. Unfortunately, this immigrant family has bigger problems than verbal abuse from a latter-day Archie Bunker. Local Hmong gang leaders are pressuring the reticent Thao to join their crew by threatening violence against his family. His initiation rite to become a member is daunting — he must steal Kowalski's mint condition Gran Torino. When the old man catches Thao inside the garage, he points his M1 Army rifle at him. When the reluctant burglar bolts for the door, Walt allows him to flee empty handed and doesn't report the break-in.

Walt is an equal opportunity bigot.

Later, the disappointed gang returns to harass the would-be thief and his sister. When the noisy commotion spills onto Walt's pristine lawn, he breaks up the fight with his trusty rifle. The gang members mock him, insisting he's too old and too timid to shoot anyone. Walt snarls, *"I could shoot a hole in your face and go back inside and sleep like a baby."* Cursing, the outraged gang-bangers back away and drive off.

Grateful for Walt's unintentional rescue, Thao's family showers the embarrassed Kowalski with food, flowers, and gifts. He defers, growling, *"I didn't save anybody. I just kept a bunch of jabbering gooks off my front lawn, that's all."*

Thao's mother, humiliated by her son's attempt at grand theft auto, insists that the teen make restitution by working for Walt free of charge for two weeks. At first, Walt refuses, then reluctantly uses Thao to clean urban blight from nearby homes. Gradually, he warms up to the hard-working boy, begins mentoring him and eventually lands him a job at a construction company run by a friend.

Slowly, Kowalski sets aside his caustic prejudice and inbred distrust. Forced by circumstances to socialize with his Asian neighbors, he notes: *"I have more in common with these gooks than my own spoiled rotten family."* Soon he is attending backyard barbecues with them and fixing broken appliances in their home. But gang violence and street crime threaten the budding friendship. In one instance, Kowalski intervenes to rescue Sue from a trio of cocky punks who've cornered her. Badly outnumbered, the octogenarian confuses the thugs with his bravado: *"Ever notice* (spits) *how you come across somebody* (spits) *once in a while* (spits) *that you shouldn't have messed with? That's me."*

Like magic, the menacing hoodlums disperse and the audience howls. **WARNING:** In case you're tempted to recite Walt's heroic speech when confronted by actual banditos, I should, um, probably mention that his tough talk was "backed up" by a giant pipe wrench stuffed in his waistband and a .45 caliber pistol bulging in his jacket.

This second rescue endears Kowalski to the entire Hmong community, who quickly deposit dozens of gaudy thank-you gifts all over the unlikely Good Samaritan's porch and lawn.

Later, Thao is confronted by the Hmong gang as he walks

home from work. Angry at his refusal to join them, they smash the carpenter tools Walt had furnished. When he resists, they disfigure his face with a lit cigarette. Thao is humiliated. Walt is outraged. He hunts down and isolates the biggest, toughest gang member to send a message to his Hmong companions. In a pulse-pounding scene reminiscent of classic Eastwood vigilantism, the old man beats and stomps the tattooed gang member into submission, making him promise to leave Thao alone.

As I watched the young gangster get smacked around by a GWA (Grandparent With Attitude), I felt a certain guilty pleasure. Justice was served. Wrongs were righted. Bad dudes got what they deserved. Tough talk and bare knuckles did what needed to be done. The audience around me rippled with murmurs of support.

In the old days, this cathartic beat-down would have been the happy ending to the movie. But in *Gran Torino*, screenwriter Nick Schenk makes the correct point that violence usually begets more violence. In ancient Palestine or modern America, the words of Jesus are still true: *"Those who live by the sword will die by the sword."* [2] Violence is seldom permanently resolved with violence. In this case, the Hmong gang quickly retaliates by savagely raping Thao's sister and terrifying the family with a horrific drive-by shooting.

The screenwriter got it right. Violence begets more violence.

The usually peace-loving Thao is furious and begs Kowalski to lead him in an armed attack to avenge his family's honor. Walt agrees that the gang must be dealt with, but insists that this kind of thing takes careful planning. The next day, he purchases a new suit, gets a haircut, and visits the confession booth for the first time in decades. The surprised priest is suspicious that Kowalski is up to something deadly but is powerless to stop him. Later, Thao keeps his appointment to visit Walt's home and *"plan the attack."* But instead of handing him a weapon, Walter locks the frustrated teen safely away from harm in his basement.

With Thao begging to join the fight, Kowalski ignores the clamor and calmly leaves the house. He walks his Labrador retriever next door and asks the Hmong grandmother to *"take care of my dog."* He drives to where the gang members live and shouts for them to come outside. One by one, the hoodlums step outside onto their porches and balconies and start taunting the white-haired man. Other neighbors venture out to see what the ruckus is about. Standing alone, Walt puts a cigarette in his mouth and asks the gang for a light. When they refuse, he whispers a "Hail Mary" and deliberately reaches his right hand into his partially opened jacket.

Thinking he is reaching for a pistol, the gang opens fire simultaneously and Walt falls to the ground, dead.

A close-up reveals his hand clutching a Zippo cigarette lighter.

Squad cars quickly roll up and Highland Park police arrest the shooters. A Hmong cop tells the sobbing Thao that Walt went for his lighter and the gangbangers shot him. Killing an unarmed man in front of witnesses will send them to prison *"for a long time."*

Earlier in the film, Walt had predicted, *"Thao and Sue are never going to find peace in this world as long as that gang's around. Until they go away, you know, forever."* Naturally, I assumed that meant Walt was going to use his military skills and vintage arsenal to blow them away in slow motion (as Dirty Harry once said, *"Nothing wrong with shooting as long as the right people get shot"*). But by tricking the gang into gunning him down in front of eyewitnesses, Walt permanently removed their threat without the chance of retributions against Thao's family.

In *Les Miserable*, the Bishop shows grace to the man who steals his prized silver. In *Gran Torino* the autoworker shows grace to the boy who tries to steal his prized car. Instead of giving Thao what he *did* deserve (going to jail for robbery), Walt gave him what he did *not* deserve (friendship, love and protection). In this modern-day parable of grace, I watched a raging xenophobe evolve from the role of angry hermit to reluctant hero, and ultimately to the sacrificial lamb who lays down his life for a friend.

Suddenly, grace had a new, flesh-and-blood, down-to-earth meaning for me.

When Walt crumples to the ground in a hail of gunfire, his body sprawls in the exact shape of Jesus hanging on the cross. And like Christ, this man who could have saved himself chose to save others by dying in their place. When I saw this powerful scene, I immediately thought of John 15:13, *"Greater love has no one than this, that he lay down his life for his friends."*

That's what Jesus did for us, and that's what we are to do for others. By voluntarily dying in our place, he not only paid the sin penalty, but set the ultimate example of self-sacrifice: *"Jesus Christ laid down his life for us. And we ought to lay down our lives for our brothers."* [3]

Some folks discover God's truth during prayer and mediation. Others by hearing a sermon. But this time, it took a cinematic curmudgeon named Walter to help me understand a powerful new paradigm: *The real hero is not one who inflicts vengeance but one who extends grace.*

> **The man who could have saved himself chose to save others by dying in their place.**

Which prompted me to scribble this entry in my journal: *Jesus Christ is not only King of Kings and Lord of Lords, but Hero of Heroes.*

God could have snuffed us out at any point in history and been totally justified. Since creation, mankind has pretty much ignored him, tested him and disobeyed him. And that term *mankind* includes me with a capitol "M."

I've ignored him by trying to be my own boss and running my life as if he didn't exist.

I've tested him by dabbling in grey areas to see how much I could get away with.

I've disobeyed him by neglecting to share his love with the people he puts in my life.

For these and a hundred other reasons per day, I'm worthy of judgment but get grace, deserve punishment but get pardon.

Here's the weird part — watching cranky old Walt Kowalski willingly take a hit for his friends helped me get my head around another mind-bending truth: *Grace is God's weapon of choice.* Throughout the Old Testament, God used floods, plagues, earthquakes, fireballs, famine, drought, enemy armies, leprosy and lightning bolts to get his wayward people's attention. But in the New Testament, grace trumps them all. Dirty Harry's .44 Magnum was a deadly weapon, but it's a pea-shooter compared to self-sacrificial love. Grace is the most dangerous weapon in the universe for fighting the revolution Jesus started 2,000 years ago.

Although Dirty Harry's famous revolver ran out of bullets, grace never does. It's the world's only inexhaustible ammunition. Grace breeds grace in the same way violence escalates violence.

Grace is the catalytic mechanism of God's upside-down strategy.

The more you give away, the more returns to you. The more you promote the happiness of others, the happier you'll be yourself. The more you extend and proclaim God's love to the world, the more if reflects back onto you. It's the catalytic mechanism of God's upside-down economy, and the Beatles described it perfectly in the last lyric of the last song on their last album: *"And in the end the love you take is equal to the love you make."*

Amazing. And even more so because it's essentially the super group's closing statement, Lennon & McCartney's musical epitaph, occurring in the last few seconds of their final collaboration, the *Abbey Road* album.[4]

In a final ironic twist, the reading of Walter's last will and testament reveals a changed man who understood grace at its deepest level. His remarkable but believable character arc is complete. His own greedy, uncaring kids (who wanted to stuff him in a nursing home) are left out completely, but his new "adopted family" is well rewarded.[5] Imagine — the man who hated religion and immigrants leaves his estate to Father Janovich's church and his beloved Gran Torino to the very person who tried to swipe it!

That's grace in action.

I don't think it's an accident that *Gran Torino* is far and away Eastwood's highest grossing movie. Debuting in 2009, it quickly earned over $263 million at the box office. And it continues to be one of the hottest rental videos in America. Why? Because as much as people like stories of vengeance (judgment), people yearn for stories of redemption (grace) even more. And although they may never admit it publically, most non-believers are hoping against hope that somewhere, somehow there's a merciful God out there who will deal with them according to his grace, not according to their actions.

Eastwood has declared that his starring role in *Gran Torino* will be his final performance in front of a camera. If so, that means the world's last on-screen glimpse of the man best known for *judgment* ("Go ahead, make my day") will be the very symbol of *grace* — a bloodied man with outstretched arms who died so others may live.

○   ○   ○

"Be ashamed to die until you have won some victory for humanity."
— Horace Mann[6]

Notes and Citations

PROLOGUE

1. Philippians 4:7 NIV
2. Romans 7:15 NIV
3. Deuteronomy 6:4-5 & Mark 12:30 NIV
4. Mark 12:31 NIV
5. Clive Staples Lewis, beloved British novelist, academic and theologian (1898-1963)

CHAPTER 1

1. See *Thayer's Greek-English Lexicon of the New Testament*, Joseph Thayer, originally published in 1885 (Grand Rapids, MI: Baker Book House, 1977)
2. Isaiah 55:8 NIV
3. Job 42:2-3 NIV
4. 2 Corinthians 12:2-4 NIV
5. Ephesians 3:2-3 AMP
6. Ephesians 3:4-5 NIV
7. 1 Corinthians 13:12 NLT
8. Anne Lamott, best-selling author, former atheist turned believer (1954-)

CHAPTER 2

1. Jerry Bridges, Christian author and speaker, vice-president of Navigators (1929-)

CHAPTER 3

1. Hebrews 9:27 NIV
2. Galatians 6:7 NIV
3. See Michka Assayas, *Bono In Conversation* (New York: Riverhead Books, published by Penguin Group USA, 2005)
4. Jeremiah 33:3 NKJV

5. Dwight L. Moody, American evangelist and publisher who founded Moody Bible Institute in Chicago (1837-1899)

CHAPTER 4

1. See Ray Ratcliff and Lindy Adams, *Dark Journey Deep Grace: Jeffrey Dahmer's Story of Faith* (Abilene, TX: Leafwood Publishing, 2006)
2. Ephesians 2:8-9 NIV
3. Titus 2:11 NIV
4. Luke 19:9 NIV
5. Romans 3:23 NIV
6. Romans 3:24 NIV
7. See David Kinnaman & Gabe Lyons, *unChristian* (Grand Rapids, MI: Baker Books, 2007)
8. John 14:9 NIV
9. John Newton, English slave trader turned abolitionist and minister. Composer of "Amazing Grace" (1725-1807)

CHAPTER 5

1. Greg Boyd, *Repenting of Religion* (Grand Rapids, MI: Baker Books, 2004) 25
2. I John 3:16 NIV
3. John 8:1-11 NIV
4. Genesis 3:5-12 NIV
5. Galatians 4:7 NIV
6. 2 Corinthians 5:17 NIV
7. Originally titled *Nachfolge* ("Discipleship"), Bonheoffer's 1937 classic is based on the Sermon on the Mount and outlines his theology of costly discipleship. In it, he maintained "Cheap grace is the deadly enemy of the church."

8. I John 3:6 NIV
9. I John 3:9 NIV
10. Romans 6:12 NIV
11. Romans 14:12 NIV
12. Romans 5:18-21 MSG
13. John 10:10 NIV & MSG
14. 1 Corinthians 8:9 NIV
15. Ephesians 4:23-14 NIV
16. Ephesians 5:1 NIV & MSG
17. Deuteronomy 6:4 NIV
18. Jimi Hendrix, Rock & Roll Hall of Fame guitarist & songwriter (1942-1970)

CHAPTER 6

1. Matthew 5:22 NIV
2. Matthew 7:1-2 NIV
3. Matthew 7:1-2 MSG
4. Matthew 7:3-5 NIV
5. Matthew 7:16 NIV
6. Galatians 5:21-22 NIV
7. Galatians 6:1-2 NIV
8. Malcolm Gladwell, *Blink* (Back Bay Books, New York 2007)194, 196
9. Philippians 2:3-4 NIV
10. Philippians 2:3-4 MSG
11. Seth Godin, *Graceful*, excerpted from *Linchpin* (Portfolio/Penguin ©2010) 3
12. Mother Teresa, humanitarian, founder of the Missionaries of Charity, Nobel Peace Prize Winner (1910-1997)

CHAPTER 7

1. Luke 15:5-6 NIV
2. Matthew 18:15-17 NIV
3. Matthew 18:17 NIV
4. James 5:16 NIV
5. Galatians 3:24 NLT

6. Mahatma Gandhi, pre-eminent spiritual & political leader of India's independence movement (1869-1948)

CHAPTER 8

1. Psalm 111:10 NIV
2. Romans 2:4 NLT
3. Romans 2:4 MSG
4. 2 Timothy 1:7 KJV
5. 2 Timothy 1:7 AMP
6. Romans 3:20 NIV
7. Romans 3:21-24 NIV
8. Romans 8:3 MSG
9. Hebrews 9:22 NIV
10. Hebrews 10:1-4 MSG
11. Hebrews 10:2 NIV
12. Psalm 103:14 NLT & MSG
13. Erma Bombeck, American humorist and newspaper columnist (1927-1996)

CHAPTER 9

1. Luke 22:4-6 NIV
2. Luke 22:47-48 NIV
3. Matthew 27:3-4 NIV
4. Matthew 27:5 NIV
5. Matthew 26:33, 35 NIV
6. Luke 22:61 NIV
7. Luke 22:62 NIV
8. Luke 22:62 MSG
9. John 6:67-71 NIV
10. Matthew 5:3 MSG
11. Matthew 5:4 MSG
12. John 15:5 NIV
13. 2 Corinthians 12:9 NIV
14. John 3:17-18 MSG
15. Alan Cohen, self-help guru and author of *Chicken Soup for the Soul* (1954-)

CHAPTER 10

1. John 8:48 NIV
2. Luke 9:54 NIV
3. John 4:39 NIV
4. Romans 3:10, 23 NIV
5. 2 Corinthians 5:21 NIV
6. Ephesians 2:8-9 NIV
7. Ephesians 2:8 MSG
8. Marvin Olasky, *World*, February 13, 2010, p.27. Interview with Michael Card, "The Life of a Slave"
9. Romans 5:6-8 NIV
10. Romans 1:17 NIV
11. Habakkuk 2:4 KJV
12. Roland H. Bainton, *Here I Stand* (Abington, Nashville, 1980)
13. Isaiah 14:12-14 NIV
14. Genesis 3:5 NIV
15. Genesis 6:5-6 NIV
16. Romans 8:5 MSG
17. Galatians 6:14 NIV
18. Matthew 6:1 MSG
19. Luke 18:9-14 NIV
20. Matthew 6:1-4 NIV
21. Matthew 6:33 NIV
22. Matthew 5:20 NIV
23. James 2:10 NIV
24. Matthew 23:27-28 NIV
25. Titus 3:5 NIV
26. Galatians 2:21 NIV
27. Romans 10:4 NIV
28. Galatians 6:2 NIV
29. Matthew 22:37-39 NIV
30. Matthew 22: 40 NIV
31. Max Lucado, *In The Grip Of Grace* (Word Publishing, Dallas 1996) 83
32. 1 John 5:3 NIV
33. Romans 10:2 MSG
34. Mark 14:36 NIV
35. Isaiah 6:8 NIV
36. 1 Corinthians 1:27-28 NIV
37. Ephesians 2:8 MSG
38. Ravi Zacharias, Indian-born evangelist. Prolific author, riveting speaker and intellectually daunting apologist (1946-)

CHAPTER 11

1. John 3:17 NIV
2. Genesis 19:23 NIV
3. Matthew 5:17 NIV
4. Matthew 5:17 MSG
5. Acts 1:8 NIV
6. Luke 18:27 NIV
7. Hebrews 12:28 KJV
8. Luke 2:40 NKJV
9. 1 Corinthians 15:10-11 MSG
10. 2 Corinthians 12:9 NIV
11. 2 Corinthians 9:8 NIV
12. Marvin Olasky, *World*, February 13, 2010, p.27. Interview with Michael Card, "The Life of a Slave"
13. Philippians 4:13 NIV
14. Acts 20:32 NIV
15. Hebrews. 4:16 KJV
16. Hebrews 4:16 NIV
17. Acts 17:34 NIV
18. Matthew 10:42
19. John 9:3 NIV
20. Paul Billheimer, *Love Covers* (Bethany House, Minneapolis, 1981) 7
21. John 13:35 NIV
22. Acts 2:47 NIV
23. 2 Corinthians 5:17-18 NIV
24. Nancy Gibbs, *Time*, September 27, 2010, p. 70. Essay, "Fighting Words"
25. John Newton, English slave trader turned abolitionist and minister. Composer of "Amazing Grace" (1725-1807)

CHAPTER 12

1. "Why Are We Here: The Great Debate," *International Herald Tribune*, April 26, 1999.
2. Matthew 23:2, 5-7 NIV
3. Matthew 23:13-14 NIV
4. Matthew 23:15 NIV
5. Matthew 23:23 NIV
6. Matthew 23:24 NIV
7. Matthew 23:25 NIV
8. Matthew 23: 27-28 NIV
9. Matthew 23:33 NIV
10. This is the only recorded instance of Jesus writing anything in the entire Bible.
11. John 8:1-11 NIV
12. Matthew 5:17 NIV
13. Luke 6:37 MSG
14. Charles Colton, British cleric, author and intellectual (1780-1832)

CHAPTER 13

1. John 8:32 NIV
2. 1 Peter 4:8 NIV
3. Fyodor Dostoevsky, Russian novelist, author of *The Brothers Karamazov* (1821-1881)

CHAPTER 14

1. Matthew 5:7 NIV
2. Exodus 34:6-7 MSG
3. Psalm 86:5, 108:4, 118:1, NKJV
4. Proverbs 3:1-4 NLT
5. Micah 6:8 NIV
6. 2 Corinthians 1:3 NASB
7. 2 Corinthians 1:4 NASB
8. 2 Corinthians 1:4 NIV
9. Philippians 1:27 MSG
10. 2 Corinthians 2:14-16 MSG
11. Matthew 5:16 NIV
12. Luke 1:46-54 NIV
13. James 5:11 NASB
14. 1 Timothy 2:4-7 MSG
15. Romans 10:13 NIV
16. Luke 6:27-35 NIV
17. Luke 6:36 NIV
18. James 3:13-17 NASB
19. Luke 11:46 MSG
20. Matthew 5:3-6 NIV
21. Matthew 5:7 NIV
22. Matthew 7:12 NIV
23. Matthew 7:3-5 NIV
24. Luke 6:35-36 NIV
25. Matthew 9:10 NIV
26. Ephesians 2:10 NIV
27. Billy Hughes, Australian Prime Minister (1862-1952)

CHAPTER 15

1. The numbers "1-8-7" refer to Section 187 of the California penal code. It's used by gangs and cops nationwide as a synonym for murder.
2. Amy Chozick, *Wall Street Journal*, September 17, 2010, p.W1. "Motown Becomes Movietown"
3. James 2:12 NIV
4. Mother Teresa, humanitarian, founder of the Missionaries of Charity, Nobel Peace Prize Winner (1910-1997)

CHAPTER 16

1. We are grateful for material extensively relied upon in chapter 16 from Alexander Solzhenitsyn, *Gulag Archipelago* (New York: Harper and Row, 1975)
2. Romans 5:8 NIV
3. Matthew 18:21-22 NIV
4. Genesis 4:24 NIV
5. Matthew 18:23-35 NIV

6. Matthew 6:14 NIV
7. Romans 3:25 NIV
8. Matthew 26:28 NIV
9. Luke 23:43 NIV
10. John 3:16 NIV
11. Luke 12:7 NIV
12. 1 John 1:9 NIV
13. Romans 5:8 MSG
14. Luke 23:34 NIV
15. Nelson Mandela, political prisoner for 27 years, toppled apartheid. First black president of South Africa, winner of Nobel Peace Prize (1918-)

CHAPTER 17

1. Mark 1:32-39 NIV
2. Romans 12:21 NIV
3. Letters written by Bonhoeffer during his imprisonment were posthumously published as *Letters and Papers from Prison.* He was executed on April 9, 1945. His last words were "This is the end — for me the beginning of life."
4. Lewis Smedes, renowned Christian author, professor and theologian (1921-2002)

CHAPTER 18

1. Business Week, August 6, 2007, Diane Brady & Christopher Palmeri
2. Ecclesiastes 2:10-11 NIV
3. Ecclesiastes 2:10-11 MSG
4. 1 Chronicles 29:12 ESV
5. Deuteronomy 8:17-18 MSG
6. 2 Corinthians 8:14-15 NIV
7. Matthew 6:19-21 NIV
8. Luke 9:24-25 NIV
9. Mark 4:8 NIV

10. Ministry & Leadership, Winter 2009 Issue, pages 14 & 15. Dr. Christian Smith
11. Luke 12:15 NIV & MSG
12. Luke 12:16-19 MSG
13. Luke 12: 20-21 MSG
14. Matthew 18:35 NIV
15. Luke 23:34 NIV
16. Winston Churchill, Prime Minister of Great Britain during WWII (1874-1965)

CHAPTER 19

1. From appendix to *Atlas Shrugged.* Published by New American Library, a division of Penguin Group (USA) Inc. New York. Ayn Rand ©1957
2. From John Galt's famous speech in *Atlas Shrugged.* Ayn Rand ©1957
3. I Corinthians 13:4-8 MSG
4. I John 3:16-17 NIV
5. I John 3:17 MSG
6. John 16:33 NIV
7. Acts 10:34 NIV
8. Matthew 8:20 NIV
9. Mark 12:30 NIV
10. Ephesians 2:10 NIV
11. Hudson Taylor, groundbreaking British missionary to China (1832-1905)

CHAPTER 20

1. Proverbs 4:23 NIV
2. Luke 6:45 NIV
3. James 3:9-12 NIV
4. Colossians 3:2-8 NIV
5. Philippians 4:8 NIV
6. Philippians 4:9 NIV
7. 1 Corinthians 13:4-8 NIV
8. 1 Corinthians 13:13 NIV

9. 1 Corinthians 13:2-3 NIV
10. Ephesians 4:31 NIV
11. Greg Boyd, *Repenting of Religion* (Grand Rapids, MI: Baker Books, 2004) 34
12. 1 John 3:16 NIV
13. 1 John 1:9 NIV
14. Eugene O'Neill, America's greatest playwright, winner of the Nobel Prize for literature (1888-1953)

CHAPTER 21

1. Matthew 25:14-30 NIV
2. Romans 5:20-21 MSG
3. Mother Teresa, humanitarian, founder of the Missionaries of Charity, Nobel Peace Prize Winner (1910-1997)

CHAPTER 22

1. Psalm 23:1-3 NIV
2. Romans 8:28 NIV
3. Jeremiah 29:11 NIV
4. Isaiah 53:2-3 MSG
5. Hebrews 2:18 NIV
6. 1 Peter 2:24 NIV
7. Hebrews 13:5 MSG
8. Romans 8:37 NIV
9. Romans 3:4 NIV
10. Luke 23:34 NIV
11. Luke 11:4 NIV, MSG & AMP
12. Genesis 3:14-19 NIV
13. Romans 8:21-22 NIV
14. Fredrick Buechner, *Wishful Thinking: A Seeker's ABC* (New York, NY: Harper Collins, 1993) Chapter 6

15. Revelation 21:4 NIV
16. 2 Corinthians 12:8 MSG
17. 2 Corinthians 12:9 MSG
18. 1 Corinthians 5:17 NIV
19. Ephesians 3:19-21 NIV
20. 2 Corinthians 3:17-18 NIV & MSG
21. 2 Timothy 2:21 NIV
22. Dwight L. Moody, American evangelist and publisher who founded Moody Bible Institute in Chicago (1837-1899)

EPILOGUE

1. *Gran Torino*, produced and directed by Clint Eastwood, written by Nick Schenk, by Village Roadshow Pictures distributed by Warner Brothers, © 2008
2. Matthew 26:52 NLT
3. 1 John 3:16 NIV
4. *Let It Be* was technically the last album the Beatles released, but it was recorded prior to *Abbey Road*.
5. God rewarded *his* "adopted family," too. His chosen people, Israel, rejected their prophesied Messiah, but non-Jews embraced him. Paul told Gentile believers in his letter to the Romans that although they weren't biological descendants of Abraham, God had adopted them as children, entitled to his full inheritance.
6. Horace Mann, Massachusetts Senator, father of public education (1796-1859)

About the Authors

JEFF PETHERICK is a portfolio manager and founding partner of an investment firm. When he's not busy picking stocks, he loves to write, travel, and serve on mission trips. He's been to India and Peru a dozen times, helping indigenous ministries obtain food, shelter and medical care for the poor. An avid outdoorsman, Jeff lives north of Detroit with his wife, Gina. He has two children, Chad and Kira. His first book, *Wavelength*, was written to show that ordinary men can do extraordinary things — when they listen and obey God's voice. Jeff founded Elk Lake Publishing for readers who are curious about spirituality but living outside the influence of traditional religion.

KARL NILSSON is the communication director at Kensington Church in Troy, Michigan. Before working at the multi-site church, he operated an advertising agency, specializing in the fitness industry. Prior to his marketing career, he was a syndicated cartoonist, newspaper columnist, and rock & roll magazine editor. He enjoys traveling, bicycling, and all things Detroit — Tiger baseball, Bob Seger tunes, and the Woodward Dream Cruise. He co-founded ELP (the publishers, not the rock trio) in 2007 to reach people who think God is irrelevant and to get free rides in Jeff's speedboat. He is married to his best friend and artistic muse, Marie. They have two children, Britt and Karl.

o   o   o

The authors have collaborated on three books: *Wavelength, Bigger Than the Sky,* and *Grace Like Rain.* All are available on Amazon.com. For upcoming works and info on speaking engagements, go to www.elklakepublishing.com.

WAVELENGTH
Turning In To God's Voice
In A World Of Static

By Jeff Petherick With Karl Nilsson

**Did God Stop Speaking?
Or Did We Stop Listening?**

Hearing the voice of God is like listening to the radio — if you're not dialed in to exactly the right frequency, you'll get nothing but static. *Wavelength* reveals what happens when a nonreligious businessman learns to tune in God's voice ... then dares to obey it. His unorthodox adventures in following Jesus will challenge your thinking and reveal how you can have your own two-way conversations with God.

"People ask me all the time, 'How can I hear and recognize God's voice?' Jeff tells us how. He's funny, he's passionate, and he's discovered the biblical pathway to intimacy with Jesus. Think of it as a spiritual hearing aid."

Dave Wilson
Family Life Conference Speaker & NFL Chaplain

"Is your Christian life so safe it's boring? Jeff takes risks for God and astonishing things happen. With fresh perspective and biblical insight, he explains how to recognize and respond to God's voice. It will yank you out of your comfort zone."

Craig Mayes, Ph.D.
Author of *Knowing God*

"Definitely not for spiritual couch potatoes. By sharing his own amazing journey, Jeff shows how anybody can learn to engage in life-changing dialogue with God. Get this book — and get ready to move from the mundane to the miraculous."

Steve Andrews
Lead Pastor, Kensington Church

Available at Amazon.com

BIGGER THAN THE SKY

By Jeff Petherick & Karl Nilsson
Illustrated by Bodhi Hill

Growing Up Is Never Easy.

Blossom lives in a cherry orchard on Michigan's beautiful Mission Point. Overwhelmed by the natural beauty and grandeur of her surroundings, she grows up questioning her self-worth, doubting her abilities, and worrying about her purpose in life. This delightful children's book helps kids and adults learn valuable lessons about patience, trust, and the importance of staying connected. Like each of us, Blossom must learn that she is a small but absolutely essential part of the Master's plan.

Lavishly illustrated in full color with 18 original creations by award-winning graphic designer and book illustrator, Bodhi Hill.

"Kids and parents both love this gorgeous book. Set near Traverse City, the story evokes a sense of Michigan's beautiful west coast. For anyone who loves nature and has a sense of wonder about God's creation, this will be a memory-maker for years to come."

Tami Verville
Children's Ministry Director, Kensington Church

"Ever wondered, 'Where do I fit in? Does God have a purpose for my life?' This charming book uses trees and animals and the forces of weather in ways I've never seen before to answer life's big questions. This is a feast for the eyes and a blessing for the heart."

Dan Kopp
Pastor, Eastside Vineyard Church

Available at Amazon.com